Policing The Bahamas
Ninteen Fifty-one and Beyond

by Paul Thompson Snr.

This book is a compilation of history, performance, achievement and loyalty contained in the writings of the author about a Police Force, that has been outstanding over the decades.

In Memory
and in Honour of
The Royal Bahamas Police Force,
Recruit Squad of April 1951

Published by: Paul Thompson and Associates
Nassau, Bahamas
Tel: 1-242-456-7909

Editorial Advisor: Dave Horsham

First Printing: 2022

*(The reader is reminded that all excerpts of any
Sections of the Laws of The Bahamas as transcribed in any page of
this book are all subject to verification)*

Preface

Policing in The Bahamas 1951 and Beyond

This book is intended to be a research document containing information about the Royal Bahamas Police Force, its many significant accomplishments, the safe and secure service provided to communities, working under the difficult and adverse conditions that existed in the early 1950's.

Readers will find it amazing that under the conditions that existed during the decade of the Fifties, in the era of Colonialism, with limited resources and ancient equipment, we in the R.B.P.F. were able to provide efficient and effective services. In 1951, we had just reached a strength of two hundred and the senior ranks were dominated by Officers from the United Kingdom. We were taught British Army type discipline, courage, fitness, integrity and teamwork, that made us the best in the public service. Training was conducted by experts and continued at Police posts with the most important on-the-job guidance by sub-officers assigned to those posts.

Readers will find that over the decades, many recommendations were made by Commissioners and Gazetted Officers to Governments for the improvement of the country and the Police Service.

A major proposal was the construction of a Maximum Secuity Prison to be built on an Island and the transformation of the prison in New Providence, to a Training Institution - UK style Borstal.

Some of the other recommendations that were more easily achieved over the years were; changes in the hours of work, introduction of Policewomen, mobile patrols, improved communication systems and more comfortable Police Stations and offices.

We had failed over the decades to get an indoor shooting range and a well staffed and equipped laboratory.

Another suggestion of major signifance was the control of the bus transportation system.

Readers will find information about the issues with politicians of every decade, the legacies of Commissioners and the famous Stanley Moir's team in the Criminal Investigation Department.

Commissioner Lt. Colchester Wemyss moved the force into a modern organization. Gerald Bartlett continued the modernization and Paul Farquharson was exceptional.

A. Loftus Roker was our best Minister.

This book contains 300 plus pages of materials gleaned from my training, local and overseas; documents received from training seminars, selected sections of criminal laws and Court decisions, including Judge's Rules and its administration.

The reader is reminded that all excerpts of any Sections of the Laws of The Bahamas as transcribed on any page of this book are for reference only and subject to verification.

Contents

Contents cont'd ...

C o n t e n t s cont'd...

In Memory and Honour of The Royal Bahamas Police Force Recruit Squad of April 1951

Ivan Beckles- Trinidad - Retired early and returned to Trinidad. Owns Beckles Studios, Camera Sales and Repairs in Port of Spain.

Steve Benacourt - Trinidad - Retired early and joined Prince George Dock as a Stevedore Supervisor. Later left the Bahamas.

David Bascombe - Trinidad - Completed service and retired

Julien Blades - Trinidad - Retired early. Retired in Chicago. Owns a security firm.

Percy Campbell - Trinidad - Retired early. Attended U.K. University. Graduated as an Economist/ Accountant. Worked for Bahamas Government, ABC Motors. Lectured at a College in the Bahamas.

James Carter - Trinidad - Baton of Honour winner 1951.

Mc Donald Chase - Trinidad - Retired as Superintendent in charge of Criminal Records Office. Fingerprint Expert. FBI rated him as being amongst the best in the region. He trained many officers in the science.

Andrew Coleby - Bahamas   - Retire Fingerprint Expert. Trained locally and overseas. He was a senior officer in the Criminal Records Office.

Jack A. Cuffy - Trinidad - Retired early and joined the Public Service.

Joseph Darceiul - Trinidad - Transferred to Ministry of Education as a teacher.

Eugene Edwards - Trinidad - Retired early. Moved to New York. Returned with a Degree in Business. Held several top paying jobs in Nassau and Freeport.

Anthony Fields - Trinidad - Retired after 18 years. Held rank of Superintendent and was first Commandant of the Police College. Managed the largest security firm in Trinidad. Returned to the Bahamas, opened a security firm in Freeport.

Cyril Joseph - Trinidad - Retired as a Superintendent of Police.

Joseph Forbes - Trinidad - Retired early. Appointed Director of Security at the Holiday Inn, Freeport. He worked there for many years.

Wilfred Jack - Trinidad - Retired. Joined John S. George Ltd.as warehouse manager for several years.

Lawrence Major - Bahamas - Retired as Assistant Commissioner of Police and joined the Bahamas Defense Force where he became Commandant. He was previously in charge of the Police Marine Division and the Air Wing.

Kenyon McDeigan - Trinidad - Retired early and started a jewellery business called 'Gold & Silversmiths'.

Joba Peterson - Bahamas - Retired. He returned to Family Island life.

Ivan Rahming - Bahamas - Retired and joined Paradise Island Resort as a Security Supervisor at Ocean Club.

Augustus H. Smith - Trinidad - Retired early. Studied Law and admitted to the Bahamas Bar.

Instructors:
C/Inspector; *Carlton Price Wentworth* - Trinidad
Inspector *Atkinson* - England and
Constable *Cyril Smith*. Police Duties & Law, Discipline & Drills and Physical Fitness, respectively.

The squad graduated in October 1951. Present were the Governor, Major General Sir Robert Neville, Ag. Commissioner Major Edward Sears and Superintendents Wenzel Grainger and Augustus Roberts. The latter recruited the Trinidadians in Trinidad in March 1951. ◼

Dedication

This book is dedicated to my Children, Grandchildren and Great Grandchildren.

Paul Rupert Thompson Jr. (dec): Assistant Supt. of the RBPF
Paul O'Brien Thompson: Security Provider/Businessman, Bahamas
Janet Thompson: Banker, Road Traffic Inspector (Ret.), Bahamas
Dianne Miller: Banker, Bahamas
Dr Raquel Elliot: University Professor, Florida USA
Judy Wooten: University Graduate, Interior Decorator, Washington, DC
Tracy Coakley: Entrepreneur, Bahamas
Gary Pratt: Retired Defence Force Officer, Building Contractor

GRAND & GREAT GRANDCHILDREN

Anika:	Chef, Bahamas
Darlene:	Graduate, University of Toronto, High School Teacher, Toronto
Andrew:	Employed in Food Services, Florida, USA
Anthony:	Employed in Food Services, Florida, USA St. Augustine's College
Andrea:	Employed in Food Services, Bahamas
Devonnia:	Executive Assistant to Chief Administrative Office, University of Toronto
D'Ondre:	Graduate of UWI, Masters in Education, B.Sc. Psychology, Mt. Allison University, Canada, Development Co-ordinator, Queen's College High School and Adult Care for Further Education
Danielle:	Attorney-at-Law, Buckingham University London, (Hons.) Admitted to The Bahamas Bar, 2021
Christopher:	Attorney-at-Law, Washington, DC

Casey:	B.Sc. University of Maryland, continuing studies for Medical Degree in Dermatology
Chase:	B.Sc. Information Technology, University of Maryland, Works in Washington DC
Jasmine:	B.Sc. International Business Finance, Seneca College, Toronto, Canad. Works in Toronto
Adrian:	Attending Seneca College, Toronto - Business and Finance
Justyn:	Graduate, St. Anne's High School Entrepreneur, Bahamas
Paul III:	Police Officer, Royal Bahamas Police Force Graduate of St. Augustine's College, Bahamas Computer Technician
Serena:	Student, Ocoee, Florida
Marco:	Student, Ocoee, Florida
Avant:	Student St. Anne's High School, Bahamas
Aaron:	Infant

About The Author
Paul Thompson Snr.

Paul Thompson Snr. was born in Trinidad and Tobago on the 19th July, 1927, in Cunupia Village and educated at Cunupia Government School, a small village in Caroni County. Most of the inhabitants were East Indian and farming was the main occupation.

He resided there until March, 1951, when he and sixteen others were recruited to join the Royal Bahamas Police Force .

In March 1981, he retired from the Police Service and joined Resorts International, Inc. as their Security Advisor. During his term of office in the Police Force he was the recipient of several training courses at home and abroad. Most significant among these courses were the Detective Training School in Westriding, Yorkshire, the Scottish Police College in Edinburgh, and INTERPOL Headquarters in Paris.

Of his thirty years of service in the Police Force, twenty-five were spent in the Criminal Investigation Department, where he started his career as a Detective Constable in June 1952 and became Assistant Commissioner (CID) in 1970. He can be certainly be proud of his record in the Police Force and of his accomplishments.

He has always been very grateful to the Force, the Government and the people of The Bahamas for providing him with the opportunities to have attained his success in the career of his choice. ◙

Awards, Recognition, Accolades
& Letters of Appreciation
RECEIVED BY PAUL THOMPSON SNR.
IN THE SERVICE OF THE PEOPLE OF THE BAHAMAS

Colonial Police Medal C.P.M. (For Meritorious Service): 1966
Queen's Silver Jubilee Medal : 1977
Queen's Police Medal, Q.P.M.: 1978

LETTER OF COMMENDATION.......*from*
> Sir Ranulph Bacon,
> Chairman of the Commission of Inquiry: April, 1967

"Paul Thompson and Prince have been with us daily over the whole period of our hearings from March 13, and I can only say they have proved invaluable. Without their help, the Commission would often have been at grave disadvantage. During a lot of times, they must have found their work tedious and even irksome. Their attendance involved long hours, but they accepted all our problems and the solving of our difficulties. Sometimes, our personal one in a cheerful spirit that I cannot praise too highly."
(Letter to Commissioner Nigel Morris, 21/4/1967)

"I am extremely pleased, and I am sure all members of the Force will share my feelings to hear of your promotion to the substantive rank of Assistant Commissioner of Police. By your own efforts and loyalty to the service; you have shown by your determination, ability and courage, that you are fully worthy of the increased trust and responsibility that will naturally follow this advancement in your career."
(Extract from a letter dated 14/3/1973 -Commissioner J.H. Hindmarsh)

"My introduction to The Bahamas has been most rewarding. Your professionalism has been a source of great strength to this office and I wish you well on your future with Intertel & Resorts International."
(Extract from a letter dated 22/12/1980 -Arthur F. Nehrbass; Special Agent in charge Federal Bureau of Investigation -F.B.I)

"Mr. Thompson received seventeen (17) commendations for outstanding performance and bravery while on duty. He spent most of his service in the Criminal Investigation Department, and he served with abounding energy. Diligence, and courage has resulted in many serious crimes being successfully investigated and the offenders brought to justice. Throughout his service, his confidential reports were of a high standard"
(Extract from Commissioner Gerald Bartlette memorandum 1980)

*Note: There were eight commendations made directly to me by Judges and Magistrates that were not communicated for Police Files)

Promotions

1/6/1952	Transferred from Uniform Branch ('B' Div.) to the C.I.D
24/12/1954	Lance Corporal
15/8/1955	Corporal
1/9/1956	Lance Sergeant
15/7/1958	Sergeant
24/11/1961	Inspector
1/10/1962	Chief Inspector
28/6/1965	Asst. Superintendent
1/7/1968	Deputy Superintendent
1/1/1970	Superintendent
2/11/1970	Actg. Asst. Commissioner

Overseas Training

1959	Westriding Detective Training School; Yorkshire, England
1970	Scottish Police College Command Course; Tulliallian, Scotland
1975-1976	Courses at INTERPOL, St. Cloud, France and INTERPOL Drug Course in Jamaica.

Many - Training Seminars with the F.B.I, U.S. Customs, U.S. Drug Enforcement Agency and U.S. Secret Service.

FOREWORD
by
MR. PAUL FARQUHARSON

I have known Paul Thompson for a long time, longer indeed than he has known me, for when I first set eyes on him, I was a recruit. He was resident in one of the bungalows near what was then the Police Training School in the back of the building, known at that time as Ranfurly House. He would pass in the morning while we were on the drill square. We would ask, who the gentleman is and the drill instructor, the late Henry Thurston would say, that is Inspector Paul Thompson leaving for duty at C.I.D. He very often had a tennis racket in his hand.

Thompson came to this country from Trinidad & Tobago to give service to our people through policing. His accomplishments were many, always working hard, eventually achieving the rank of Assistant Commissioner. No one who has worked with him walked away without knowledge of policing. Our paths crossed when after 20 years in the Criminal Investigation Department he was transferred to the Uniform Branch as Assistant Commissioner, New Providence District, where I was assigned to clerical duties as a Constable at age 22. His favorite suggestion to young Policemen was that they must use their notebooks and record their actions when reporting an offender or investigating a crime scene. He stressed, that it is a tool that helps when in court, giving evidence.

All of us knew that Paul Thompson's first love was policing and his love for our Royal Bahamas Police Force, is unquestioned. Whenever he had a mic in his hand, he was sure to defend the Police at all cost. I could hear the late Mrs. William, who worked in the office saying; *"Mr. Farquharson, we have to help Mr. Thompson."* His success was attributed to his humble approach to the staff. He got people to work longer and harder, than they would normally do. Three things I learned from him: (1) never send an officer out on assignments, that you are not prepared to do yourself, (2) as the boss, treat your staff good, and show concern for their welfare, and (3) correct and discipline when you must, but be fair and reward good work. With these principles under my belt, I emulated him to the best of my ability and I believed he was influential in my first promotion to corporal at that time.

Paul eventually retired from the Force and went to Resorts International, Paradise Island as their Corporate Director of Security. During the tenure of the late Commissioner Mr. B.K. Bonamy, he returned to the Force as a Training Officer. He was able to share his knowledge and experience with younger officers, and was instrumental in starting the Detective Training School. Knowledge acquired by him in the field of Private Security is huge.

We were all aware of his love for sports; cricket, soccer, tennis, table tennis, all of which he played for Police teams. He is still active in dominoes, loves Trinidad Soca music, and his favorite artiste is the Mighty Sparrow, a personal friend. With his sharp mind Paul continues to make contributions to our society. There are times when you would hear him on the Radio Talk-Shows addressing Police topics, such as minor crime, traffic offences, and corruption. He made suggestions concerning the arrests of immigrants, their court appearances, and the prosecution of the landlords of the Shanty Towns. Very often at Dominoe games the late Jack Bethel, Superintendent of the Police Ret. would say; "You are no longer a policeman. Stay off the radio with your advice. You had your time." We would all laugh. The arguments and sparring between the two was entertaining. As Commissioner of Police, Paul would drop by the office at any time he wished. I used many of his brilliant ideas. His silent footprints are on the Paul Farquharson building. 'Self Help' was his mantra.

He and I wanted to bring all of the Private Security Services together for proper training and swearing-in as District Constables, which would have given the Police many more eyes and ears to render assistance. The plan failed due to the lack of full cooperation from the Security Firms. Paul's contributions to Community Policing efforts were cemented by his support and confidence. We won four international awards as a result of his input. As my inspiration - we agreed, that good policing results are achieved when the service is closer to the citizens. ◼

MR. PAUL FARQUHARSON
Commissioner of Police – Ret./
ROYAL BAHAMAS POLICE FORCE

FOREWORD
by
Keith V. Mason O.D, MBE, LVO, QPM

Paul, I wish to congratulate you on another book on the requirements of 'Good Policing'. Your ability to write this book at this age is remarkable and a testimony to your tenacity, passion, and dedication to your policing career. Your recall and knowledge of police work, especially in the art of investigation and, a police officer's conduct in court, are admirable.

It is my hope that every person engaged in professions related to peacekeeping, security, and court prosecutions would have an opportunity to read and apply the information and nuggets shared in this book.

Having had the privilege and opportunity to work with Paul Thompson as a colleague in Policing, his years of experience in Law Enforcement, Investigations, technical competencies; knowledge and exemplary performance as a Security Technician qualifies him, with the credentials found in the pages of this Resource Publication.

Sincerely,

Keith V. Mason O.D; MBE, LVO; QPM
Deputy Commissioner of Police (Retired)

FOREWORD
by
Sam Springer

He was recruited from his native country, Trinidad & Tobago, for the Bahamian Police Force in March, 1951 and arrived in Nassau, N.P., Bahamas on Easter Monday of 1951. He attended the Police Training School at Police Headquarters on East Street, Nassau, N.P. under the Director of Training; Chief Inspector Carlton Price Wentworth, who was recruited from the Trinidad & Tobago Police Force to head the training school. Thompson took his training seriously and at the end was posted to the Uniform Branch ("B" Division) under the command of the Assistant Superintendent Wenzel Grainger, a distinguished Bahamian, who served in the British West India Regiment and attained the rank of captain.

Thompson took his training and duty assignment assiduously and after six months was posted to the Criminal Investigation Department under the tutelage of the then Sargent Salathiel Thompson (Commissioner of Police) and Sargent Albert Miller (Deputy Commissioner and Sir Albert Miller). He worked earnestly and honestly, thereby increasing his knowledge, experience, team work, leadership, criminal investigation techniques, report writing, evidence presentation, case building and management.

Thompson's educational training was elementary at the Cunupia Government School in Cunupia Village where he was born. In the absence of a college education, he became an avid reader, greedy listener, and a gluttonous absorber of information on intelligent subjects. Upon joining the Trinidad Government Railways as an apprentice, he had to attend the Royal Victoria Institute to further his education.

Thompson's hard-work, discipline, dedication, and successful results in investigations assigned to him, gained a particular advantage over most of his occupational competitors and rewarded him with well-earned mobility up the ladder of promotion. He was also the recipient of local and overseas training, notably the FBI, DEA, US Secret Service, US Customs, the West Riding Detective Training School (UK), the Scottish Police College (Scotland) and INTERPOL (France).

In 1970 he attained the rank of Assistant Commissioner of Police and was transferred to the Uniform Branch after nearly 20 years in CID. During his tenure in the Police Service, he was the founder of the Police Staff Association, the Crime Prevention Unit, and the Traffic Citation INTERPOL-BAHAMAS. Most of the Crime Prevention Unit and INTERPOL were under directions from Commissioner Salathiel Thompson, who also commandeered former Deputy Commissioner Dudley Hanna and Thompson to write a disaster manual, which we did and was approved.

The manual encompassed various forms of disasters, including hurricanes and aircraft accidents. The manual was tested twice with mock air-craft crashes at LPIA. Thompson received a total of 25 commendations and congratulatory letters. Notably among them are; Edgar Hoover and William Webster (Former directors of the FBI), her majesty the Queen, Queen's Police Medal, Colonial Police Medal, certificates from the USA, Drug Enforcement Administration, Judge and Magistrates of the Courts, and Commissioners of Police.

After leaving the Force Thompson was employed in the following positions; Corporate Director of Security, Paradise Island Resort Casino (Resorts International/ Kerzner International), Director of Complex Security at the Nassau Marriott Resort and Crystal Palace Casino, Force Training Officer at the Police College where he assisted the consultant of the Detective Training Manual, General Manager and Consultant Restaurant Service Limited. He is also the founder of Paul Thompson & Associates, a Security and investigation firm.

Thompson was a founding member of the Bahamas Football Association, Executive Board Member of the Bahamas Cricket Association, Executive Member of the Trinidad & Tobago/Bahamian Society and Deputy Commandant of the Police Reserves. Thompson was very active in sports; such as cricket, soccer, table tennis, and track for Police teams. He also took Commonwealth Wanderers Cricket team on overseas tours annually from 1970 through 1990. Thompson has written two books, thus far, namely 'Basic Training for Security Officers' and 'A Policeman's Story', both of which have sold well here and overseas.

This book, entitled 'Policing The Bahamas 1951 and Beyond' Issues, Ideas and Information' contains: information from his training and experience as a Police Officer, extracts from his training materials, court decisions, the Constitution of The Bahamas, the Penal Code and other Laws of the Bahamas. Also, documentation of many recommendations made to Governments and the Royal Bahamas Police Force. The book could be educating to Police Officers and serve as a Research Manual when necessary. It could be his final contribution to his Alma Martyr; The Royal Bahamas Police Force. ◼

Sam Springer, of Barbados.
Now deceased served in the Grenada Police Force, The Trinidad and Tobago Prison Service, The Bahamas Prison Service, The Bahamas Civil Aviation Service and The Royal Bahamas Police Reserves.

The Royal Bahamas Police Force

OATH OF OFFICE

I do swear that I will be faithful and Bear True Allegiance to her Majesty Queen Elizabeth, Her Heirs and Successors according to law.

MISSION STATEMENT

'The force in partnership with all citizens, residents, and visitors exists to provide a quality of law enforcement service with emphasis on the maintenance of law and order; the preservation of peace, the prevention and detection of crime and the enforcement of all laws with which it is charged. We will perform our duties in a manner which reflects fairness, sensitivity and compassion. Yet, we shall be in firm pursuit of all offenders of our laws, so as to ensure a safe and just society where neither crime nor fear of crime adversely affects the quality of life. We shall accomplish these goals with a high degree of professionalism through leadership and teams of individuals who are competent, ethical and dedicated. We shall discharge our duties with courage, integrity, loyalty and being ever mindful of a changing environment with willingness to embrace justified criticism and the need for change.'

The Royal Bahamas Police Force

The R.B.P.F is a law enforcement agency that is respected and admired by its counterparts in the U.K., U.S.A., Canada, and in particular the Caribbean Region. We have received commendations from Directors of the F.B.I. and Drug Enforcement Administration for outstanding Police work and cooperation extended.

Prime Ministers of the U.K. have commended us on the manner in which we handled Royal visits here, the security provided and most importantly the admirable performances of police officers on the military parades, commanded by senior police officers; Seifred Wilson, Keith Mason and Kemuel Hepburn and others.

The Force was given the distinction of being the Royal Bahamas Police Force.

During the decades of the Fifties through the Seventies our police officers were photographed and pictures displayed on billboards in the U.S.A. by the Ministry of Tourism, advertising The Bahamas. Sir Stafford Sands had police officers and entertainers accompany him on trips promoting our Country.

Cay Lobos was invaded by Cuban Nationals, who arrested the Bahamian Official there, took down the Bahamian flag and replaced it with the Cuban flag: The insurgents were crushed by police officers under the command of the Commissioner of Police Lt.Col. E.J.H. Colchester Wemyss. The armed contingent landed and arrested the invaders, freed their prisoner and replaced our flag. A United States Navy destroyer was steaming offshore when our police officers landed. There was no resistance.

Investigations involving criminal complaints in which politicians were suspects, were efficiently investigated and files presented to the Attorney General for advice on prosecutions. We had a politician arrested and charged with sedition. He was tried and acquitted. A politician was charged with election bribery. He was tried and acquitted. There were two M.P.s. charged with fraud and stealing. One was not prosecuted. The other was acquitted and we had a politician charged with an attempt to bribe a Magistrate. He was convicted and imprisoned.

During the decades of the Fifties through the Seventies, Police Officers were assured of complete support from Police Executives when performing their duties, lawfully, politely and firmly.

When the Progressive Liberal Party appeared on the scene and in particular when Sir Lynden Pindling became leader, Police Officers supported the movement, but it did not in any way interfere with their performance as Policemen.

The UBP removed the Police barracks from the city consistency as a result of the Police support for the P.L.P.

A prominent senior politician remarked that the large number of persons arrested for the 'numbers' racket were members of the P.L.P.

He was promptly told that our political support did not influence us in the performance of our duties.

In the decades of the service there were two occasions of so called "scandal". A Commissioner, from the UK was accused of gross misconduct by the U.B.P. Government. Their efforts to remove him through a Commission of Inquiry failed. He however, resigned.

The other incident: another Commissioner purchased land from the Grand Bahama Port Authority in Freeport at a very low price. He resigned when the matter was disclosed and became a political issue.

The Force has grown and there are discipline problems, which must be corrected if the legacy we established over the decades is to be maintained.

Women of
The Royal Bahamas Police Force

Police Women have been included in Police Forces all over the British Commonwealth and the United States for several decades, since the Second World War. In Trinidad & Tobago they enlisted in the Police Service there in the late Forties. In The Bahamas the idea to recruit females to the ranks of the Police Force started with the arrival of Lt. Col. Colchester Wemyss as the new Commissioner of Police. He came from Barbados where women were a part of the Police service. Wemyss was appointed by the Bay Street Boys/UBP Government to develop the Police service. Prior to the recruitment of women, we used a matron and nurses at the hospital to search females, arrested for crime.

Wemyss at an early stage began a transformation of the Police service. The recruitment of Police Women was notable in his plans. In those years we patrolled on foot and bicycles. I frequented a bar on Baillou Hill Road, that was owned and operated by Mr. Spurgeon Bethel, a former Police Officer. We always engaged in conversation about the Police service and topics such as; Police Women, Police Dogs and improved Mobile Patrols.

Bethel became a Member of Parliament for Grant's Town and gave his full support to proposals for improvement to the Police Service. He strongly supported Police Women, Police Dogs and Mobile Patrols. Mr. Roy Solomon, M.P., nicknamed "Commissar" was the Parliamentarian assigned to work with the Commissioner for the development of the Force to make it a more efficient, and modern Public Service Unit.

On the 23rd: November, 1964 six females, namely; Anita Bethel, Theresa Baker, Norma Clarke, Alsada McFall, Hildred McClain, and Esther Stubbs started training under the command of Sergeant Weigh, a female officer from the Metropolitan Police Force in Yorkshire, England. Inspector Cyril Joseph was responsible for recruit training.

Weigh's experience in policing was obvious and it was put to the test when the cruise ship S.S. Yarmouth Castle was on fire in waters outside of New Providence. Weigh brilliantly and effectively commandeered personnel and vehicles at Prince George Dock, where tourists evacuated from the ship were being landed, to be taken to hospital and other locations. Weigh left the Bahamas in 1966.

Police women had become an important part of the Police Service. The pioneer group completed their training in 1965 and were attached to Police Divisions as a group for exposure. On the day of their arrival at the C. I. D. they reported to Detective Sergeant Anthony Fields. He was about to go to the mortuary at the hospital to have a dead body identified and witness an autopsy. Fields took the women with him. The visit and experience did upset them as a few vomited. Fields told them that the experience would prepare them for scenes of violence they will have to visit as Police Officers, where blood wound and dead bodies will be seen.

During their attachment to the C.I.D. they were very useful in areas, such as clerical duties, searching prisoners, interviewing the victims of sexual offences and interrogating juvenile offenders. We were impressed with the performances of these pioneers. I recall Esther Stubbs, Norma Clarke and Theresa Baker being retained on the CID staff. The recruitment and training of females for the Force continued. We got our share of female officers in the C.I.D. I became very familiar with their performance for which they were frequently commended by me.

Allardyce Strachan, who retired as a Superintendent of Police was an important fixture to the C.I.D. Her record keeping diary, crime book, property book and other records, was efficient. She displayed discipline and encouraged others to do likewise. Her interviews and interrogation methods were effective and professional. Many of the younger staff looked to her for guidance and assistance in areas such as report writing and making appropriate entries in records. Sheila Armbrister (deceased) was a quick learner and was a very reliable officer. Her interrogation and investigation skills were excellent. She was able to act for civilian secretaries and performed exceptionally well in all sections of the C.I.D. Armbrister became the first officer to head the newly formed Crime Prevention Office, a unit of the C.I.D. INTERPOL duties were added to her responsibilities in the same office. She eventually relocated to the Police College where she became Commandant. Later she was the OIC of the Mobile Division. Her work in the Force was commendable.

The pioneers and those females that followed, by their performance, discipline, competence and integrity, confirmed the need for females in the

Royal Bahamas Police Force.

Among the other female officers I got to know and appreciate their performances were: Dorothy Davis, a well-educated lady, who was disciplined, and outspoken. I recall her accompanying us to a murder scene where Rev. Wingsinger had killed his wife. She found the murder weapon in a garbage bin in the yard. Being outspoken and her verbal abuse of a very senior officer, who attempted sexual advances, retarded her progress. She had made some powerful foes. Davis reached the rank of Inspector and was an excellent Court Prosecutor. She was the first female officer to attain the rank of Inspector.

Delmeta Turnquest, fingerprint expert spent all her years in the Criminal Records Office. She was trained at the Durham Constabulary in Durham, England and retired as Assistant Superintendent of Police.

Rubie Collie Saunders was our first female motorcyclist. She drew a lot of attention from motorist as she was an attractive woman and looked good in uniform. Collie Saunders became a target for tourists taking photographs of our Police Officers.

Other female officers contributing to the success Police Women were; Denise Tynes, Inspector, recruited and attached to the Police Forensic Science Laboratory, Pauline Ferguson, first female Dog Handler, Killy Heastie, attached to the Air Wing and W.P.C. Douglas ,the first to enter the Police Band.

During my decades in the Police Service I found the Police Women to be very reliable, responsible, competent, and very efficient at recordkeeping and communications. In the United Kingdom we observed, that Police Women used for crowd control and access control were very effective. We were told by our U.K. Police instructors, that Police Women on crowd control duties have the support of the crowd, if anyone became aggressive or abusive. Persons in the crowd would come to the defense of the female officer. In the case of males, the crowd looks forward to confrontation for entertainment when they make an arrest. In the case of access control the female officer stands in the entrance and denies entry. There is no argument or abuse. With the male officer it could be the opposite. Police Women have made massive progress in the ranks of the Force. They are in every gazetted rank and for the first time we have a female Deputy Commissioner of Police, who has served with distinction.

Our Police Women are assets to the Royal Bahamas Police Force. ◧

The Police Staff Association
(A BRIEF HISTORY)

The existence of Police Staff Associations (P.S.A.) and their importance to Police Forces were revealed to me in conversations and discussions when I attended overseas training courses in England and the U.S.A. During these discussions I learned of the conditions of Service, that existed in Police Forces in the U.K. and the U.S.A., Canada and the Caribbean. It became clear to me that almost all of the countries in the British Commonwealth welcomed P.S.As in their Forces. Needless to say the conditions of service enjoyed by officers were a great deal better, than what we had in the Police Service here. It was at this stage that I began to educate our police personnel about the need for a P.S.A., to advance the need for the improvement in our working conditions. I obtained correspondence in the form of literature, published by the P.S.A. in the U.K., Trinidad and the U.S.A. At the time, being in the lower ranks of the service I had to be discreet, but found support from many of the serving officers. The following are some of the conditions, that existed for Police Personnel in the Fifties through the Eighties.

- On duty for 24 hours, off 24 hours, Sleeping arrangements at the Police Station.
- C.I.D. personnel worked 60 hours per week on day shift and 84 hours per week on night shift.
- No compensation when attending the Courts during off duty or vacation time. No 'time back' policy.
- Clothing allowance for detectives was inadequate.
- Bicycles were the transportation and there were no hand radios.
- Wives/Families of Officers, who died in the execution of duty/ other causes, were entitled to one year salary and funeral expenses. There was a limit to the payment, which would be supplemented from the one year salary if more than the amount entitled.
- here was no insurance, group or life.
- The Officers from the U.K. occupied rent free accommodation in

and around the barracks, with all utilities paid for and a car provided for their duty and personal use. In the late sixties when the U.K. Officers contracts were discontinued and local qualified personnel applied to occupied the residences, they had to pay rent and utility charges. They were also required to pay for the car. (The Jamaica Constabulary retained all of the conditions enjoyed by the U.K. Officers for their Officers after their departure)

- Transfers to Family Islands were mandatory. Reasonable excuses such as :
- Children in High School and Wives in lucrative jobs did not matter.
- The wages for Police Officers were very low. These are some of the conditions, that encouraged me to pursue the introduction of the P.S.A. Many officers who supported my efforts, made a complete turnaround after promotion for the gazetted ranks.
- During my movement into the gazetted ranks I became more open with my quest for the P.S.A. I did not get much support from my colleagues in the upper ranks. In fact a serving Commissioner told me, Prime Minister Sir Lynden Pindling was not in favour.

We subsequently had a visit from the Inspector General of Police Forces from the U.K. He was conducting an inspection of our Force and making arrangements for overseas courses for our Police Officers. During his question period I asked about the P.S.A.: He expressed his favour and added, that the associations are good for Police Forces and Governments, as there is communication among the ranks up to the Commissioner, that provides very valuable information relating to conditions of service, morale, training and most importantly advice and recommendations for the improvement of the service. He highly recommended, that our Force consider the formation of a P.S.A. I continued to talk and write about P.S.As. The opposition political party FNM became interested and promised to support the venture. Two years after their election to office I heard nothing. I approached The Hon. C.A. Smith (present Governor General), who was a Minister in the Ingraham Government. He was a personal friend, whom I knew when he was a Customs Officer in Grand Bahama. He promised to assist. A short time thereafter we had legislation introduced and a Constitution drafted0. Commissioner Gearld Bartlett gave his full support to the organisation and provided office accommodation at Central Police Station. The P.S.A was born. - The P.S.A. Act., 6February, 1997. ◙

The Royal Bahamas Police Force's Honourable Citizens of Prominence

The Hon. Sir Lynden Pindling - Father of our Nation, who was Prime Minister for decades was the son of a Policeman of our Force.

Sir Sydney Oakes was one of the first to enlist in the Police Reserves and frequently went on mobile patrol with officers. Commandant of the Police College, a PhD. Police instructors with degrees in education.

POLITICS:

Mr. Spurgeon Bethel (Deceased)- Member of Parliament for the Southern District of New Providence was a policeman in our Force. He served with distinction before retiring and opening a liquor establishment in Grants Town.

Mr. Errington Watkins (Deceased) - Member of Parliament for Abaco, Leader of the URP opposition in parliament, political activist and Party Chairman. He served as a police motorcyclist for decades with distinction.

The Hon: Marvin Dames - Minister of National Security, joined the Force at the Inspectorate level and progressed to the rank of Deputy Commissioner of Police.

Senator Keith Bell - Served with distinction before entering politics. He introduced and supervised the Statistics Unit of the Force, with a very modern computerised system, that is very useful to the Force in its allocation of resources etc.

The Hon: Frankie Campbell - Minister of Social Services and Urban Development was a policeman in our Force.

Mr. Audley Kemp - Businessman and Liquor merchant.

Sir Albert Miller. - Former Deputy Commissioner of Police served with distinction before joining the Grand Bahama Port Authority

Messrs Freddie Munnings of the famous Cat & Fiddle Night Club.

Mr. Henry Wemyss - Proprietor & C.E.O. of Wemco Security & Collections Ltd., the largest security firm in the Country.He served on the

Force and became the first Caribbean Officer to emerge first in final exams at Hendon Police College in the U.K. He remains a strong supporter of the Force.

A SENIOR MAGISTRATE AND A GROUP OF ATTORNEYS ARE ON THE LIST.

THE CLERGY -
Apostle Leon Wallace, Bishops Hulan Hanna, Smith and Bodie. Frs. Turnquest, Goodridge and Burrows.

THE TAKE OVER (SUPER TEAM OF DETECTIVES)

The Team I inherited, that continued the progressive work and exceptional performance of the C. I. D.,

McDonald Chase - aka 'Porog'. - He was rated by the F.B.I. as being one of the leading fingerprint experts in the region. He was very thorough at crime scenes; also a good photographer.

Supt. Ret. Basil Dean - aka 'Shaft' - one of a youthful group assigned to C.I.D., a quick leaner, courageous, hardworking, patient and thorough. He developed a cadre of informants and got good results.

ACP (Ret) Douglas Hanna - aka 'Dougie' - one of the youths sent to C.I.D. An East Street resident, with good contacts, that helped him to develop as a detective. Courageous, hardworking, reliable and sociable. He always got good results in his investigations.

ACP Ret. Garth Johnson - Displayed leadership qualities, ourageous, and hardworking. He got excellent results. He was promoted to Inspector and posted to the uniform branch. He was very often recalled to C.I.D. to lead major investigations. He was commended for his success in the serial killings called, 'the hacker murders'.

Supt. Ret. Ormond Briggs. - Photographic memory, excellent teacher. Directed detectives and supervised their performance. He was an excellent investigator and demanded efficiency from his subordinates. Great interrogation skills. Excellent knowledge of the criminal law and police procedures.

ACT Ret. Milan Gittens. - Very thorough. A disciplinarian. Good investigator, with great interrogation skills.

Supt. Ret. Anthony Fields - aka "Dog". First Commandant, Police College. Courageous, hardworking, great leader, with uncanny instincts, a very suspicious mind, a good teacher, excellent interrogation skills, a great sense of humour, that endeared his colleagues to him. He produced excellent results as an Investigator, teacher and leader.

Supt. Ret. Louis Hemmings - aka 'Takashimar' - One of the best Investigators on staff. He got good results and was commended many times. He was a search specialist. It was said; 'If Hemmings doesn't find it, it is not there'. He developed great techniques searching buildings for evidence. He found Rolex watches in a rice container, jewellery in a flour container, a gun taped to the cover of a toilet tank, drugs taped inside the cover of a cesspit tank and a suspect hiding in the ceiling.

Supt. Ret. Allardyce Strachan - She did a magnificent job maintaining files and records. In addition, her successes in investigating sexual offences was well recognized. Her leadership qualities and discipline kept the young detectives in line.

Supt: Ret. Sheila Armbrister - aka 'Auntie Sheila' - Exceptional in clerical duties, quick learner, reliable and hardworking. She was put in charge of our first Crime Prevention Office. She conducted Crime Prevention lectures in public places. She was eventually assigned to our first INTERPOL Office. Commandant of the Police College and Officer in charge of the Mobile Division were assignments held by her.

Supt: Ret. Allan Gibson - aka 'Gipple' - Excellent investigator. Good leadership skills, courageous, hardworking and reliable, organised raids to arrest wanted criminals, .

Supt. Ret. Arthur Yearwood - He was very conversant with the laws of the Bahamas. He studied Law and was eventually called to the bar. He excelled as our fraud investigator.

Supt. Ret. Garbo Saunders - aka '121' - An East Street resident, who had several disciplinary convictions for gambling, was sent to C.I.D. after being rejected by other units. He became an asset. Garbo was able to frequent bars on East Street and Grants Town and be accepted by customers as one of them. He was able to gather intelligence from conversations there about crime and develop informants among the associates there. We sometimes provided him with cash from the C.I.D. to treat his associates in the bars. Garbo was able to serve summonses, on persons we had difficulty locating, and locate persons wanted for crime. He went out daily on bicycle, visiting bars and very often would return with wanted suspects. Promotion to Detective Sargeant was swift. After retirement he joined Bahamasair.

OTHERS ON THE TEAM, WHO MADE VITAL CONTRIBUTIONS FOR AN EFFICIENT AND EFFECTIVE C.I.D.:

Lincoln Hercules, Joe Clarke, Egbert Eastmond and ***Ronald Coleby*** of Criminal Records Office.

Hercules was an exceptional investigator, who was used often in difficult cases with success.

Messrs: Turnquest (now Fr. Turnquest of the Anglican Church), Ferguson and Pennerman were also part of the team and made valuable contributions.

The drug Enforcement Unit was formed as a part of the C.I.D. It was headed by ***Mr. Coutney Strachan*** and included ***Wilton Strachan*** and ***Bernard K. Bonaby.*** The Unit was very effective in the enforcement of drug related offences. Both Strachans retired as ACPs.

Bernard K. Bonaby became Commissioner of Police.

Wilton Strachan headed the Unit for several years after Courtney Strachan moved to Special Branch. ◼

Outstanding Bahamians
PRODUCTS OF THE ROYAL BAHAMAS POLICE FORCE

Prime Minister Sir Lynden Pindling was the son of an officer of the Royal Bahamas Police Force.

Prime Minister the Most Hon: Hubert Minniss is the son of an officer of the Royal Bahamas Police Force.

RELIGION

Bishop Delton Fernander- President of the Bahamas Christian Council
Jumper Baptist Church, East St. Nassau. N.P.,
Bishop Hulan Hanna - Deputy Commissioner, Ret.- *Baptist Faith.*
Bishop Arnold Josey - Baptist Faith
Apostle Wallace - Baptist Faith
Bishop John Rolle - Baptist Faith
 Bishop Leon Smith - Baptist Faith
Bishop Frederick Newton - Baptist Faith
The Reverend Fr. Rodney Burrows - Anglican Faith
The Reverend Fr. Roland Pierre -Baptist Faith, Trinidad & Tobago
Stephen Turnquest - Anglican Faith.
Fr. Cyril Paul - Roman Catholic Church. (USA)

THE CONSULAR CORP

Mr. Carlton Jones∗   - Counsel of Barbados
Mr. Patrick Hanlan∗∗   - Counsel for Jamaica
Mr. Paul Farquharson‡ - Bahamas High Commissioner to U.K.
Mr. Ellison Greenslade‡ - Bahamas High Commissioner to U.K.

∗Jones was a traffic officer (motorcyclist),
∗∗Hanlan served as a detective in the Crime Investigation Department.
‡Farquharson and Greenslade were retired Commissioners of Police.

POLITICIANS (All outstanding former Police Officers)

Mr. Spurgeon Bethel — M.P. Member of Parliament, Grants Town
Mr. Errington Watkins — M.P. Abaco - Former leader of the UBP
The Hon. Marvin Dames — Former Minister of National Security, M.P.
Deputy Commissioner of Police, Retired
The Hon. Frankie Campbell - M.P., Former Minister of Social Services
The Hon. Keith Bell - M.P., Minister of Labour & Immigration

PRIVATE ENTERPRISES

Sir Albert Miller, former Deputy Commissioner of Police joined the Grand Bahama Port Authority and eventually became its President and CEO. He owned and operated several businesses in Freeport, Grand Bahama.

Mr. Henry Wemyss, President & CEO of WEMCO Security and Collections Ltd., the largest such firm in the Bahamas,

Messr. Grafron Ifill, Anthony Fields, Stephen Seymour, Carl Glinton and a few others were involved in the Security Business, providing security officers and conducting private investigations.
Mr. H.L. Rolle was involved in Service Stations, Garages and a Retail Business.

Many of the former police officers are engaged and or employed as Security Directors by Casino Resorts and Hotels. The, present, Vice President of Security at the Atlantis Resorts & Casino was the former Assistant Commissioner, (CID) Mr. Douglas Hanna. He replaced the late Mr. Basil Dean.

Paul Thompson & Associates is a security and investigations provider, operated by retired Assistant Commissioner, Paul Thompson and former associates.

Constable No.216 Charles Ashley Edwards & Police Dog 'Charley'

LEGENDS, THAT MUST NOT BE FORGOTTEN

Charles Edwards aka "Charlie" entered the Royal Bahama Police Force as a cadet in 1969. He was just a boy weighing less than 100 pounds, but his ambition was to be a Policeman. After a period of eighteen months he was accepted, in a recruit squad for training. He completed training, placing second in his class. He was posted at Southern Police Station. The Airport Police Station and Cable Beach Police Station. After a period of about nine months he was posted to Abaco. While in Abaco he applied for motorcycle training and was sent to Nassau to be trained. He returned to Abaco and engaged in motorcycle patrols. He reported a high profile public servant in Abaco for a traffic violation and was posted to the traffic Division in New Providence.

Apart from his work as a traffic officer, he showed interest in crime and was very observant. I first got to know him as the arresting officer in a rape case in western New Providence. A woman was raped by three men. She called the Police immediately after they left. Police Control, broadcast the information. Edwards, on his motorcycle saw the three men running from the scene. He gave chase and was able to arrest two of the men. W hen I saw him at the C.I.D. office I asked him if he was crazy chasing three criminal by himself, armed only with his baton.

He was commended. While in the Traffic Division he applied to the Canine Section, which was a small unit then. He was accepted and sent for training in England.in March 1975 together with Constables, Samuel Roberts and Raymond Murphy. They returned to New Providence in June, 1975 with three German Shephard Dogs. Edward's Dog was name "Charley". Edwards was a dog lover and the upkeep of a dog was nothing new to him. He was a large, heavy beautiful dog, that came to The Bahamas well trained and attached to his handler Charles Edwards.

In the C.I.D. we soon realised, that we had an efficient and effective canine team. They were trained in operations involving assailants, armed or thought to be armed. We were proven right by "Charlie & Charley".

I recall several push snatchings on East Bay Street. The victims were visitors walking to and from Paradise Island from their yachts and the Pilot House Hotel. Our efforts to catch these fleet footed criminal failed. We posted Edwards and Charley in hiding in the area. In the first two nights there were four young men arrested and some property recovered. The attacks on visitors suddenly stopped. There was an incident when Drug Enforcement Unit personnel arrested a driver and vehicle on Peter Street for possession of a large amount of ganja. A group of young men surrounded the vehicle obstructing the officers and making threats. The officer called for assistance. I arrived on the scene at the same time as Edwards and Charley. When Charley jumped out of the vehicle the group disappeared. We were able to make arrest of those who fell in holes in a yard and two whose necks got cut by clothes lines.

In another incident, there was an armoured car robbery. We made some quick moves and got information leading to a white young Bahamian. We got to him early and recovered some of the money and a revolver. He told us, who the second man was in the robbery. This man we knew to be a dangerous criminal, who had served time, both here and in the United States. He was a deportee.

It took us a few days, but we got his address. We put together a team, that included Officers, Fields, Briggs, Garth Johnson, Allan Gibson and Douglas Hanna. Edwards and Charley accompanied us to the residence, arriving there at 4:00 a.m. We sneaked up and covered the doors and windows. We banged the door open, the culprit arose with a gun in his hand. Charley rushed in; when he saw the dog moving towards him at such a pace and growling, he dropped the gun and hollered "get this dog off me". Charley had the wrist of the hand that held the gun between his teeth. He held the man there until Edwards gave the command to release.

The C.I.D. was provided with a very large Station Wagon. We hardly used it during the daylight as parking was always difficult. We formed a group in the C.I.D., that reported at 3:00 a.m. for the purpose of arresting wanted criminals. I drove, with two detectives in front, Edwards and Charley in the back. Officers in the day would compile information with the addresses of wanted persons and those with outstanding warrants.

We would make the arrests in the early morning hours. We carried revolvers and a shotgun. It was the era of the home-made and sawed-off shotguns. The criminals gave the vehicle the name War Wagon. I recall an occasion when Inspector Fletcher Johnson was jumped on, when the criminal went out the back door, Johnson's leg was broken. A short time later, we heard the call for help from a nearby cemetery. Charley had chased the man, and had him on the ground. terrified.

I would say, that during the reign of that canine team, there were about seven hundred arrest for various crimes. The dog saved Edwards' life on two occasions, that I recall.

We were tracking Victor Storr in bushes after a robbery when he shot at Police. Edwards and Charley were closest. Charley was released and with speed he ran at Storr. His weight knocked him to the ground down and we did the rest. On another occasion when the Penny Savings Bank was robbed, Edwards encountered the robber in the Regency Park. The man pointed the gun at him. Charley jumped on the man. The weight of the dog knocked the man down. Whenever Charley knocked anyone down he would grab a hand and hold it between his teeth and howl for the handler.

Edwards left the Force in 1981 and joined me at Resorts International, Paradise Island. I had recommended dogs for patrols on the island. We were having some night robberies and on a few occasions personnel moving money between hotels were robbed. We got dogs from the U.S. and Edwards put together a canine team with handlers Curtis, Bowe, Donna Saunders and others, Escorts and the canine patrols were in operation. The street robberies ceased.

Charley's untimely death could have been avoided. The dog became so attached to Edwards, that he would not work with anyone else after Edwards resigned. The dog even refused to eat. Edwards had to visit and feed him. Edwards asked the Force to sell him Charley. I am told, that he was given to someone on the Eastern Road and died The of starvation.

Edwards continued his work with dogs and attracted many persons on Paradise Island by his ability to train dogs. It is my opinion, that Charles Edwards is the best Dog Trainer in this region.

The Royal Bahamas Police Force should reward Charlie and Charley with a photograph of them somewhere in a suitable location. They deserve to be remembered. ◙

Police In Sports

The Police Sports Club was formed shortly after our arrival as recruits. Gerald Bartlette, Inspector Wentworth Training Instructor, Sargent Stanley Blair and Sargent Roy Armbrister were instrumental in getting the club started with a Police Cricket team. Among the recruits from Trinidad were a number of good cricketers, namely; Joseph Darcuiel, Gussie Smith, Cyril Paul, Percy Campbell, McDonal Chase, Curil Joseph, Joe Forbes, and Paul Thompson. There were officers here from Guyana, who were good players in per of Reginald Dean-Dumont and Seifred Wilson and Jamaican Harold Lecky. Roy Armbrister was appointed to lead the Police Cricket team. He became my sports mentor. At the time Armbrister was light heavyweight boxing champion O.G. The Bahamas, a top sprinter and swimmer, who competed with distinction in an annual swim meet from Prince George Dock to Fort Montagu. He eventually represented The Bahamas in both cricket and soccer. He is in the Ministry of Sports Hall of Fame.

In our first yean 1951 the Police cricket team won the Bahamas Cricket Association title with a perfect record of no losses. In 1952 we won again, with one loss and in 1953 we had another perfect record. Armbrister was magnificent as a leader and his contribution as a player was massive; batting, bowling and fielding. It was our opinion, that if this man had the opportunity to play in the West Indies he would have made the regional team. Jamaicans, who saw him play here and in Jamaica concurred. WE engaged in friendly soccer with teams from British ships arriving here and with the Sea Scouts F.C. The Bahamas Football Association was founded we played soccer with good results, winning the championships of two occasions in the 'fifties. The Police Club participated in table tennis at the YMCA and latter championship tournaments at the Catholic Priory. There were annual tournaments for team, which we dominated. The singles tournament was won by Paul Thompson for five years until the return of Dr. Francis Adderley, who dethroned Thompson.

The Police Sports Club also participated inTrack & Field, with limited success. Constable Cyril Paul was our greatest achiever having won the sprint events on a number of occasions. Paul Thompson was also a participant second in the sprints and 400 yards at one of the annual sports meets. During the short period of our arrival here as recruits and later policemen we socialized and made many friends. I am sure, that in those early year sports involvement helped to mend gaps and improve public relations. The Police Cricket team is the only team in any sports in The Bahamas that competed for seventy consecutive years, uninterrupted and is the most winning team in cricket. ◙

From The Arrest To The Trial

This chapter provides information and material for the continuing education of Police Officers, in particular those involved in criminal investigation. Contents are from my training in the Royal Bahamas Police Force, The Westriding Detective Training School, The Scottish Police College, INTERPOL and several U.S. Law Enforcement Agencies including; the FBI, DEA, US Customs & US Secret Service. Also, my 25 years of experience as a CID Officer.

The Bahamas is a democratic society where Law Enforcement has the awesome responsibility of assuring that citizens and residents have their freedom to live, remain free, pursue happiness and to have due process of law.

Law Enforcement has also been charged with the society-freedom from crime and violence as well as abuses of power by law enforcement officers who are trained and expected to act and fulfill their responsibilities, but always within the constraints of the law.

The Constitution of The Bahamas (Article 19)

Protection of the Fundamental Rights and Freedoms of the individual states that, no person shall be deprived of his/her personal liberty unless in those cases stated in the Constitution. For the purpose of this chapter paragraph (d), this states: *"Upon reasonable suspicion of him/her having committed or about to commit a criminal offence."*

Arrest is the most important power Police officers possess. In a criminal sense, it is the taking and restraining of a person from liberty by apprehension or taking into custody to answer according to law, some specified or alleged offence. In brief, it is to restrain a person from liberty. The arrest should be carried out as quietly as possible. The approach and method depend on: the crime, the environment, circumstances, and most importantly, the conduct and demeanor of the person to be arrested.

The Officer must identify himself/herself and it is mandatory that persons be informed of the reason for their arrest. All necessary force may be used to affect an arrest. Handcuffs may be used at the discretion of the arresting officer, who is responsible for securing the prisoner. Officers must read and digest the contents of those sections of the laws of the Bahamas, relating to 'Justifiable Force and the use of Deadly Force.' In all instances where an arrest is resisted and officers are assaulted, reports submitted must include such conduct and injuries sustained by the officer and the prisoner. It is advisable that the appropriate charges of assault and resisting be laid, in particular, when the person arrested is injured. A complaint of Police brutality by the prisoner is likely to fail.

The Search

The person arrested must be immediately searched by the arresting officer to; (a) seize anything of evidential value and (b) locate anything that could be used to cause personal injury or death to an arresting officer.

On a training course in the U.K., students were told of the murder of a Detective Sergeant from Scotland Yard. He had arrested a German national, who was wanted for several crimes in England. The arrest was at a train station. He handcuffed the prisoner in front and went into a phone booth to call for transportation. The prisoner, who was not searched, took a gun from his waist and shot the officer dead in the telephone booth. This and other important cases are used in Police Schools to emphasize the importance of the immediate search of persons arrested and the securing of prisoners.

In Nassau, two Police Officers responded to information that a food store on East Street South was being broken into. It was during the hours of the early morning. This particular store had been the target of criminals several times before. The officers arrived on the scene and saw a man at the store's back door. He was so occupied trying to pry the door open, that he did not see the officers approaching. After he was arrested, he was immediately identified as a serving Police Officer. Apparently, the fact that he was a colleague caused them to omit the procedure of searching and securing the prisoner. The prisoner was placed by himself in the back seat of the Police car. Before they could leave, he shot the driver dead and injured the officer in the passenger seat. The latter was able to draw his revolver and shot the prisoner dead. The failure to promptly secure the suspect resulted in two deaths.

At Police Station.

Recordings are made by the by the Station Officer, e.g. name, address, antecedents, and a more diligent search is conducted. Prisoner's property should be appropriately checked, recorded, and secured. The prisoner must sign the book confirming the property listed. The Station Officer notes the physical condition of the prisoner and records the statements made by him/her. This is done each time a prisoner is moved from the cell and returned. It is a form of protection against the complaint of Police Brutality in later days, notably in a Court of Law.

Interrogation & Search of Premises.

At this stage of an investigation a decision has to be made on how to proceed with the interrogation of the suspect, or the search of all premises occupied by him/her. Experience has taught me that it is wise to execute search warrants as quickly as possible after an arrest. The administrative process in acquiring the search warrant must be discreet. Should the investigating officer be satisfied, that the suspect is about to confess to the crime, the taking of the suspect's statement must take precedence. A search team, that is familiar with the crime and the evidence being sought, can proceed to execute the search warrant in the absence of the suspect, provided, that there is available, a responsible adult who resides at the premises.

During the search, delays in conducting such searches have been known to contribute to the removal of evidence from the premises. Search teams from the old CID was so efficient, that a saying was coined - *"If they didn't find it, it is not there."*

It is said, that during a search the suspect's demeanor must be constantly observed as he/she becomes nervous when a search is ongoing in the area where evidence can be found. Such observations led us to a large quantity of jewelry found in a container of rice, a quantity of stolen watches were found in a container of flour, and a murder weapon found in the garbage bin. OBSERVE the suspect during the search.

Officers must be aware, that the law provides for the Commissioner of Police to authorize a search, without a search warrant, under certain circumstances and conditions. Under the Firearms Act the Commissioner of Police can authorize a search for firearms and ammunition without a search warrant.

In conducting interrogations of a suspect, the investigator must be familiar with the administration and implementation of the Judges' Rules. Officers must be able to recite and write the cautions. Their knowledge will be tested in the Courts when they have to present accused written or verbal statements. We carried a copy of the rules and cautions in our pocket notebooks.

Confessions by accused persons could be omitted from evidence by Judges and Magistrates if the Judges' Rules are not properly administered.

Officers involved in the interrogation of a suspect must have certain skills, which would have been acquired through experience and practice.

For example:

Observe changes in the mood/demeanor of the suspect, in particular when certain questions are being asked and should pursue this line of questioning. Sweating in a cool atmosphere, stuttering or taking long to respond to questions, refusal to look at photographs connected with the crime, becoming abusive, experiencing difficulty providing an alibi, and being pleasant or hinting to tell the truth. In the case of multiple suspects being interrogated it works to have an officer hint to an interrogator in another room that can hear the suspect confessing.

This has been used with success in many interrogations. The criminal believing that his partner is confessing to the crime will sometimes decide to confess as well. Confessions must be recorded immediately and must be in accordance with the Judge's rules. All pages must be signed and corrections initialed. The statement must be recorded in the exact language of the suspect. Any phrase or word used, that is not known to the officer, the latter will ask the suspect for the meaning and write it in brackets following the actual phrase or word.
The statement must be read over either by the SUSPECT OR THE OFFICER AND MUST BE WITNESSED. In case of juveniles, a parent or guardian must be present during the interview and statement taking.

Police Notebooks & Report Writing.

Investigating officers must maintain the Police Notebook by recording the time of arrival, names of officers on the team, and the persons found on the scene that may be able to provide information about a crime. Conditions at the scene must be described in the notebook and when necessary photographed. Names of persons providing information about the crime are to be recorded with addresses and telephone numbers. Exhibits found at the scene must be noted and collected. The Police Notebook is intended to be the memory of the Police Officer. Officers are expected to record, in brief, all of their activities, in particular, as it relates to crime and arrest. Also include Identification Parades, Search Warrants, and items found.

The Policeman's notebook is the most important tool he carries. In Court, three or four years after an arrest, when giving evidence he can be authorized to read notes from his notebook, provided the notes were made at the time or shortly after. The report written and submitted is likely to be very accurate, when written from the notes made in the notebook. It is certainly an essential tool and is used by police personnel worldwide.

Herewith are embarrassing moments for officers neglecting to use their notebooks:
- Two officers in the same car arrive at a crime scene. In court, their arrival times differ by a half-hour.
- Two detectives search a premise and find stolen items but, the location differs for where the particular items were found.
- Two officers search a car and find a gun. A man was arrested. In court, they could not identify the gun when shown to them by the prosecutor.

Criminal Charges and Court Dockets.

Officers must learn to prepare dockets by writing criminal charges as they will have to do so when posted on Family Islands.

Security of Case File & Exhibits

In felony cases it is advisable that a copy of the case file be retained by the officer in charge, along with the original of any written confessions. Copies of the latter are to be sent to the prosecutors. Court exhibits are to be properly listed on the case file, delivered to and signed for, by the prosecutor or exhibits officer.

The Constitution of The Bahamas provides for attorneys to visit and counsel persons in custody for crimes. However, there is a provision that authorizes an investigating officer to decline the attorney's request if meeting with the accused would hamper the process of the investigation. (Judge's Rules)

Example:

An officer is about to execute a search warrant on the accused premises. If the accused meets with his attorney, information could be leaked to persons at the premises to be searched. If the accused is about to take me to a location where a kidnapped child, stolen property, a murder weapon, or guns and drugs are, seeing his attorney will very likely prompt him to change his mind. ◉

Judges Rules Restated

All Police Officers, in particular those involved in investigations must be familar with these rules and their administrative procedures. Knowing the rules could be an asset when testifying in court.

INTRODUCTION

The Rules do not affect the Principles

(a) that citizens have a duty to help a police officer to discover and appre-
hend offenders;
(b) that police officers, otherwise than by arrest cannot compel any person against his will to come to or remain in any police station;
(c) that every person at any stage of an investigation should be able to
communicate and consult privately with a solicitor. This is so even if
he is in custody, provided that in such a case no unreasonable delay or
hinderance is caused to the processes of investigation or the administration of justice by his doing so;
(d) that when a police officer, who is making enquiries of any person
about an offence, has enough evidence to prefer a charge against that
person for the offence, he should without delay cause that person to be
charged or informed that he may be prosecuted for the offence;
(e) that is a fundamental of the admissibility in evidence against any person, equally of any oral answer given by that person to a question put
by a police officer and of any statement made by that person to a question put by a police officer and of any statement made by that person,
that it shall have been voluntary, in the sense that has not been obtained from him by fear of prejudice or hope of advantage, exercised
or held 0ut by a person in authority, or by oppression. the principal
set out in paragraph (e) above is overiding and applicable in all cases,

within that principle the following Rules are put forward as a guide to Police officers conducting investigations. Noncomformity with these Rules might render answers and statements liable to be excluded from evidence in subsequent criminal proceedings.

ADVICE TO POLICE OFFICERS, IN PARTICULAR DETECTIVES INVESTIGATING SERIOUS CRIMES.

It is mandatory, that Officers read and study the Administration of the 'Judges Rules' .It is vital that the Police Officers investigating crime, conduct themselves in accordance with these Rules. ◼

Post Retirement Recommendations to Government and The Royal Bahamas Police Force

1981

Presentations to P.M. Sir Lynden Pindling after meeting with Ret. ACPs Courtney Strachan, Ret. ACP Lawrence Major, & Ret. ACP. Paul Thompson Sr.

Should a poll be taken among the residents of New Providence, it will reveal that crime is considered to be the worst problem in our nation's communities. This would be in sharp contrast to any similar poll taken prior to 1980, when crime was given secondary consideration among other items on the list of social problems. It was there, but many of us did not discern it and there were those of us who did not wish to admit its presence. We all hoped that in time the problem would disappear, however lawlessness had reached unprecedented heights over the past three years and the volume of serious crimes, in particular those crimes involving firearms and other deadly weapons has risen awesomely. It is surprising, but mostly encouraging to police officers and those of us involved in security. To observe the public's awareness of the present trend and seeing that it is being given low priority convinces me that the public is troubled and alarmed by it.

There is every reason to be alarmed, when factual reports from the police disclosed that most of the crimes of violence are being perpetrated by our teenagers and other young people. An alarmed public such as ours, could well be a blessing in disguise, for it is in their attitude that crime will find the environment to flourish when we are unconcerned with lawlessness on our doorsteps. When we patronize illegal activities, condone wrong doing, consciously break the law ourselves, fail to come forward and testify concerning witnesses and give little or no support to our Law Enforcement Agencies. Crime will subside, when we express our outrage and report its occurrence promptly, co-operate fully in its investigation and prosecution, and give our unflinching support to the police and other Law Enforcement Agencies. Our demands for more realistic punishment and our leadership by example at being law abiding citizens must be a continuing exercise. We must all become involved in correcting the inequities that may exist in our communities.

Our tasks, Police and Public, are to enforce the law in a constitutional manner. We can accomplish this through dedication, co-operation and professionalism. We can be tough and effective within the law.

Over the past two decades, budget and manpower limitations have forced the Royal Bahamas Police Force to function with less than it needs. Its efforts to stem the tide in the increasing wave of crime have been frustrated. Combating increasing crime with static or decreasing resources is a challenge, which required Police Officers to work harder. Our Police Force is divided into divisions, among which particular responsibilities are shared.

Following are examples of the divisions and their responsibilities:

- Headquarters Administration, Finance, Personnel, etc.
- Radio & Transport Mobile Patrols, including the 919 system
- District HQ Licensing, Administration of Uniform Police in New Providence and the Family Islands except Grand Bahama
- Traffic Division, traffic control and enforcement of uniform of traffic laws.
- Internal Security Division, security of official residences and certain offices training and administration of the strike force.
- Security & Intelligence
- Branch - V.I.P. Security, and other security & intelligence functions.
- Training College, training and recruiting
- CID Investigation of CDU

As expressed earlier, crime is the worst problem facing the country today. I have therefore decided to comment on the role of the CID in dealing with the subject; "The Enforcement of Law and Order" over the past decade, the CID has not been given the priority it deserves, and has not been provided with the resources to fight rising crime. In the broadest terms, personnel in these sections are limited and have been this way for several years. The shortage of manpower has resulted in:

- Detectives having to work twelve hours per day or night

- The lack of follow-up investigation in criminal complaints
- Inefficient and shoddy preparation of court cases
- Lower percentage of crime detection
- Lower percentage of recovery of stolen property
- The inability to institute certain investigation i.e. surveillance etc.
- Less through examination of crime scenes by fingerprint personnel
- Lower percentage of detection by fingerprint
- An unusually high case load per detective
- Public criticism of the department (unaware of its problems)

The lack of sufficient equipment, in particular, transportation has contributed even more to the department woes. There is such a shortage of vehicles that detectives have to await the return of vehicles before proceeding on assignments. This shortage has also contributed to some of the deficiencies mentioned earlier.

How can the finger print officer be expected to get around to the various scenes of crimes without a vehicle assigned to his section? With more equipment, more fingerprint officers can be sent out to crime scenes. Fingerprints are still the most important clue to search for at a crime scene. Proper accommodation is lacking, and overseas training for detectives and fingerprint officers have decreased. In conclusion, I wish to suggest to you some possible solutions to the problems of the C.I.D.

The suggestions have been made before to previous Police administrators, but there has been no effort made to implement any of them. In fact, I do not think that the suggestions received any reasonable consideration or discussion by the administrators. The conditions remain the same and the suggestion are still the same. The challenge of decreasing resources requires the Police not only to work harder, but to work smarter to reach its goal providing a safe and comparatively crime free environment for the public it serves. The police can more effectively meet this challenge by sharing experiences, by sharing information about what works and what does not. Information is available from other Police Forces, from Police management, in effectively dealing with reduced or inadequate budgets.

For example:

Motorcycle Response for Congested Areas

Response time to priority calls in congested areas can be enhanced by assigning motorcycles units to respond to non-traffic as well as traffic calls for service in congested areas during the peak traffic hours. Due to their maneuverability in heavy traffic, they can respond faster than radio cars. e.g. a bank robbery on Bay Street during peak traffic hours.

Increased use of search dogs

More Police Dogs trained to search for narcotic drugs would decrease the time spent searching by officers.

On call Court System

Significant Officer time is spent in court waiting for cases to be heard. Many Police Forces have arrangements with the courts to have officers placed on call. This provided for more officers to be in field and cut the time wasted around the courts waiting to be called.

Civilian Personnel

Most Police Departments in the UK and USA are expanding the replacement of trained Police personnel with civilians, particularly in the areas of: records, courts, communications, secretaries, clerks, mechanics, vehicle maintenance, canteens, payroll, stores and supplies etc. Personnel trained to perform these auxiliary and support functions require less salary and could provide savings in the Police budget, which could be used to provide more equipment. Some Forces are even using Manpower Supplements, such as; citizen volunteers, student workers and scouts to assist in some of the non-police jobs.

Leasing and Buying Equipment

Some Police Departments are finding that funds are no longer available for the outright purchase of vehicles. They have resorted to leasing which is often a way of avoiding the initial outlay and a means of survival. Leasing should be considered, if it could be from a Manufacturer or big dealer.

Finally, I would like to ask that the Public be aware of its right to question those who are responsible to provide the basic manpower and equipment resources for the Police, to carry out its tasks. The public also has a right to lobby for changes in administrative techniques, which could provide for better policing in their communities. The public must also realize that the Enforcement of Law and Order is not only a Police responsibility, but of all of us who reside in this beautiful country. ◙

Resorts International (Bahamas) Ltd.

May 5, 1983

The Rt. Hon. Sir Lynden O. Pindling
Prime Minister
Commonwealth of the Bahamas
Churchill Bldg.
Nassau, Bahamas

Dear Mr. Prime Minister:

Enclosed herewith is a copy of the F.B.I. Law Enforcement Bulletin for April, 1983. You may find the article on Police Management entitled "Facing Increasing Crime with Decreasing Resources" to be very interesting and informative.

You will note that I have marked the paragraph entitled Civilian Personnel. It supports my recommendations of "Civilianization" which I have been advocating since the early seventies after my Police Management training course at the Scottish Police College and the University of Strathclyde in Scotland.

During the seventies my efforts to have our Force consider employing civilians to perform certain tasks were frustrated by those persons who were not receptive to modern ideas.

If one would take a close look at the number of trained police personnel deployed in non-Police tasks, I submit: a) that the shortage of manpower can be considerably reduced should civilians be employed to replace these Police Officers and b) that such a move would help the Police budget and create employment for capable young people in clerical positions on the Force.

Here are some areas in the Force where civilian personnel would operate efficiently and more economically:

> Paymasters Office
> Police Certificates (Receptionist)
> Police Canteens
> Police Stores
> Switchboard Operators
> Vehicle Maintenance Crews
> Clerks and Copy Typists
> Prosecutors Clerk

Our Pay Office is crowded with trained police personnel. The patrol cars are being cleaned by trained Police Officers. Youngsters can be hired at half the salary of a Police Officer doing this job.

For many years I have been recommending that civilian mechanics be hired for the Police Garage. I did not include the garage in the above list as I expect good mechanics to be costly but in the end the cost would be justified by the efficient service.

I implore you to give some consideration to the recommendation of employing civilians for non-Police tasks.

Should you feel, Sir, the need for further consultation with me I should be only too pleased to make myself available at your convenience.

I remain,

Yours most respectfully,

Paul W. Thompson

PWT/gc

PRIME MINISTER'S OFFICE
P O Box N7147
Nassau, Bahamas

9 May, 1983

Dear Mr. Thompson:

Thank you so much for your letter of the 5th instant and enclosed magazine.

There seems to be merit in your suggestions and I'm passing them on to the Minister.

Yours sincerely,

PRIME MINISTER

Mr. Paul R. Thompson,
Resorts International (Bahamas) Ltd.,
P. O. Box N-4777,
Nassau, The Bahamas.

The Challenges Confronting Us

'Nothing discourages and disheartens law enforcement officers more than the knowledge that their efforts in apprehending criminals are too often no more than a useless expenditure of time and money - useless because unwarranted leniency in the form of suspended sentences, parole, or probation so frequently makes a mockery of good Police work. Assuredly, we must strive to rehabilitate those persons, who have strayed from lawful ways. On the other hand, consideration must be given to protecting society by isolating depraved individuals who have no respect for law and order or the rights of others. The scales of justice must be balanced,'

'We are confronted by criminals - a criminal class of older seasoned offenders as well as a crop of blood-minded juvenile offenders and thugs, who seem to believe, that they can evade the rule of law with little or no regard for life and other people's property'

'We owe it to our youth and to all God-fearing citizens to reassert all that is good and decent in our heritage and to unite to stop those who seek to disregard and destroy that goodly heritage.' 'We did not arrive at this grave state of affairs overnight. Still our dual challenge is to the immediate effects of crime as well as the longer-term causes and solutions to violence and antisocial behavior.'

'We are a blessed people, a people of hope and resilience, faith and fortitude. In the spirit of Psalm 121, just as another people did at another time of lamentation we pray':

> *"I will lift up mine eyes unto the hills, from whence cometh my help. My help cometh from the Lord, which made heaven and earth"*

With God's guidance, unity of purpose and unyielding resolve we will ensure greater law and order, we will ensure greater peace in our Bahamaland.

J. Edgar Hoover - Director of the Federal Bureau of Investigation.
Hubert A. Ingraham — Prime Minister of the Commonwealth of the Bahamas ■.

Adequate Security For Hotels

4th September, 2003

In recent weeks there have been criminal acts perpetrated against visitors to Nassau. The rate of such attacks is not alarming, but we must take steps to ensure that statistics for such crimes do not rise. I was not surprised to hear of the sexual assault of a young female on an upper floor of a 'West Bay Street Hotel' as reported in the press as I am aware of the lack of interest in providing adequate security at that hotel. The attack on the upper floor of the hotel was perpetrated by armed/masked bandits, who robbed and raped her in the presence of her parents.

Since leaving the Police service I spent fifteen years in hotel and casino security. First, at the Paradise Island Resort & Casino/Kerzner's Atlantis Resort. During my time there, we were able to build a professional security team, ensuring the security and safety of our guests. When I left, the resort continued to invest in technology and training. They can boast that security at their resort is amongst the best in the region and the Americas. The owners of the resort always demonstrated a profound concern for security and safety at Paradise Island.

There are improved conditions of service, better wages, rewards for outstanding performance and incentives to motivate the security officers to perform at a continuously high standard.

Upon my departure from Atlantis, I was retained for eighteen months at the Crystal Palace Resort & Casino. I was mandated to take whatever measures necessary to improve security. I acquired the services of Mr. Lawrence Major, a former Assistant Commissioner of Police to be my deputy, responsible for casino security.

With years of combined experience, we understood what had to be actioned. First we reviewed all personnel, eliminating those persons we assessed to be 'unfit'. We then tried to retain the services of a higher caliber of personnel.

We knew that security officers had a major role to play in all resorts. Unfortunately, the management of this resort did not see security as a money earner, just something that may be necessary. As far as they were concerned; as long as nothing happens, the place is secure.

We had asked for patrol stations to be installed on all of the floors of the hotel. Up to the time of my departure it was not done. The strength of our personnel dropped by 10% and I found that whenever I discharged a security officer, I did not get a replacement. I also found that the management wanted me to investigate casino employees, suspected of stealing, which I was prepared to do in a lawful manner. I was asked to include set checks of croupier's bank accounts as part of my investigation. This I refused to do, as it is against the law. My refusal annoyed upper management and at the end of one year my position was made redundant. I had to seek legal action to get my rightful separation renumeration.

If a security survey was done of those hotels on the Cable Beach strip, with the exception of the Radisson Resort, it would have been discovered that security was grossly inadequate. The owner/management was only concerned about security when a major incident occured.

In the mid-nineties while at the Crystal Palace there was a casino robbery and $879,000.00 was stolen from a safe. Two armed bandits escaped. The Police was at the scene within seconds of their departure and chased them through bushes, in the area of the old Hobby Horse Hall. The bandits escaped, but later the Police recovered all of the stolen money in the bushes. The owner of the Crystal Palace was so pleased with the Police work that he offered to donate $10,000.00 to the Police Dependent's Fund. The two men who were later arrested were tried and acquitted, but all of the money was returned to the original owner. I was asked by the owner to arrange the presentation of the reward to the Police. To date the presentation has not been made. I have written to the owner and his seniors on occasions over the past decade, but there has been no response.

There is a famous case that I have quoted to Hotel Managers in the past to get their attention regarding security at their properties. In 1994 a Federal Jury ordered the Las-Vegas Hilton and its parent company to pay $6.7 million to Navy Lt. Paula Coughlin for failing to provide adequate security during the 1991 Tailhook Association convention, at which Coughlin and 82 other women were allegedly assaulted or harassed by drunken conventioneers. There was $1.7 million in compensatory damages and $5 million in punitive damages. The case was based on the fact that the hotel did not provide adequate security for the protection of its guests. The record shows, that the Jury's decision to award punitive damages, was significant, not only for the Hilton but for other hotels. This helped to establish that similar acts would not be tolerated. The only way you can communicate with a corporation that has disregarded the safety of the public is to affect its profit line.

It is my opinion that the Ministry of Tourism and the Ministry of National Security should conduct security surveys of hotels in New Providence, in particular those hotels on the Cable Beach Strip. There must be patrols inside and outside of the hotels; on the floors as well as the grounds. There must be equipment installed to ensure that such patrols are taking place. Masked men should not be able to get to the floors of a hotel apparently unseen to be able to rob and rape guests.

Note: Just a few nights ago the manager of Quality Inn was robbed of $15,000.00 inside the hotel by a masked gunman. It was fortunate that no guests were in the lobby at the time. This is a 200-room hotel. They do not have security personnel on staff.

Mandatory Security at Hotel and Guest Houses

I wish to refer to an article on the front page of the Tribune, dated 24th: May, 2004, giving the sordid details of a sexual attack on a female visitor residing at the Poinciana Villas on Paradise Island. Some weeks prior to this attack there was a similar sexual assault on another female visitor in the area of Sunrise Beach Villas and the Sheraton Grand Hotel. She was a guest at Comfort Suites.

It is my humble opinion that all hotels and guest houses that cater to our visitors must be compelled to provide adequate security and safety for their guests and persons visiting their premises. It is also my opinion that the Government Authority responsible for licensing these establishments ought to include security and safety as criteria for approval.

Hotels and Guest House's owners and managers must be made to understand that Security is a Cost Center not Revenue Center. Without it, lawsuits can prove that the property was negligent about security and damages awards and bad press can result in serious damages to business and our industry.

Can you imagine, that with the crime trend in the world today, we still have hotels and guest houses in our country without any security personnel on staff? Many of these businesses do not take security and safety precautions.'

Many years ago, there was a double murder in a hotel room at a prominent hotel resort in Bimini. The victims were visitors from Europe. Police investigation resulted in the arrest of an ex-cop, known for his violent ways, who upon his release from prison in Nassau was residing in Bimini. Shortly after the incident, I was visiting Bimini and had the opportunity to investigate the security and crime prevention measures at the hotel resort. On the night of the murders there was one security officer on duty at the Yacht Haven on the opposite side of the street. There was no security officer on patrol at the hotel. Lighting between the beach and the hotel was poor and, in some places, non-existent. The sliding door of the room occupied by the victims could not be locked. It is through this door the murderer gained entry.

Some years ago, there was an incident, a rape in a room at a Cable Beach Hotel Resort. The culprit entered at night from a door adjacent to the beach that should have been locked, but was not. He made his way up to the floors and attacked a couple in a room. The wife was raped in the presence of her husband by the gun wielding bandit. Visitors in neighboring rooms, who suspected something was wrong, called for security personnel. The delay in the arrival of security personnel was notable. I learned, that the resort had only two security officers on duty at the time, one posted at the checkout and the other the lobby guard, who was not available he was on his 'break'.

Hotel Fire In Puerto Rico.

It was on a New Year's Eve Night. The Casino, on the ground floor of the hotel hosted a New Year's Eve Party that was being attended by several hundreds of paying guests.

This hotel and casino were not built to our standards in The Bahamas and the materials used not as fireproof as ours. It was a disaster waiting to happen and it did happen. A disgruntled former employee started a fire in a storage room inside of the casino. The fire fuelled by paint explosions spread rapidly into the ceiling of the casino and upwards into the hotel floors.

Persons attending the function in the casino had paid a large fee to enter. Security personnel in an effort to prevent persons from sneaking in, had locked the fire exit doors. The only point of entry and exit was the front door. As the fire moved swiftly in the ceiling and floor of the casino, guests ran towards the fire exits, but they were locked and security personnel had difficulty getting to the doors with the keys to open them as the crowd pushed on the doors. Several persons sustained severe burns and broken limbs in the rampage to get out. The fire spread swiftly into the hotel floors immediately above the casino. Guests and employees had to proceed to the roof where they were rescued by helicopters. It was New Year's Eve night and patrons visiting the hotel/casino were in large numbers.

The parking of vehicles was not controlled, which caused very long delays in the arrival of Fire Engines and Ambulances. In order for emergency personnel to get to the scene, wreckers had to be used to clear the Fire Lanes and make entry possible. It took hours to do so.

The hotel/casino was destroyed. Lives were lost and there were hundreds of persons injured. The disaster was investigated and the report condemned the planning and performance of the Security Management team. The report also criticized the building code, that allowed the use of certain materials in the construction; the paint room in the casino and the ancient Fire Exit doors.

The report reached us at Paradise Island Resort & Casino in the form of a film describing the incident and a warning to us, that fire regulations and parking rules must be strictly enforced. Do it firmly but politely.

Major Incident at a Kansas City Hotel

At a New Year's Eve gala function there were too many persons on a balcony extended over the hotel lobby. Patrons were being entertained in the lobby and on this verandah over the lobby. The weight of the patrons on the upper verandah caused it to collapse on persons in the lobby and fall on those persons, crashing with it. Several persons were very seriously injured. Medical response by ambulances and staff were delayed due to illegal parking, blocked streets and fire lanes. The injured suffered for the want of rescue and medical attention. Security Managers and the local police were blamed for the situation that delayed the arrival of the medical crews.

Insurance companies used the above incidents to warn hotel executives and security managers of the need for proper parking arrangements that must include Fire Lanes and Signage and most importantly Enforcement of the rules, firmly and politely. These incidents are examples of the lack of enforcement by those responsible.

Plan for Hotel Fires

When proceeding to your rooms after check-in look for the Fire Exit Signs. You will know where they are in the event you have to leave the room in an emergency. Place room key in a particular spot at all times so that it can be easily found when leaving the room.

Remember, that in the event of a Fire the Hotel Elevators cannot be used. Elevators may take you into the area of the fire. In many hotels when a Fire Alarm is activated the elevators automatically proceed to the ground floor and remains there.

If the Fire Alarm is activated it is likely, that in addition to the sound, you will be notified by telephone or Television. DO NOT PANIC. Follow these instructions:-

Get your door key. Do not leave the room without it. It is very likely, that your room may be the safest place.

Before leaving the room touch the door. If it is hot, the fire is outside. It would be best to remain in the room.

Fill bath tub and facebasin with water. Wet the door and the floor in front of it.

Cover vents with wet towels to stop smoke from entering the room,. including the space under the door.

Hang a sheet on the balcony. It is an international sign recognized by Firemen that someone is in that room.

Should smoke enter the room, lay on the floor where there is oxygen. The smoke will rise.

If you are able to leave your room do not use the elevator. Proceed to the Exit Stairs. If the Fire is on floors below, proceed to the roof where you would be rescued. Most hotels have flat roofs with an exit to get there.

Crime & Tourism in The Bahamas
**Prepared by Bahamas Ministry of Tourism for
CTO Crime & Tourism Conference
April 26 & 27, 1993 In St. Lucia**

The Bahamas receives over 3.5 million visitors per annum. Approximately 80% of these visitors are from the United States of America.

In 1988 a survey was done on the American warm weather destination market by an American based company. This segmentation study revealed that safety was the most important factor for Americans when choosing a vacation destination.

The Bahamas Ministry of Tourism and the hospitality industry have therefore placed very strong emphasis on crime prevention and stabilization. Crime committed against visitors in the Bahamas range from housebreaking/stealing to murder.

The escalation of crimes against visitors over the past three or four years is believed to be directly related to a decline in stopover arrivals with the subsequent increase in unemployment in the Bahamas.

The most common offenses are stealing and robbery. There are several areas in which the Government and the private sector are working jointly to prevent or minimize the level of crime committed against visitors.'

Visitor Relations Unit - Ministry of Tourism

In 1972 the Bahamas Ministry of Tourism created its visitor relation unit to deal with visitors' complaints. Typically, dissatisfaction with our product (i.e., hotel issues, transportation, overcharging, harassment, etc.

More recently, however, the visitor relations unit has been involved in issues related to crimes committed against visitors, as we accepted that we have to play a bigger role in offering damage control.

Crime issues are brought to our attention by the Criminal Investigation Division of the Police Department, the American embassy and other consular representatives and the local newspapers, on occasion.

A relationship has been established with the CID and the consular representative so that crime issues are brought to our attention as quickly as possible after the commission of these crimes so that we can render assistance where possible and where appropriate.

Typical responses/assistance offered in cases of murder, attempted murder, assault, robbery etc. is as follows:
- moral support from the highly trained and empathetic staff of the visitor relations unit — hospital visits, flowers, etc.
- the use of a telephone to make long-distance calls to relatives/ friends back home - facilitating police assistance
- assist with arranging undertaker services
- notifying consular representatives to assist with providing temporary identification and travel documents
- complimentary accommodations
- prevailing upon the airlines to waive cost of airline tickets
- payment of Bahamian departure tax.

Not surprisingly, most crimes are committed against visitors staying in hotels as against cruise visitors (this does not mean that most crimes are committed in hotels). In an effort to provide even quicker responses to visitors, should they be the victim of a crime, the Bahamas Ministry of Tourism has installed a helpline service, where assistance can be had during normal working hours.

Security Managers Forum

The security manager's forum was established a few years ago. It comprises the heads of security departments of hotels & resorts, as well as Government representatives. The Police Department is often called in to offer special assistance or advice, the primary objective of the forum is the sharing of information relative to crimes against hotel guests, i.e. crimes committed in and around hotel properties. The group accepts that it has a vital role to play in the continued development and improvement of the tourism product, and has recently renewed its efforts to develop to the extent where it can become an effective lobby group. The group meets once a month.

Hospitality Leadership Conference

The Ministry of Tourism spearheads the organization of the Annual Hospitality Leadership Conference. This conference draws participants from all sectors of society — hoteliers, retail merchants, restaurateurs, bankers, attraction owners, straw business persons, college lecturers, Government representatives from the Ministries of Tourism, Education, Transport public personnel, the Police Department, Defence Force unit, and in 1992 the quincentennial commission's objective of the conference is to secure commitment from all segments of the industry to take immediate action to improve the quality of service and products provided to our guests.

A significant part of the fourth Annual Conference held in 1997 was the crime presentation which focused on the impact of crime in the Bahamas. This initiated discussion among participants on joint efforts which could be implemented to combat crime; these efforts would help provide a safe environment for visitors and residents alike:

- The Police Department renewed its commitment to step up its efforts in the areas of crime prevention and detection with special emphasis placed on matters related to hotel security personnel's ability to assist the Police Department; this involves improved training to monitor/and document suspicious actions of visitors and employees on the properties.
- The Police Department was urged to improve its enforcement of the vagrancy act as a large proportion of vagrancy offence victims are tourists who are frequently approached by vagrants disguised as peddlers or hawker to sell drugs.
- It was recommended that consideration should be given to the integration of white undercover Police Officers within the rank of the police force to be assigned to tourist areas.
- Other recommendations for crime prevention included increased use of paid local informants, installation of S.O.S. telephones on the outskirts of towns for emergencies as well as the installation of metal detectors at all sea ports to detect weapons.

Liaison Between Ministry of Tourism and Police

The Ministry of Tourism liaises very closely with the Police Department on the issue of safety for tourists at large planned events or festivals, e.g., Goombay, Bay Fest, Junkanoo parades, spring break events, etc.

Additionally, whenever there is a security breakdown in any tourism area, the Ministry of Tourism will initiate meetings, involving the police and all parties concerned, to develop action plans to deal with the situation, e.g., harassment of visitors by jet ski operators on beaches. ◉

Recommendations to Governments

22nd September, 2011

I wish to record for your information, recommendations that I have made in the past, which could be of major assistance in our battle with the criminals terrorizing our beloved country. I hate being repetitive, but I am convinced, that the introduction of these measures would be extremely helpful.

(a) GPS systems in Police vehicles would enable a timely response from the Command Centre. I have seen the system at work in Detroit and Chicago. The staff in the Centre is constantly aware of the locations of all Police vehicles. On many ocassions they have been able to respond in 3 minutes, resulting in averting a crime: moreso in situations of armed robbery. Similarly, our response time could be significantly reduced, achieving the same success. It would also save on fuel consumption as patrol vehicles won't have to be moving constantly.

(b) Protecting our borders. The law enforcement agency responsible for this task could consider my previous recommendation to develop outposts at strategic locations around New Providence, to be manned by the Defence Force; equipped with special binoculars for night vision, with 24/7 postings. This would provide the information needed to intercept the vessels and illegal immigrants at sea; in particular those from Haiti must be of major concern to our law enforcement agencies and health authorities. It is known that these vessels have been used to smuggle guns and drugs into our country. Some of the illegal immigrants may be from criminal elements in Haiti and we are aware of the health problems that exist there, with cholera, malaria and dengue fever as the most notable.

(c) Increase Police ability to provide for more expeditious examinations of recovered firearms and comparison of bullets from scenes of crimes and the bodies of victims. It could be a major thrust in our detection efforts. It is one of the areas in which overseas assistance is required. Each weapon seized by the Police has to be examined and the comparison made.

(d) Police Prosecutors and the Attorney General Office must endeavor to get early trials on all high-profile gun cases such as the recent arrest of persons with 16 guns and ammunition. I have been very critical of the lengthy adjournments for gun case. There is a 2006 case, that was completed in August 2011 and a 2008 case (bullets in baby clothing at Kelly's Dock) not yet completed.)

A gun possession case is what can be called a 30-minute case. The prosecution witnesses, who consist of three officers at most times can be concluded within 30 minutes, yet attorneys, have been able to secure adjournments for several months. It is also notable that the work being done in the 'Gun Court' is not being publicized. The sentences meted out in that court should be a deterrent, if disclosed by the media.

(e) Encourage the Bahamas Chamber of Commerce to accumulate from its member's money for rewards for information on murders, armed robberies and firearms possession. They must also encourage merchants to take precautions and preventative measures at their places of business. Reading some of the crime reports reveals to me that many persons are talking about the crime trend, but are making themselves victims by their carelessness. Crime Prevention Experts must be given more media time to educate our people about crime prevention. Insurance Companies should encourage persons to use available technology to prevent car thefts by reducing the premiums of those who comply.

(f) There is a need for regular training of our law enforcement officers in the use of firearms, which must include: shooting practice and the care and safety of their weapons. I had recommended many years ago and I continue to do so, that the Force undertakes to procure an indoor range in a location of Arthur House at Police Headquarters. I had taken the liberty to get specifications from a Police source in South Florida. The information was sent to the Ministry of National Security and to the Commissioner. The range would be for all law enforcement officers to practice under the guidance of an expert (former or serving Police Officer) which could be done on their own time as in the U.S.A. and the requirement that they become certified to carry a particular weapon. In addition to law enforcement officers, those persons, who apply for gun licenses could be trained and also certified at this venue before obtaining approval.

It is my hope, that some of these recommendations would receive consideration. Please be assured of my cooperation in all matters of mutual interests. ■

Police Commissioners
(Post 1951)
Administrative Ability, Discipline & Morale,
Public Relations & Legacy

The situation that presently exists with our Commissioner of Police and the Government is nothing new in our Bahamas. In the following paragraphs I will provide information on past political interference and direct attacks on our Commissioners and senior Police personnel.

In 1951 when I enlisted in the Police Service, Major Edward Sears was acting Commissioner of Police. He was a disciplinarian, an ex-Army Officer and a man of integrity. He did not get the support from the then Bay Street Boys to many of his proposals for the advancement of the service and he was never confirmed in the rank of Commissioner.

I learned from my Bahamian colleagues, that this was due to a report he wrote in the Oakes Murder investigation, which differed with an alibi given by notable suspects in the case, who happened to be a part of the Bay Street Boys. The latter governed the country. Sears retired as acting Commissioner of Police.

Lt. Col.E.J.H. Colchester Wemyss was appointed. He arrived here from Barbados. Wemyss, supported by Mr. Roy Solomon of the Bay Street Boys made an impact immediately. He was able to get salary increases, modern equipment, more vehicles, better Police Stations, Police women, Police Dogs and improved training. He was able to move the Force from an ancient back woods organization to a modern and effective unit.

During his reign the Force engaged in sports and social events, such as the annual Christmas and New Year's banquets in the Police Barracks.

We also saw an invasion of English Officers arrive for senior positions in the service. Cottages were built for them and their conditions of service were of the best. Solomon, who was called by Police personnel the 'commissar', for some reason fell out with the Commissioner. There was an inquiry, that caused some embarrassment to the Commissioner and he resigned. He left a legacy of a greatly improved Police Service.

Mr. Nigel Morriss was appointed. He was a part of a senior Police Organization in the U.K. that traveled throughout the British Commonwealth inspecting Police Forces. He had visited and conducted an inspection of our Force before his appointment as Commissioner of Police. Nigel Morriss was a good administrator. He organized overseas training for our police officers in the United Kingdom and improved our relations with law enforcement agencies in the U.S.A. He resigned when politicians discovered, that he had purchased property in Freeport, G.B. and had been given a huge discount in the price.

Following Morriss, there were Commissioners *Cluney and Hindmarsh*. Cluney's administrative ability was questionable and caused a decrease in morale among the ranks. He was constantly criticized by his senior officers and was replaced.

Many of us could not understand why Bahamian Officers were not being considered for the post of Commissioner of Police.

We had *Mr. Wenzel Grainger,* a former British Army Officer, who acted as Deputy Commissioner of Police on numerous occasions and who was a mentor to many police officers. We had Mr. Augustus Roberts, who also served in the British Army and was an efficient Police Officer. Both Cluney and Hindmarsh were recruited from England by the Pindling Government, before Independence. At the time of Hindmarsh appointment

Mr. Albert Miller was Deputy Commissioner of Police. Miller had received overseas training in Police management. We presumed that he would have been our next Commissioner of Police. His ambition was to be Commissioner of Police. He had all the qualifications, training and most importantly the support of the Force. The politicians denied him. It was disclosed, that the friendship existing between his families the Solomons and the Symonettes made him untrustworthy by the Government of the day.

The Government legislated for the Force to have two deputy commissioners and appointed *Mr. Salathiel Thompson* as the second deputy. Mr. Miller, who was senior to Mr. Thompson, was banished to Grand Bahama District and Thompson was promoted Commissioner of

Police shortly after Independence. It was a sad blow for Miller and the Force. This dreadful act eventually turned out to be a blessing for Miller, who after resigning from the Police service was grabbed by the Grand Bahama Port Authority. He eventually became a millionaire and was knighted by Her Majesty the Queen.

Mr. Salathiel Thompson was a brilliant policeman. He was well versed in the laws of The Bahamas, Police Duties and Investigations. Most importantly, he was excellent as a training officer in the Criminal Investigation Department. The Force continued to perform efficiently and effectively, but the environment suffered. This caused a decline in morale.

Thompson was a 'do-as-I-say' Commissioner, who abused his power in the promotion process and even in transfers to Family Islands. Police personnel, who asked not to be transferred due to the jobs held by wives or the high schools being attended by children were told, 'when you enlisted your wife and children did not enlist with you'. Thompson's legacy was his complete support of the government and the politicians. But he opposed wrong doing by politicians and supported investigations of them. He denied a Minister of National Security, his wish to ride in a police car on patrol. He told the minister, that he would get in the way if the officers had to act in a violent situation.

He reported a Cabinet Minister for sending a man to get changes made on a Police character certificate to help him get a job. He called the minister and warned him about trying to corrupt his officers. Many Police Officers were happy when he resigned. I will always be grateful to him for my training and development and the personal interest he demonstrated in me.

Mr. Gerald Bartlette in my opinion was the best we had. He immediately started by improving the environment in which we worked and built morale by way of his personal approach, the manner in which he discussed assignments, allowing you to speak and give your opinion. Morale was enhanced. He was the polite but firm, friendly leader.

Commissioner Reginald Ferguson was posted to the criminal investigation department as a very young officer. He immediately displayed that he was willing to learn and work hard. He was very polite and responsible and very soon became a skilled investigator. His performance and record resulted in rapid promotions. As commissioner of Police, he demanded discipline, decorum, honesty, and promoted training with special courses for officers.

He was criticized by some Government Officials for facilitating the arrests of several LPIA employees by the DEA in the United States of America. There was evidence of drug trafficking against them. The employees were sent to the U.S.A for training when they were arrested. Some government officials believed that the government should have been informed, as it was of National Interest. We rid our airport of persons who aided and abetted drug smuggling into the USA.

Mr. B.K. Bonamy left a legacy of educating Police Officers. He encouraged all policemen to pursue education. Many followed him and acquired law degrees. His problem was his demand for educational capability in the promotion process. Officers undermined him with frequent complaints to politicians of the FNM government and he was eventually asked for his resignation. Bonamy did not go easy. He made certain financial demands, which cost the Government of the day and the public treasury. Bonamy was a man of integrity and fearless.

Mr. Paul Farquharson will go down in history as one of the best Commissioners. He continued to maintain the environment. Build morale to its highest, community policing was his thing, for which he was commended at home and by other Police Forces, who learned from him. He had a background in Police administration. He made the Police Force a place persons loved to work. He remained close to the Police Reserves and with former Police Officers, whose advice he occasionally sought. The Paul Farquharson Convention Centre was built by him and the Police Staff Association received his full support. Commissioners of Police all over the Commonwealth respected Paul Farquharson. He too, became the target of politicians when he accepted the position of High Commissioner to the United Kingdom.

Messrs Greenslade and Dames were sent to Canada for training and were attached to the Royal Canadian Mounted Police for one year. On their return and the banishment of Paul Farquharson the Government appointed Mr. Greensladeas Deputy Commissioner. I am told, that the fact Mr. Greenslade came through the junior ranks of the Force, played a role in his appointment. Mr. Dames was always respected and admired by me, and at the time, I thought the Government could have considered an increase in wages and have him oversee crime management along with his position as Deputy Commissioner, which is mainly administrative. Dames eventually resigned and took jobs in the private sector, finally at Bahamar. I am told that when he resigned from Bahamar it was his desire to return to the Police service, but this was denied. This information is well known throughout the Force.

Mr. Greenslade had been an efficient and effective leader. He had built an organization, starting with trusted and outstanding senior personnel in the executive grouping of the Force. He had improved the work in the divisions and units of the Force and added other units that exceled in crime detection. Over the years there have been a decrease in certain crimes and an increase in the detection rate. Murders have become the major problem and it appears that the Commissioner of the Police and the Force are being blamed for the murder rate. It is my opinion, that we were fortunate to have had a Police Force that was proactive and committed in the struggle to eradicate crime. Murder is not a preventable crime. The murderer will pick the place, the weapon, and the time. He has motive. Detection and punishment are important factors to be considered by the Police and the State respectively. Mr. Greenslade was well liked in our communities. We saw the results of his administration and enforcement.

Our communities and the church should get involved and find ways to stop unfair treatment of this Bahamian.

The change in the Police Act, that took away security of tenure from the Commissioner, was a major mistake made by the former Government. At the time I had criticized the move in a letter to the Tribune. I pointed out that the change would make the Commissioner of Police beholden to the politicians in power, as they were the ones, who dictate and control the security of that position. It was my opinion at that time, that the Police Staff Association should have challenged the change and taken legal action to prevent it. At least an effort should have been made.

Prior to Independence we had the British Commissioners, who had security of tenure. There was no need for the Commissioners to fear the politicians. They performed their duties without fear of reprisals from politicians.

During the governance of the Bay Street Boys and the United Bahamian Party, detectives were sent to the Eastern District to investigate reports of election bribery, involving Sir Roland Symonette. Frank Russell, a former Officer of the London Metropolitan Police was in charge of the Criminal Investigation Department. It was apparent that he had received reports, that we were harassing voters in the Eastern District to acquire information about bribery in the elections. We focused our efforts on 'cash for votes' and favors with regards to mortgages.

In a meeting with Mr. Russell, he commended us for our performance in the field and informed us, that our efforts were putting fear in some persons, who had complained to the English Commissioner of Police.

I was sent to Abaco on a similar investigation, which resulted in the arrest of Mr. Frank Christie, UBP politician, who was charged and prosecuted for election bribery.

During the governance of the Progressive Liberal Party, there were investigations conducted against Sir Randol Fawkes, who was arrested and charged with sedition. At the time Mr. Fawkes was the Labor Leader and a strong supporter of the P.L.P.

There were also investigations against two P.L.P. Members of Parliament, who were involved in fraudulent and criminal activities at the National Insurance Board and the Bahamas Broadcasting Corporation. The Superintendent of the C.I.D. directed me to conduct these investigations. The Members of Parliament were arrested and charged before the Courts.

There was never any concern about reprisal.

The British Commissioners and later the Bahamian Commissioners all had security of tenure. There was no need to be concerned about the politicians. In the case of the Member of Parliament, who attempted to bribe a Magistrate, Detectives conducted the needed surveillance exercises and investigations, which resulted in the arrest of the Member of Parliament, who was a member of the governing party.

As Police Officers and Public Servants, our training at home and abroad, commits us to supporting the policies of the Government of the day. However, what the Police Commissioner discloses to politicians must never be detrimental to any investigation or hazardous to personnel conducting investigations or any Police Operations.

Police to Police cooperation internationally was always great, in particular with the United States, Canada and Jamaica. We worked secretly on information involving a boat load of ganja at Eleuthera, all persons involved, which included close relatives of a Government Minister.

The criticism of a Commissioner of Police, who did not disclose to the Minister of National Security, that there were persons employed in the airport, who were suspected of being involved in the export of narcotics and that these persons were being sent to South Florida for training. The persons were arrested in South Florida, where law enforcement agencies had the evidence required for the prosecution of these persons.

The Commissioner of Police was under heavy fire from politicians for not disclosing to his Minister, that these persons were engaged in criminal activities at the airport.

Politicians, some media personnel and even a former Commissioner of Police were of the opinion, that the arrests of these persons in South Florida were of security interest, internationally, and that the Commissioner should have informed the Minister of the investigation and the pending arrests. I supported the Commissioner of Police in keeping the operation secret to accomplish the desired result: exposing the criminal activity in our airport.

We had a Commissioner of Police, who distinguished himself to be a man of integrity, a decent hardworking man, who had been well trained and had the experience, coming up through all the ranks and educating himself for the job. His performance thus far had been magnificent. He had been able to continue the rebuilding of morale and the discipline started by Paul Farquharson. He had been able to continue the socialization and public relation exercises.

He was a student of technology and the Force benefited from his knowledge. The Royal Bahamas Police Force improved under the management of the Commissioner and his executive staff. Prisons overcrowded, Courts having difficulty coping with the number of trials and most importantly the attacks on illegal firearms and drugs.

It was hoped by many of us, that the Deputy Prime Minister's promise to revoke it, is related to the Commissioner's tenure before the end of 100 days.

Let the Commissioner perform his duties and responsibilities without fear. ◘

Commission of Inquiry into Drug Trafficking in The Bahamas

Statement of Paul Thompson

All the information I propose to give in this statement may be considered relevant to paragraphs (b), (c) & (d), of the Royal Commission's terms of Reference. I have no information on paragraph (a), except for my suspicions of corruption in the Police Force, which has been proven in numerous cases where Police Officers and other civil servants have been involved in drug trafficking. During my years of service in the Force, in particular those years spent in the gazetted ranks, I have never received any information from anyone pertaining to corruption of Government Ministers or Members of Parliament acquiescing or participating in any activities, promoting or facilitating the transshipment of dangerous drugs.

During the late 1950's and early 1960's as I moved into the senior ranks of the Police Force (CID), I met and worked with several Law Enforcement Officers from overseas, in particular from the USA. Apart from the working relationship, which was excellent I also developed a personal relationship with many of them. There was mutual trust for each other, a desire to help and learn from each other the varying techniques of the profession, but most of all I was able to develop a close friendship with them and learned quite a lot about policing.

I worked very closely with Agents of the FBI, DEA, US Customs, and the US Secret Service and Treasury Department. Also, Police Personnel in Canada, Jamaica, Bermuda, Haiti, Trinidad & Tobago, and several other Caribbean Countries. The relationship worked well for our Police Force. The exchange of information and ideas, providing literature for training, and even arranging training courses were some of the benefits derived from the relationship. Most important was the type of international co-operation which circumvented the "red tape" and enabled all of us to get the job done expeditiously and in confidence.

Prior to the 1960s' Drug Abuse in the Commonwealth of The

Bahamas had been confined mainly to possession and use of ganja within the Country. Trafficking had been minimal and the persons involved were mostly foreigners, Americans and Jamaican. The statistics in the Police Annual Reports for the years, referred to as the early sixties, will show that there had been a steady rise in the number of Bahamians being arrested for drug offences, and the problem became more serious as ganja became identifiable with the cult known as the Rastafarians; whose adherents considered the use of ganja complementary to their religious beliefs.

The cult was spreading slowly in the Bahamas, where over-employment existed and Jamaican nationals were arriving here in large numbers for work. As our Country grew more prosperous, drug trafficking and related crimes became more sophisticated. Improvised packages of ganja began to be detected by Customs Officials at the Nassau International Airport, and to a lesser degree in Freeport, and at the local Post Offices.

In the year 1968, the Drug Squad was formed in the CID. I subsequently increased the number of personnel and changed the name to Serious Crime & Drug Squad. I was satisfied that the increase in violent crimes in the country was associated with drugs. It must have been obvious to all Police Officers that we were in for some hard times.

Drug Abuse, firearms being frequently used in holdups, plus a vast increase in rapes and an appearance of lawlessness among the youth, should have convinced anyone that something had to be done with the Police Force and the law of the land. Yet frequent requests to Police Administrators to increase the strength of the CID and provide us with the equipment to fight this cancer in its early stages apparently fell on deaf ears. My advice to the Commissioner of Police and his very senior Officers, were not being taken seriously.

At the start of the 1970's the trafficking south of the U.S. border in drugs between the cultivating and manufacturing countries in South and Central America and the USA, had been suppressed by U.S. Law Enforcement Agents in a prolonged operation called, "Intercept".

The routes between the U.S.A. and Mexico were closed and alternative routes were necessary. Jamaica and the Bahamas had become transshipment ports. The harder drugs - cocaine, hashish, heroin etc., were being introduced. The geographical position of the Bahamas with its vast archipelago and total land area of about 5,400 square miles of Islands varying in size made it ideally suitable as a transit point between the countries in South and Central America and USA, and was therefore prone to be a haven for the runners. The task of providing even superficial Police coverage throughout the Bahamas, stretched Police resources to the limit. Statistics for 1972 will show that of the 273 persons arrested for drug offences, 76 were Bahamians and of the 306 persons arrested in 1974, 146 were Bahamians.

By this time the Police Force was receiving support and collaboration from law enforcement agencies in the USA and Jamaica. There were information exchanges, undercover investigations, joint surveillance exercises, air and sea patrols, and electronic surveillance of certain landing strips. The DEA provided training for Police, Customs and Immigration Officers, both here and at schools in the USA. Our Police Force co-operated with the DEA in its efforts in this area. However, there were two requests made to us by the DEA which were declined.

The DEA asked for permission to use our Police radio frequency when operating in The Bahamas, so that they could communicate directly with our personnel, when on Sea and Air patrol: The request was denied. The DEA also suggested that all uncharted air-strips on those islands used by aircraft transporting drugs, be damaged, by blowing large holes with explosives. The DEA offered to provide the equipment and expertise. The request was also denied.

At that time Mr. S.H. Thompson was the Commissioner of Police. He had been appointed to the post in 1973. We had expected vast improvements from him in modernizing the Force, and improving working conditions. We knew that Government had a lot of faith in him and it was our opinion that he would be able to get things done. The Force needed a 'Shot-in-the arm' and we thought this was the man who could provide it.

The decisions made in the DEA request, created some doubts in my mind about the type of administration I expected. In the early 1970s I was transferred from the CID to the Uniform Branch, where I acted as Assistant Commissioner in charge of New Providence District and the Family Islands. I was later transferred to Freeport, Grand Bahama, as Officer in charge of that district.

In 1974, I was returned to New Providence where I became Assistant Commissioner in charge of the CID. I immediately embarked upon a program to strengthen relations with foreign law enforcement agencies, in particular, the FBI, the US Customs, and the DEA. The response and the subsequent results were excellent.

In the CID, we observed that the crime trend had continued. There was no change. Firearms were most frequently used in robberies, rapes and other violent crimes were on the increase. We were satisfied that many of these crimes perpetrated by juveniles and young adults were drug related. We had made it our business to question youths arrested, about drug abuse and in most cases, they were admittedly 'high' when committing crimes. In the CID the cases per man was exceedingly high, the working hours exceedingly long, and the general conditions in the offices deplorable. These conditions were having an adverse effect on the CID. Detectives were short cutting investigations resulting in poor presentation of evidence in the Courts. There were numerous accusations of Police brutality and several accidents due to tiredness and long working hours.

Police Headquarters, through my reports were made aware of these problems. In fact, I had discussed manpower needs with some of the Senior CID Officers and made recommendations to the Commissioner. No reply was ever forthcoming. The serious Crime and Drug Squad was overworked. This affected our ability and commitment to deal with the drug problem. The Police Administrators appeared to be unconcerned about the escalation in crime and the drug traffic. It appeared that top priority was being given to the needs of the Security & Intelligence Branch (SIB) where some of the best investigating officers were being posted. The CID lost top personnel to that Branch, whose duties included VIP Security, political and civil investigations. I never saw the need for such a large SIB staff.

The Bahamas is a peaceful Country, no civil unrest and the Government of the day is the popular choice. It was always my opinion that crime and drug trafficking should have been given top priority. I was very vocal at Senior Officers conferences about these matters. Police Headquarters eventually abandoned the idea of the conferences, which had been going on for several years.

In March 1975, I was selected to attend the Interpol Caribbean Conference in Kingston, Jamaica. On my return a report was submitted to the Commissioner, dated April 4, 1975. It was my hope that this report would have convinced the Police Administrators of the need to effectively increase the strength of the CID and to improve our communication with other Police Forces in the region. My presence at the Conference helped to improve my relationship with other Police Officers from various countries. During these years as the drug traffic grew, the need for joint undercover operations was necessary, if we were to arrest major offenders.

The Head of the DEA in Miami was interested in assisting. Undercover operations arranged by us in the past had been very rewarding, resulting in several arrests and the seizure of large quantities of drugs.

The success of undercover operations depends a great deal on secrecy and speed of execution. It would be a dangerous exercise if all such matters had to go through the administrative red tape of other departments. Too many persons are likely to know of the operations and there could be leaks.

As a result of the escalation of the drug traffic, we were making large seizures of tons of ganja in the Islands. The large loads were being brought to Nassau for storage and subsequent destruction. The drugs were stored in old buildings in the Headquarter's compound and later at Oakes Field. These unsuitable buildings were then targeted by criminals to retake the drugs. It appeared obvious, that Police Officers were involved.

After the very first attack on one of the buildings, I suggested to Police Headquarters that I place a select team of armed detectives to maintain surveillance on the buildings to capture the burglars.

I was satisfied that Police personnel were involved. My request was denied. The Commissioner instructed that a uniformed Officer be posted at the buildings. The theft of large quantities of ganja continued.

We lost a lot of respect from the public during this period. The DEA had offered to have the large seizures taken to Miami by a Coast Guard Cutter, periodically, to be destroyed. This offer was declined.

Our senior officers were of the opinion that the DEA did not trust us. I was all for it as I was aware of the amount of work involved in the destruction of ganja. This was being done by serious crime personnel who could be doing other work instead. I had requested the purchase of an incinerator for burning the ganja. I never got it. I recommended that we ask Government to provide us with the old Customs warehouse building on East Street as a storage place. The plan was to renovate the building, strengthen the ceiling, close off the doors on the roadside and create an entrance inside the Police Compound. I had asked that alarms be installed that would signal in the Police Radio Control Room and the Quarter Guard. This plan would have eliminated the need for Police Officers to watch the drugs and the temptation of corruption in that area would have been eliminated. The building was being used by the Ministry of Education. We never got the use of the building. The theft of drugs from the Police storage areas continued.

From the mid 1970's onward the transit traffic grew. Ships and aircraft used our Islands and Cays at regular intervals for refueling and for storage. Among the Islands being used were, Mayaguana, Inagua, Bimini, Andros, the Berry Islands, the Exuma Cays, Cat Island, Acklins, and the infamous Gorda Cay in the Abaco Cays. Drug wars had started between local residents who began stealing shipments from the runners. High powered automatic weapons were being used.

There were a number of drug related murders and gangland style killings. The local residents involved, purchased high powered boats and guns. Sea piracy became a new type of drug related crime. Bimini was the worst of the Islands. There was evidence of Police corruption there. The population at Bimini seemed to favor the traffic. Several prominent persons were arrested in a raid, that led to that Island by me. When we were leaving with those apprehended, rocks were thrown at us by adults as well as small children.

The raid was a success because of the complete secrecy and assistance of Defence Force. The team was not told where we were headed until late at night, when out at sea. It was known that the smugglers paid handsome bribes for information on Police movements. The charter of a plane or boat by the Police, would touch off a network of messages to the criminals.

I am sure that Government did not get any of the recommendations we were making. ◙

Police & Policing (Issues & Ideas)

The performance of our Police Force continues to be outstanding. We must continue to be supportive and express our gratitude for their performance. The executive management of the police service is in capable hands. Morale is high and support for ovine initiatives is overwhelming. As in most law-enforcement organizations there are the problems of corruption and discipline, which always seem to be present. Eradicating these problems will depend on the efficiency and effectiveness of the middle management officers, who will encounter the problems. Support from the public and the dedication of the Police complaints unit to expedite the investigation of complaints made against Police personnel and to ensure, that persons, who complain were made aware of the outcome of those investigations. I am convinced, that personnel in the Police Complaints Unit conduct their investigations fairly and efficiently and that those Police Officers found liable are made to appear before Police Tribunals or in the Criminal Courts.

I continue to be critical of the Police in the areas of discipline as I am fully aware of what I had (British Army discipline) and what we have now. I have often recommended, that we make a united effort to restore the discipline we once had, in all ranks. It could be accomplished if the middle managers of the Police service commit themselves to the task. Such an undertaking would be rewarding and further enhance Police Public Relations, which is so important at this time.

Police performance has been effective and deserves commendation in the area of major crime; the same cannot be said of the work being done in the area of minor crime. I am aware of the concern of some senior Police Officers about the huge backlog of cases pending in the lower courts. It is my submission that a concerted attack on minor crime would (a) help to restore order, the order we once enjoyed in our communities and (b) identify and expose those involved in major crimes, caught committing the minor offences. It is called 'Zero Tolerance'.

It has been a very effective weapon used by the Police in the large cities of the world. There are examples such as, (a) the arrests of the key suspect in the bombing of the FBI Office in Kansas City. He was stopped by Police for a traffic violation. (b) The wrests of suspects for the bombing of the bullet-train in Japan occurred when he exceeded the speed limit. There have been several similar situations here where persons stopped for minor offences were found to be in possession of drugs, guns or stolen property. The 'Zero-Tolerance' concept was in operation here for a period and proved to be a success.

The minor crimes frequently encountered on the Island of New Providence are recorded for information; Parking on the sidewalks made for pedestrians. It is dangerous to pedestrians, damages the sidewalks and the environment which is costly to repair and replace. I recollect that the bicycle is a vehicle and should adhere to the rules of the road. Bicycles are ridden on sidewalks and against the flow of traffic on one-way streets. Running the red light is very prevalent in certain locations on the Island. There is an increase in street vendors and those who sell food in the area of our schools. Are these food vendors in possession of current medical certificates? Motorcyclists riding dangerously with no licenses, no insurance, and no helmets etc.

The efforts of the Traffic Division needs to be supported by all officers, in particular those on foot patrol.

The Ministry of Home Affairs convened a meeting to discuss law enforcement action to 'close down' Bimini. The meeting was attended by Customs, Immigration, Police and other Government officials.

The Permanent Secretary chaired the meeting. After several subsequent meetings we produced a plan which, I am told was for the Cabinet. No more was heard about our plan. The cost would have been phenomenal, which apparently caused the lack of action.

DEVELOPMENT OF THE CAYS

In May 1979, I attended the INTERPOL Caribbean/Central American Regional Conference in Bermuda along with Mr. Avery Ferguson, the new A.C.P. in charge of the CID. On my return I submitted a report on the findings of the conference which dealt with drug trafficking in the region.

I had only visited Norman's Cay on one occasion. I was sent there by the Commissioner to see what was going on. There was information concerning transit traffic in drugs.

Upon my return, I reported to the Commissioner that the infrastructure was there for such traffic and the absence of any law enforcement on Norman's Cay made it a haven for any type of smuggling and drug trafficking.

I knew that Joe Lehder owned the Cay. I had noticed a lot of Latins on the Cay together with a few Bahamians working there. I am unable to remember when I visited the Cay, but it may have been either after some disclosure was made by the DEA or by Mr. Norman Solomon.

In the last paragraph of my report, I advised that Government should consider establishing a physical prescence in the Cays with infrastructure to house Police and Customs personnel, then attempt to attract big investors to our Islands and Cays.

I have seen Robert Vesco on occasions in Nassau. On one occasion I was asked to accompany an Immigration Officer to deliver a letter to him. I have never heard of any involvement in drugs by Mr. Vesco.

FORENSIC LAB

For several years the RBPF used the laboratories of other Police Forces, namely the Jamaica Police, Dade Country Public Safety and the FBI. As the drug traffic grew, so did the need for our own lab. We were eventually able to use a Government Lab in Nassau to analyze drugs.

The Police Force recruited Mr. Carey at the rank of Inspector and sent him to the UK to study forensic science.

While Mr. Carey was away, I wrote to Police Headquarters, reminding them that we would need an equipped lab before Mr. Carey's return. I had been lecturing regularly to the service clubs in Nassau and solicited their assistance in getting a lab for Mr. Carey. I told the Commissioner of Police of the progress I made and a Mr. Jones visited him and told him that his club would be prepared to provide the funds for the equipment, provided that a suitable building could be found.

The Commissioner sent me to Miami to get prices and ideas on how to equip a lab. I returned with a full report from my friends at the Dade County Lab; I heard no more about the lab. We could not produce a building and the club dropped the idea.

Mr. Carey returned here with honors. Several years have passed and there is no lab. The analysis of drugs is creating hardships in getting cases completed before the courts. It would be interesting if the correct statistics could be obtained about the number of cases pending for months, awaiting lab reports, and the number that has been dismissed due to the lack of the lab report. One may find that Mr. Carey is being overworked and is frustrated by the lack of concern with respect to providing him with proper facilities and recognition.

I continued to make other recommendations from time to time, but with varying degrees of success.

I am satisfied that the Administration of the Police Force at that time had little intention of implementing any new ideas corning from its younger Officers. Many of us were too scared to press for reforms or challenge any decisions made at Police Headquarters. I was subsequently branded as being disloyal because of my struggle to implement modern methods of Policing and better working conditions. With a majority of cowards who would never have challenged his decisions or indecisions, there was fear in the hearts of the men who worked with him. I am sure that Government did not get any of these recommendations.

RAPID RESPONSE
5th October, 2011

In Law enforcement organizations around the world, it is accepted, that Rapid Response, early detection, effective prosecution and appropriate sentencing, contribute to crime prevention. The criminal, who becomes aware, that he is likely to be caught is likely to consider the risk of going to jail. Crime Prevention Education and Crime Watch Programs are very important weapons in the fight against crime. The public needs to be educated on the 'do's and don'ts' in communities where there is rampant crime. The public must support its law enforcement agencies and adapt to the slogan; "Notify, Identify, and Testify".

The first response to crime, request for assistance or information on criminal activity requires Rapid Response and decisive action. The crime scene must be secured, the safety of witnesses and victims be assured and information about the incident or suspected criminal activity collected. There must be the assurance of anonymity and confidentiality, as required.

Rapid Response is a goal that our Police service has been trying for decades, to achieve. It is noted, that when our Police personnel can get to the scene of a crime; in particular, crimes against the person, such as armed robbery and rape, quite often the criminals are encountered at the scene or nearby, resulting in arrests. It is known to Police personnel that past Commissioners have been aiming at a three-minute response.

The recent signing of a contract between The Bahamas Government and Motorola will introduce a new and modern 919 system to our Police arsenal in the fight against crime. The new system will enhance the Rapid Response concept and would be a major weapon in the war on crime. One of the features of the new technology will allow the Commander in the Police Control Center to be able to locate, observe and direct the movement of all such vehicles to respond to crime scenes. The Commander will know, which is the nearest vehicle to any crime scene and dispatch that vehicle for immediate response. He will also know of other vehicles in the area should additional assistance be needed.

The Government has added yet another crime fighting tool. It is very likely that the importance of this new technology will be discussed with the public in due course after the Police training has been completed.

There is another feature, that allows the personnel in the Police vehicle to listen to the caller or the victim of the crime while en-route to the scene. The new technology will also improve public relations.

In recent years the Police have increased their efforts to provide Crime Prevention Education to our public, through the media, advertising, lectures/seminars and crime/neighborhood watch programs.

It is evident, that some of the victims of crime are not taking heed of the Police advice and are making themselves victims. Car thefts have increased as owners decline to have anti-theft equipment installed and Insurance Companies are not encouraging them to do so. Home invasions, many of which are due to negligence, poor locking devices and the neglect of those who can afford alarms, to have them installed. Drivers, in particular females not taking precautions to lock doors when driving along city streets and having valuables exposed on their persons or on the front seats. The business owners, large and small, who neglect to install available crime prevention and detection equipment on their premises. Criminals target the large sums of money they retain in their businesses and on their persons.

The negligent conduct by many victims reveals that the Police message on crime prevention is not sinking in.

Recent examples:

(1) A female returns to her residence and immediately observes, that her front door, which she left locked was unlocked, she also heard noise inside the house. Yet, she enters and is accosted by two armed men.

(2) A female business woman is driving on Wulff Road with her bag on the front seat of her car containing cash assets for banking. The car is not locked and the window is down. She stops on the traffic light at Market Street, a man takes the bag from the seat and flees the scene.

(3)A man goes to a bank and collected a large sum of money to pay his employees. His car is parked a long distance away from the ban,: he is walking to his car with the cash in a bag with the bank's name. On arrival to his car, he placed the bag on top of his car to search his pockets for his keys; the bag of cash was removed by a pedestrian, who seized the opportunity.

The Community Policing philosophy, which is extensively used in our communities, emphasizes the importance of problem-solving partnerships. Crime and disorder are most efficiently solved when all stakeholders are represented in the solution.

POLICE CONTROL CENTRE

23rd September, 2011

It is the place that we call when we need help in any emergency; criminal attack, fire, accidents and any other emergency requiring immediate attention. The center is staffed by mostly female officers, with good communication skills, who are computer literate and have a good understanding of the laws of The Bahamas and Police Duties. Some of them can speak and understand a second language. The Officer in charge of the Control Centre has to be experienced in police duties, the laws of The Bahamas as he is expected to give directions to Police personnel proceeding to scenes of crimes or fires etc. On occasions he has to act as a counselor giving advice to persons who call for same. He is the man, who controls the movement of patrol vehicles. He has to ensure that proper records are maintained and that the senior management of the Force is kept informed. I have suggested on previous occasions, that the Commanding Officer there ought to be of the rank of Assistant Superintendent.

It is notable, that whenever the Police are able to respond rapidly to calls for help, the criminals or intruders are captured at the scene or nearby. It would be an asset if the Police can develop its Rapid Response initiative and be able to respond within three minutes, which was the goal set by Mr. Paul Farquharson years ago. It would be a major accomplishment, which would enhance the capability of the Force to respond promptly to calls for help and to act on information. Public confidence in the Police Force would also be enhanced.

It is my opinion, that the Rapid Response initiative could only be accomplished if the Commander in the Control Centre can be aware at all times of the exact location of all Police vehicles. The Commander will be able to direct the nearest vehicle to the location. There is technology available to provide the equipment required. I had the opportunity to visit Police Control Centers in Detroit and Chicago. The Commander has a large map on the wall. On the map there are lights indicating the street location of all of the Police vehicles. He can direct the nearest car to the scene and also set up road blocks with other vehicles if deemed to be necessary.

There is available in The Bahamas, security companies that can provide merchants, businessmen and even householders with a "panic button", which is very useful in communicating information in the event of a situation such as an armed robbery. The victim does not need to use a telephone, just press the panic button, which alerts the security company, that then calls the Police. The panic button can be carried in the holder's pocket and can be activated by just pressing their pocket.

"We Served with Honor — we remember with Pride."

REWARDS FOR GUNS, in particular reporting the importers of the weapons. The rewards must be substantial and could be in partnership with the private sector.

Finally, in spite of the criticisms of politicians and others the morale of the Force is high, its Commissioner and his executive are popular.

The prisons are overcrowded and the backlog in the Courts continues to grow. With this in mind I am pleading for the overtime pay or 'time back' on vacations to be consirered, as we once did. ◼

"To my former colleagues, keep the pressure on the criminals, attack the minor crimes, BE SAFE."

The War on Crime

We are engaged in a war against criminals, who are getting bolder and more violent in carrying out their unlawful acts against us. Most of the murders appear to be emanating from organized criminals, involved in drug trafficking and the assassination of those who betray them or are operating on their turf. There are also the gang killings, the revenge killings, and the killings in the course or furtherance of other crimes; rapes and armed robberies and to a lesser extent domestic violence (altercations, arguments and uncontrollable tempers).

In a War such as this, it is expected, that the Good Guys (us) will use all the weapons at our disposal to defeat the enemy and could result in victory in a short period of time. Some of the weapons available to us may be considered to be outrageous, inhumane, demanding and may be deemed to be Police harassment. Some may suggest that we are moving towards a Police state. We (good guys) must consider any action taken against a persistent violent murderous enemy, necessary to reach the desired objective. There will be criticism, but success will prevail.

In the following paragraphs I will discuss those areas in which we (good guys) are making remarkable progress. Our efforts, however, are finding hurdles in other areas of the system. There are also some major weapons available to us, if used consistently would have a major impact on the conduct and operations of the bad guys.

Police activity in removing guns off the streets is commendable. There have been many arrests, but prosecution, conviction and sentencing are being delayed by attorneys requesting and obtaining long adjournments. The Gun Court was introduced and was successful in providing speedy trials, but was eventually discontinued. It was a form of swift justice, a concept, that provided for short adjournments (weeks), in particular in those cases involving the most dangerous weapons.

It is constitutional and lawful for any law enforcement officer having reasonable grounds to suspect that someone is engaged in criminal activity to: Stop, Question, Search, Seize and Arrest. This has to be the focus of all Law Enforcement Officers in this war. It must not be left to just a few. All must be involved. We must proceed politely but firmly. This course of action would assist in removing even more weapons, not just guns off the streets. It would help if all such persons could be exposed to swift justice. Immigrants, who are involved in criminal activity, must be identified and ordered to leave the country or deported. Those immigrants suspected of being involved in criminal activity, must be vigorously investigated and reports submitted to Immigration for consideration of their forced departure from our country. This course of action would rid the enemy of some of its financing.

Tracing Firearms: It is important, that we continue our efforts with the assistance of U.S. law enforcement to trace the origin of firearms found in our country. We must upgrade our efforts in firearms examinations as an important measure in obtaining evidence that could identify and convict violent criminals.

Firearms examiners resident in the Bahamas would be a massive asset. Skillful interrogation of persons arrested for possession of firearms would be effective in gaining information about smugglers, vendors and the methods being used to get such weapons into The Bahamas.

It is believed, that finance used by organized crime to engage persons to perpetrate violent criminal acts against their competitors and opponents, comes from this source. The enforcement of the law related to the tracing and forfeiture of the 'Proceeds of Crime' is enforced by those officials, authorized to do so.

It could be a massive weapon in the fight against crime in the Bahamas and even overseas.

Vagrancy and unlawful possession were laws used effectively by the Police in the maintenance of law and order and in particular the detection of crime. It is important to note, that the person charged with unlawful possession has to satisfy a Magistrate, that the possession is legal. The person arrested for loitering and charged with vagrancy has to satisfy a Magistrate that he had a satisfactory reason for being where he was found loitering. Both laws were effectively used by the Police in the past. Unlawful possession could be effectively used against the purchasers of gold, silver, copper and vehicle parts.

Shanty Towns were to be eradicated shortly after the appointment of Mr. Salathiel Thompson as Commissioner of Police. He was very concerned about the large numbers of immigrants residing in such places whose names or antecedents were unknown to us. He spoke about the Shanty Towns as a major security threat. His plan to demolish was stopped. In recent months we have erred in the manner proposed to deal with Shanty Towns. Law enforcement Officers should have been told to deal with the problem as they would with any other criminal act. Prosecution of the landlords and an order for them to demolish the buildings would have come from the Courts. A Committee was not needed. All of the offences committed by the landlords and occupants would have been dealt with by our law enforcement agencies.

Criminal Intelligence: It is important to policing and could be enhanced here, if the Police would obtain passenger manifests from airlines. In those documents Police may find the names of the numerous persons, who are ignoring traffic warrants or who are wanted by the Police. Knowing the movement of known criminals between our islands could assist in the detection of crime on the Islands.

Capital Punishment: I recall the failure of the West Indies Federation, which was buried in the ballot boxes of a Jamaican referendum decades ago, when Dr. Eric Williams, Prime Minister of Trinidad & Tobago coined the phrase "one from ten equals zero." Jamaica and Trinidad & Tobago, the first to shed the yoke of colonialism and the Privy Council as their final Court of Appeal. Our politicians here continue with an endless word game about accessing the Caribbean Court of Justice. (We contribute to it). This is not a legacy that Eric Williams, Norman Manley, Grantley Adams and Lynden Pindling would have wanted to perpetuate, but it remains the political burden sustained by politicians of several CARICOM nations. There appears to be reluctance to being judged by our own people. The Privy Council decision in the "Max Tido" murder case has convinced me that Capital Punishment would never be enforced as long as the Privy Council remains our final Court of Appeal.

Police Corruption: There are a number of factors, which render Police organizations worldwide, vulnerable to corruption. Many of those Police Organizations that we hold in the highest esteem have their problems with corruption. A Police Force is composed of people who constitute a cross section of the community, which the Force exist to safeguard. The commonplace values of that community, its norms of behavior, are inevitably reflected in the minds of Police Officers, even though Police Officers are expected, and themselves expect to live up to a higher standard of behavior than most people.

We have all seen the disastrous effects of having Police Officers enforce laws, which do not have the support of public opinion. Legislators are much to blame when they pass or do not pass laws, which take little account of human nature. In the Bahamas we had laws, which were systematically broken by a great many people of the working class, who place bets with bookmakers and web shops. The betting service could not be so extensively provided unless the Police turned a blind eye. Where corruption is known to exist in any part of a Police organization the mischief goes far beyond the depredations of the individuals concerned. I do not believe that there is very much corruption in our Police Service. I have a great deal of confidence in the organization. I am convinced, that a high proportion of our Police personnel would be glad to be relieved of the burden of knowing, that a minority exist. The Force is doing its best to rid itself of that minority.

The Commissioner of Police should have the authority to interrogate Officers regarding property suspected of being acquired by means of corrupt practices.

Commendations: Implement a system of commendations and rewards.

Incentives for Police Officers; Higher wages, and other incentives such as mortgage loans, car loans and scholarships would assist their financial security. A Reward Policy may also be considered, such as; if a Police Officer is offered a bribe and makes the arrest. His reward would be of a sum similar to that of the bribe.

Our Customs Department over the decades has been actively involved in the detection of crime. Customs Officers have been commended on numerous occasions for their skills in detecting contraband, in particular drugs and guns concealed in strange places. They have been magnificent. Resources should be provided for the detection of firearms and explosives arriving in the country. Officers should be rewarded for their discoveries. The performance of the Police has been remarkable. Police Officers seem to be undisturbed by their critics throughout the media, in particular where Police bashing is frequent and most of what is disclosed is untrue and/or malicious.

The Force has been accused of doctoring crime statistics, using excessive force and the 'covering up', even though officers have been prosecuted and convicted, making it known to all, that such conduct is not condoned. I do not recall reading or hearing of any praise being given to Officers, who are exposing themselves to grave danger to make our country a secure place to live and to visit.

The shooting of a criminal, who attempts to kill a Police Officer would-be front-page news. The criminal, who shoots an unarmed citizen in a robbery, is not given the same publicity. I continue to say; 'Police Shoot to Live Not to Kill'. As an experienced observer I am pleased with the performance of my former colleagues. I have observed the attacks on minor crimes and the improvement in the aggressive style of enforcement with commendable results. In recent years the Force has been engaged in areas, where it had to provide increase resources, such as; policing schools, policing 'Urban Renewal', and the Courts, to name a few, resulting in the removal of personnel from certain areas to supplement the above. Police Officers are working longer hours and much harder, morale however is still high.

Loyalty is at a high level and most importantly public relations is at an acceptable level. The Force is dedicated to eradicating crime in our country. The reports disclosed in the media, the huge backlog existing in our Courts and overcrowding in the prison, together with recent statistics have convinced me that we are winning the War.

The Force's Mission Statement; *The Force in partnership with all citizens, residents and visitors, exists to provide a quality of Law enforcement service, with emphasis on the maintenance of law and order, the preservation of the peace, the prevention and detection of crime, and the enforcement of all laws with which it is charged. We shall perform our duties in a manner which respects individual human rights and which reflects fairness, sensitivity and compassion. Yet we shall act in firm pursuit of all offenders of our laws, so as to ensure a safe and just society, where neither crime nor fear of crime adversely affects the quality of life. We shall accomplish these goals with a high degree of professionalism, through leadership, teams of individuals, who are competent, ethical and dedicated. We shall discharge our duties with courage, integrity, loyalty and being evermindful of a changing environment with willingness to embrace justified criticism and the need for change'*

The Politicians must provide their needs without interference, the media must deter from destructive criticism designed to discredit the executive team, and the public must provide support.

> *'The enemy must be engaged as a single*
> *unit in our quest for victory'.'*

Community Policing is just one of those concepts being used by Police Forces at present to enlist the partnership of the public in crime prevention and crime detection.

Police efforts in Community Policing must be extensive and there must be interaction by all ranks. One aspect of the concept that must not be overlooked is the 'walks', through communities and the personal one on one chats with residents. In some Forces the religious leaders in the District accompany the Officers. Elected politicians for the communities have also been active. The Police very often arrange lectures and social events so as to meet more of the people of these communities. One Police Force has been known to organize clean-up campaigns in communities, coach teams, supply sporting apparrel, and hold band concerts in crime plagued areas. These measures have resulted in some success.

The public must become more security conscious and take reasonable precautions to protect themselves and their property.

The public must be convinced that their full cooperation with the Police is the only way to eradicate the crime problems we now have in our communities. Failure to cooperate with the police is giving the criminals the upper-hand and eventually all of us may become victims.

Crime in general has had a chilling effect on all citizens and residents. While this has given rise to the level of fear in our communities and the obvious impact it is having on the quality of life of The Bahamian public, it is believed that many crimes against the person and property can be prevented. Crime Prevention Education and Neighborhood Watch programs must be accepted by the public as the way to go, in the fight against crime.

Our Police Service is dedicated to ridding our country of this evil. Most of the officers and men are honest, hardworking, and courageous and determined to win the war against the criminals. One only has to look in the media for the results that support the fact that our Police Service is standing firmly in the midst of the battle against the criminals of our country. They are to be commended for their courage and dedication. But what we see quite often are criticisms, blame and insults even in the editorials of some of the daily newspapers. The public must give the support needed to motivate the Police and let them know that their efforts are appreciated. We must realize that the law enforcement agencies in our county stands between us and a takeover by the criminals.

In all law enforcement agencies throughout the world there are those negatives that exist; corruption, gross misconduct, poor attitudes, physical abuse, and a host of others. The Police Service has to eradicate these negatives, but can only do so with the help of the public, who would have information on the so called 'bad cops'. It is necessary that the public support the Police to expose those individuals, who by their conduct and greed, destroy the good name and excellent work being done by the majority.

The public must have the assurance that confidential information will be treated as such and the source would never be disclosed. However, we must realize that on most occasions confidential information may not be sufficient to expose the criminal.

'Notify, Identify & Testify': - a slogan that is visible in many cities in the United States is applicable here.

The public must be prepared to take the stand, identify and testify against the criminal. The public must have the assurance against possible reprisal. (The Government and the Police through Witness Protection Programs could give that assurance.)

Crime Prevention Education: - Produce crime prevention education programs for radio and television. Promote group lectures to residents, businesses and schools in addition to distributing printed material.

People have to be taught how not to make themselves victims of crime. With the crime trend today, citizens must develop a heightened sense of awareness; always ready to take preventative action to protect themselves from becoming victims. It is said that a man's house is his castle, therefore he should be able to live there with little or no fear of crime. No building could be considered crime proof. Hence, householders and business owners should be made aware of the latest technology available to improve security to their properties.

Neighborhood Watch: - 'Neighbors watching out for neighbors'. This program is a proactive concept to reduce residential 'break and entry' as well as other property crimes within a community. Through increased awareness and crime prevention education provided by the Police, participating community members are encouraged to develop good security habits and to watch out for each other's property.

A Police Officer patrolling a community may not recognize a stranger in a yard or a strange vehicle in the neighborhood, but his neighbors would. A recent publication of statistics by a Police Force indicated that at least 70% of the crimes reported for the period of one year were preventable. That Force has launched an extensive crime prevention education campaign and increased its activity in helping communities to get involved in Neighborhood Watch. Our Police Force must take the lead in developing such programs.

Anti-Corruption Legislation to assist investigations:

Investigation of corruption must be intensive and fully supported by the Government.

The Criminal Investigation Fund: - Used to pay informants and for crime information.

New Legislation: - Consider what new legislation can be of use to the Police in the war on crime. (Bail, Search Warrants, period of detention of suspects and search and seizure.)

Speedier Trials: - for certain crimes, such as kidnapping and possession of firearms.

Rapid Response is a very effective Police measure. It could be very effective in serious crimes provided that notification of the police is prompt. The Rapid Response Unit should not be the only unit expected to respond. Any Police Unit in or near the scene of the crime must respond immediately. Rapid Response properly administered could help to develop public trust in the Police Service. The Police must work on achieving a response time of three to five minutes.

Public Relations: - There is a lot to be done if we are to succeed in eliminating the, existing division between the Police and Public. The Police must intensify its public relations efforts by the extensive use of the media, in particular the electronic media to produce programs that would generate public understanding of the Police Service and solicit their full cooperation and participation in the fight against crime.

All honest law abiding citizens and residents must stand firmly behind the Police. Communities must remain close and supportive of the Police Service, but must lobby and agitate for better service where needed. Persons making complaints against Police personnel must follow-up to ensure that such complaints are investigated thoroughly and that they be informed of the results.

Police conduct, is an area that all Police Forces must address. In one Police Force the term 'Polite, but Firm' is being drilled into its officers. There is another complaint heard very often from customers and that is, the long delay experienced in getting the Police to respond to house 'break-ins', burglaries and thefts. The victims lose faith and often have no hope of their complaints being successfully investigated. It may be good procedure to advise the customer when the investigators could be expected to arrive. Another area of public concern is the run around one gets when going to one Police Station to make a complaint and then being told that one had to go to another Station. The public does not understand why the complaint could not be taken at any Police Station and the statements etc., sent to the appropriate station ◙

Police Prosecutors
October 1st, 2010

Their performance over the decades of the Fifties to the present and their continued efficient performance in our Magistrates' Courts must be recognized.

In most countries in the Commonwealth, Police Prosecutors continue to provide this service. The amount of work done by our Police Prosecutors is accomplished through their dedication and devotion to duty. The long hours of reading and studying case files, lend testimony of their dedication. They occupy small cubicles in the Prosecutions Department where space and comfort are lacking, but as Police Officers, they make do with what they have available to them. Most importantly they save our Government millions of dollars by providing this service.

Police Prosecutors of the past, namely; Salathiel Thompson, John Crawley, Cyril Joseph, Summer Bannister, Chilean Turner, Keith Mason, and Grafton Ifill, retired DCP & ACP respectively were excellent in their presentations and examination of witnesses in our Courts. The Honorable Eugene Dupuch in describing Salathiel Thompson stated that he is 'a worthy advocate'. I have to be extra prepared when defending in his Court.

The Prosecutions Section of our Police Force is one of the most efficient units of the Force. Its personnel continue to provide efficient and effective service in the Justice System. With the addition of Police Officers with Law Degrees and Legal Training, performance in the unit has improved immensely.

I recall my training at the West Riding Detective Training College in Yorkshire, England; it was made very clear to us that Police Prosecutors are not expected to respond to legal submissions made by Defence Attorneys, in particular when it is on a point of law. Magistrates must deal with such matters. If the submission is about evidence or Police procedure, there ought to be a response from the Police Prosecutor. I would suggest that the Honorable Attorney General and other authorities, considering the change from Police Prosecutors to Attorneys at Law, visit the Police Prosecutions

Department for information on the following:

(a) Accommodation: Will the small cubicles presently in use be acceptable to Attorneys? Consider the cost of providing more suitable and acceptable office accommodation. The cost of upgrading the offices.

(b) Will a single Attorney in each Court be capable of and prepared to undertake the volume of cases being dealt with by Police Prosecutors? The average being about 25 cases per day, including; trials, bail hearings, first appearances and pleas. Attorneys from the Attorney General's Office attend the Supreme Court with one case file which they could have had for weeks of preparation.

(c) Deals between Police Prosecutors and Defence Attorneys are very unlikely.

(d) Calculate the difference in the earnings of Police Prosecutors and Attorneys.

(e) Interview Police Prosecutors on their case load and the number of files that are taken home to be read and prepare for presentation in Court on the following day. "If it ain't broke don't fix it."

I recall a case in which I was involved in the arrest of a man in possession of a large number of Quaaludes, a prohibited drug. The case was heard by a female Magistrate and Mr. Grafton Ifill ACP, Ret., prosecuted. The man was acquitted and the Magistrate ordered that the Quaaludes be returned to him. Mr.Ifill refused to carry out the Magistrate's order and consulted me on the matter. We called the Attorney General's Office. There were consultations between the Attorney General, the Chief Justice, and the Magistrate. The Quaaludes were eventually destroyed. Prosecutors in the Force have always been efficient and effective. The legacy continues today. ◼

Traffic Control & Enforcement

15th March, 2010

The number of traffic deaths and the increase in road accidents must be of concern to all of us. In the past I have written about the laws we have on the books, the laws we don't have, those that we should have and the failure of the Police to enforce some of what we have.

Our citizens and residents must lobby with their representatives for new laws and sustained enforcement of the traffic laws.

Speed is one of the causes.
The Police must use the speed guns and prosecute speed violators. If we need more speed guns, get them.

Drunk driving is dangerous.
We need a law that would enforce the breathalyzer test. The test must be mandatory. The penalty: heavy fines or imprisonment or both.

The breathalyzer test is being enforced in Trinidad & Tobago. Any suspicion that a driver may be intoxicated, the Police enforces the breathalyzer test, which cannot be refused by drivers. In all instances of road accidents, the drivers must take the test. The Police reported a 40% decrease in road accidents and 27% less fatal accidents. The fine for driving drunk is $5,000 to $8,000 dollars. Just two weeks ago a drunk driver involved in a road accident was sent to prison for two years.

Seat Belts save lives.
The law needs to be revisited, enacted and enforced.

Helmets for motorcycle riders.
The law is there, but is not being enforced. Check out a dead biker's funeral. The bikers are there by the score. No helmets and many without license plates. Many of the bikers do not have their bikes insured. They defy the law. Don't chase them on the streets; just get the unlicensed bikes when they are parked. Many of these bikers are the criminals moving the drugs and guns.

Inspection of vehicles.

The Road Traffic Department has to consider implementing a more intensive inspection of vehicles. Check wheel alignment, brakes, steering system and shocks etc.: as is done in most countries. While doing so check engine and chassis numbers. The latter would help in the search for those stolen vehicles which have been 'cloned'. In some countries the inspection of vehicles is contracted to qualified garages, where equipment is available to carry out the required checks. Road Traffic personnel can be sent abroad for the training. I have been told that some road traffic personnel have been trained, but the equipment is not available to conduct the proper examination of vehicles.

Review the Traffic Citation process and make it possible for the ticket to be sealed to the windscreen of the vehicle in the absence of the driver. Distribution of the duplicates should be to the Court, the Public Treasury and the Police Traffic Division. Enforce the arrests by warrants on those drivers, who ignore the tickets.

Zero Tolerance.

Motivate Police Officers to crack down on the law breakers racing during the late-night hours on JFK Drive, West Bay Street, Carmichael Road and the Eastern Road. The motor cycles, and bicycles being driven against the flow of traffic on one-way streets.

The condition of our country today can be described in these words; discipline, supervision, enforcement, transparency and accountability. We are sadly lacking in all these areas. ◼

Criminal Offences Overlooked by Police Officers.

30th April, 1979

Please note that any excerpt of any 'Act' as reproduced in any page of this book cannot be taken as read and the author takes no responsibility for its accuracy.

1. Section 230 of the Penal Code Chapter 48

Every person shall be guilty of an offence if -

Sec. 230(3)   Being the owner or occupier of premises in any Town or Settlement knowingly permits any disturbance to the public peace by loud shouting or otherwise in, or upon such premises. (This offence can extend to the owners of dogs, who knowingly permits their dogs to bark after a complaint has been made. Sec. 230(2) - In a public place in any Town makes a bonfire, or sets fire to, or throws, when lighted any fireworks, commits an offence.

Sec.230 (4)   In any street or place of public refills any kit or plays at cricket or any game to the annoyance or danger of passengers or residents.

Sec.230 (5)   In any part of any Town or Settlement or any place immediately adjacent to, makes or causes to be made any fire in the yard or other part of any house or premises except the kitchen whereby the Town, or any house or building, in or near it may be endangered.

sec. 230(6)   In any part of any Town or Settlement or any place immediately adjacent thereto, lights or causes to be lighted any fire or carries any lighted torch, candle or lighted thing or any fire through the same, unless secured in a lantern or some other safe thing in which it may be conveyed.

Sec. 230 (7)   Wantonly extinguishes the light of or destroys or interferes or meddles with, any public or street lamp.

Sec. 230 (11) Having custody of any child above five years, permits it to go naked.

Sec, 230(18) Rides or drives furiously any animal or vehicle, so as to endanger the life or limb of any passenger.

Sec.230(31) Begs for alms, or annoys any person by Importuning, soliciting or asking for custom for any purpose whatsoever on any highway or public place or upon any private premises, or causes or procures or encourages any child or young person so to do

Sec.230(33) Holds or takes part in any procession in any public place or street without the previous written permission of the Commissioner of Police.

Sec. 230(34) Washes any vehicle or motor vehicle in Rawson Square or in any part of May Street, which is within the City of Nassau as defined by the Interpretation Act Chapter 3. (Section 232(2) protects any peace officer in respect of any matter arising out of a breach of Section 230 whereby no action shall be brought against any peace officer provided that such officer has acted bonafide in the execution of his duty.

Sec 210 of Chapter 48 (Penal Code) - False Fire Alarm Whoever by means of any telephone message or otherwise maliciously gives or sends a false alarm of fire to the Fire Brigade or any member thereof commits an offence.

Sec: 229 of Chapter 48.-Stowaways

Sec. 238 of Chapter 48. Offences against Sanitation.
Whoever throws or causes to be thrown into any harbor or other waters adjacent to any Town or settlement with in the Colony, any putrid hides or the carcasses of any dead animal or other rotten substances commits an offence.

Sec.245 of Chapter 48 — Cruelty to Animals.
Whoever cruelly beats, ill-treats, starves or over-rides over-drives, overloads, abuses, tortures, or otherwise maltreats an animal of any species whether wild or domesticated whether a four-footed animal or not shall be guilty of an offence.

Sec. 250(1) Chapter 48. Whoever:
- In any manner encourages, or assists at the fighting or baiting of any bull, cock or other animal or bird, whether domestic or wild

- Keeps or uses or acts in the management of, any place used for the purpose of fighting or baiting or baiting any such animal or bird as aforesaid;
- Allows any place to be so used, shall be guilty of an offence.

Sec. 262 of Chapter 48 - Smuggling.
The Liquor Licenses Act — Chapter 291.Sec. 23
Any person who is:

- Holding a proprietary club license only either personally or by his servant or other person on his behalf sells by wholesale any intoxicating liquor;
- Holding a wholesale license, either personally or by a servant or other person on his behalf, suffers any other person to whom he has sold or disposed of any intoxicating liquors to drink such intoxicating liquors or any part thereof on the premises.
- Being a licensee refuses to produce on demand his license to any peace officer when in the execution of his duty.
- Being a licensee either by himself or his servant permits to be or be used as a brothel;
- Being a licensee, either by himself or his servant sells any intoxicating liquor to any person who is under 18 years of age or sells any intoxicating liquor to any drunken person to remain on the premises;
- Being a licensee under the Act fails or neglects to post his license in a conspicuous place on the licensed premises;
- Being a licensee knowingly sells or allows any person to sell to be consumed on the premises any intoxicating liquor to any person less than eighteen years of age.
- Being a licensee other than the holder of a hotel proprietary club, or restaurant license and except provided by this Act, either by himself or his servant, sells or exposes or offers for sale any intoxicating liquor, or opens or keep open any part of his licensed premises in which the intoxicating liquor may be sold, or permits any person to be or remain in such part on any night after the hour of nine o'clock or on any morning before the hour of seven o'clock unless such hour are extended by the licensing authority; shall be guilty of an offence.

Ministry of Works (New Providence) Rules (Chapter 14 of the Subsidiary Legislation.)

Rule 3 (1) - No person shall either, partially or entirely stop up, obstruct, alter or encroach upon. Or in any manner damage or render inconvenient to passengers, any public road or place. 3 (3) - No person shall deposit, place or discharge or cause to be deposited, placed or discharged in any public road or place; (a) any stone, sand, lime, timber, wood or material of any kind; (b) any barrel, box, case or other package or goods of any description whatever, except for removal at the earliest opportunity within the space of six hours; (c) any fruit skins, stones, earth, weeds, sweeping of any kind, paper, rags, rubbish, filth or any substance or any liquid; (d) - Stand, sit or lounge on any wall, fence, post or chain enclosing any public square or place or damage or interfere with any plant, tree or bush growing there on.

The Marine Products Fisheries Rules (Chapter 25 SubsidiaryLegislation)
Rule 9(1) - From and including the 16th day of March to and concluding on the 31st day of August in any year no person shall fish for take, capture, destroy or kill, or have in his possession any live or fresh crawfish without first having obtained the written permission of the Minister.

The Water Skiing and Motor Boat Control Act 1970
Section 4(1) - No person shall water-ski or drive any motor boat, whether or not with a water-skier in tow within 200 feet of the shoreline in any are to which for the time being, this section applies, except when the motor boat or water skier is either: -
(a) approaching or leaving a marina, dock, jetty, wharf or other installation of a permanent nature intended for the reception of boats;
(b) proceeding at a speed not exceeding three knots and with due caution and circumspection in the most direct line consistent with safe navigation between the open sea beyond the restricted zone and the shore or any mooring within the restricted zone
(c) towing a water skier in a lane clearly marked off with buoys and ropes of an approved pattern between the open sea and the restricted zone
(d) in distress or rendering assistance to some other person in distress (Restricted Zone means that area of water lying within 200 feet of the shoreline in any part of the Bahamas Islands to which for the time being Section 4 applies)

Sec. 5(1) No person shall drive a motor boat or manipulate any water ski within the territorial waters of the Bahama Islands: -
  (a) in willful and reckless disregard for the safety of another person or property.
  (b) without due caution and circumspection; or
  (c) at a speed or in a manner likely to endanger life or limb or to damage the property of or injure any person.

The Explosive Regulations 1969
Regulation 11. Every vehicle used for the transport of explosives other than fireworks shall affix to it at each side, so as to be distinctly visible from the front and rear, a red flag of at least eighteen inches square.

Regulation 12. No person shall drive or allow any other person to drive any road vehicle conveying explosives other than fireworks at a speed exceeding 20 mph.

Regulation 13. No person shall smoke or allow any other person to smoke or whilst on, in or attending any vehicle containing explosives or whilst acting as a watchman over explosives.

The Immigration Act. 1967.
Section 8 - If any Immigration Officer or Police Officer has reasonable cause to suspect that any person other than a person who is deemed to the Bahama Islands, has committed an offence under this Act or any regulations and if it appears to him to be necessary to assist such person immediately in order to secure that the ends of justice for the purposes of this Act shall not be defeated, he may arrest such person without a warrant whereupon the provisions of section 45 of the Magistrate Act shall apply in every such case. (Section 45 of the Magistrate Act is now repealed by virtue of Criminal Procedure Code Act, 1968.

Section 11 — It shall be the duty of every Police Officer and Customs Officer to aid and assist generally in carrying out the provisions of this Act; and if any contravention or failure to comply with; any of the provisions of this Act or any regulations shall become known to any Police Officer or Customs Officer. It shall be his duty to report the same forthwith to an Immigration Officer.

Outstanding Warrants

14th September, 2011

During the period when Messrs. Farquharson and Ferguson served as Commissioners. I had made a recommendation to them for consideration relating to the thousands of outstanding arrest warrants, mostly for traffic (citations) offenders. I never had any response and am not aware if the recommendation was considered. I am not aware of what is the present position regarding outstanding arrest warrants, but I wish to once again, make that recommendation for consideration.

Prepare a document listing all outstanding warrants of arrest in alphabetical order. Apart from the names of persons, include date of birth, place of birth, address given to the Police, driver's license, insurance company, description of vehicle and license number. All of this information should be available from the files held by the Police for prosecution.

Distribute copies of the document to all Police Stations, including the Family Islands for access by all Police personnel.

Consult with the various Government departments for assistance of their personnel to cross reference e.g., Road Traffic Department where persons visit to have their driver's licenses renewed, and vehicles inspected for licensing. Personnel can be asked to check the document for the names of these persons and if found on the list, to call the Police. Bahamas Customs and Immigration Departments where so many persons have to pass through when travelling and in the case of foreigners, visiting the Immigration Department for work permits etc., Airlines, local and foreign; to be asked to provide to the Airport Police, copies of passenger manifests daily for checking of the names with those on the warrant documents. Passport Office for the checking of the names of persons, who apply for passports or renewals. Voters Registers and Jury Lists are also sources for checking for the names in the document.

In my work I find them to be very helpful when trying to find missing persons or persons to be interviewed in private investigations. There may be other sources to be considered in this exercise.

Additionally, the Ministry of Foreign Affairs could be asked to negotiate assistance from the United States Preclearance personnel here and in Freeport in the identification of persons listed in the document.

The document should be printed so that names could be added when additional warrants are issued.

I know that something similar was being done in Toronto, Canada, with great success; an associate of mine did not pay a traffic citation on time. He went to license his vehicle. The officials checked the copy of the manual, found his name in it and called the Police.

TRAFFIC CITATIONS

3rd April, 2012

The traffic citation was recommended to Government by me when I was in the Police Service. It helps to enforce the traffic regulations expeditiously. There were to be four copies. The original issued to the driver, a copy for the courts, a copy for the public treasury and a copy to remain in the citation book for the Police records. In addition, a small coloured sticker was to be placed on the windscreen directly in front of the driver to inform him that he was ticketed for a traffic violation. This was to be done in the event that the citation left on the windscreen blew away or the driver claims that he did not see it. Legistation was to be introduced that would have required that the driver/operator of a vehicle, upon seeing the sticker, to inquire from the Police about the citation left on the vehicle and obtaining, a copy.

Inquiries made by me, revealed that there are thousands of arrest warrants existing in New Providence for persons, who have not paid their Traffic Citations. Although several arrests have been made, many of these persons have been able to prove that the fines were paid, either by receipts or other means. There appears to be a lack in communications between the Court receiving the payments and the Police Warrants Section. Communication on the receipt of payment for a fine should be immediate so that the arrest warrant could be canceled. A person wrongfully arrested can institute civil action, that unfortunately, could be costly to the state.

The arrests of persons wanted on outstanding warrants, in particular for traffic violations would boost Government's revenue.

Executing this large number of outstanding Warrants would enhance Police effectiveness and boost public confidence.

Road Traffic in Cuba.

In August and October 2019, I spent several weeks in Havana, Cuba. During my daily travel on the streets of the city, I observed the cleanliness of the environment, which was very impressive. I also observed an orderly movement of traffic not usually seen in large cities. The drivers of large buses, trucks, taxi cabs and motorcycles all appeared to be compliant with the traffic laws. Buses only stopped at bus stops, motorcyclist and passengers wore helmets, speed limits were observed, in particular in school zones.

During the visit I did not see a single traffic accident on the streets I had the opportunity to speak to a senior Police Officer of the Cuban Police Service. He told me that in Cuba the holder of a driver's license has a number of points allocated to him/her. Convictions for traffic violations results in points being deducted from the quota, the amount depends on the violation. If and when the quota of points is exhausted the driver's license is suspended for one year. Driving without a driver's license is serious offence for which the offender is arrested. During the late Fifties an attempt was made to introduce legislation approving a similar system for The Bahamas. It failed. In addition, mandatory breathalyzer tests for drivers suspected to be under the influence of alcohol and drugs would have been included. ◙

Recommendations to Government and The Police Force 2010-2011

December 15th, 2010

It is evident that law enforcement agencies have increased vigilance in our country and are being rewarded with the much-needed success in the war on crime.

Caribbean nations are hoping that with gun legislation and increased vigilance they can combat crime, in particular violent crime, a regional menace which is threatening the tourist industry. Some of the Islands have enacted legislation that denies bail for firearm crimes, with quick trials and mandatory prison sentences of three years minimum.

It is accepted by the leaders and residents of these Caribbean countries that crime impacts on the perception of safety, a crucial element influencing a person's decision to travel. Unless travelers feel a certain sense of security in making a trip, they will not embark on a journey.

An upsurge in crime, a growing trend in the Caribbean within the last few years should be of grave concern for regional tourism and hoteliers. Many are worried that declines in tourist arrivals to their respective countries will result, unless measures are taken to reduce violent criminal activity. Recent attacks on tourist in small island nations in the South Caribbean have been alarming. Some Islands are looking towards Canada and the UK to supplement their Police Services with the much-needed expertise.

As Caribbean countries are so dependent to a large extent on foreign exchange generated by the tourism industry, negative developments such as, increased violent crimes could have devastating consequences for their individual economies. In the Bahamas we are fortunate that violent crimes against visitors are occasional and our Police Service has successfully brought the criminals to justice. We are fortunate to have a Police Service that is well trained and equipped with vehicles, communication systems, modern technology and most importantly the qualified management and technical expertise which are tops in the region.

The problem in The Bahamas is guns, big guns, small guns, all sorts of guns. If we can eradicate the guns, violent crimes would be reduced. The Police are doing remarkably well with the number of arrests for firearms possession and recovery, the present system is frustrating their efforts, as those violent criminals are granted bail and back on the streets with other guns. This is a fact: the Police find themselves engaging the same criminals in battle. There are those who have been killed in gun battles with the Police who were out on bail for gun crimes. There is a dire need for legislation that would;

    (a) Authorize a special court for gun cases.

    (b) Deny bail for persons charged with gun crimes.

    (c) Mandatory imprisonment for those convicted of gun crimes.

RECOMMENDATIONS *January 4th, 2011*

1. A Gun Court to expedite trials for persons arrested for possession of firearms and ammunition.
2. Mandatory imprisonment upon conviction. (Would remove these criminals from our streets eliminating re-engagement with the Police, as is presently the case.)
3. Private Sector to be encouraged to support the efforts of the Police by offering rewards for information leading to the arrest, conviction and recovery of firearms and ammunition. Rewards to be extended to Police Officers in deserving cases.
4. The TASER and other non-lethal, but effective weapons to be made available to Police Officers. Training could be arranged with the manufacturer or agent. It could reduce the need to use deadly force in some instances
5. Make more bullet proof vest available.
6. Indoor shooting range needed for use by all Law enforcement officers. It would improve the ability of officers in the USE and SAFETY of Firearms. It would also encourage officers to use off duty hours to practice and develop themselves, provided the range is centrally located. It would also save working hours. The Private Sector may wish to share the cost. Possible venue: Upper floor of the Old Prison Building (Arthur House) at Police Headquarters. A brochure with information has been submitted to the Commissioner of Police and the Ministry of National Security.

7. Install GPS in Police vehicles, in particular patrol vehicles for better control by the Duty Officer in the Police Control Room. The rank of Duty Officers should be elevated. By knowing where Police Vehicles are at all times Duty Officers would be able to improve on the response time, organize road blocks, when necessary and eliminate the abuse of such vehicles. Such a measure could also reduce fuel cost.

8. The Police must motivate officers to do more with the ZERO TOLERANCE concept of enforcement. (traffic violations, liquor license violations, loitering, begging alms and the abuses of the Health Regulations by food vendors, nudist clubs, prostitution, etc.)

9. Police Officers, in particular the Staff Association must work towards eliminating corrupt practices. Give support to the efforts of senior management to do so. Private engagement of Police Officers is a privilege that must not be abused: adhere to the rules. Officers must attend Court when required to. Rudeness and misconduct must be discouraged and good work commended and rewarded.

10. Background investigation of recruits for law enforcement agencies could include the publication of photographs etc. with request for public information regarding their suitability. All information received to be investigated prior to confirmation.

11. All illegal immigrants must be photographed, fingerprinted and properly documented for Law enforcement Records. Assistance could be forthcoming from Retired Officers, who qualify.

12. Monthly or Quarterly Meetings by the Heads of Law enforcement Agencies and their assistants would be a major asset in the efforts to eradicate crime and restore the orderly society we once enjoyed. The Agenda for such meeting could include: The need for the united effort by all forces. Prison assistance in obtaining criminal intelligence from inmates and Prison Officers. (In the old days we got a lot of good information about crime and criminal activity from HMP). Immigration's joint efforts with other law enforcement. Assisting Police with information on wanted persons, who may be here illegally. Police information on Permanent Residents involved in criminal activity. Defence Force, protection of borders, Nassau Harbour and the theft of boats from Nassau Harbour. The exchange of information. Such meetings could include senior security personnel from government departments to remind them of their enforcement authority, to provide crime prevention education and training for their staff. ◼

The Licensing of Firearms
17th June, 2011

The licensing of firearms is the responsibility of the Police. It has always been the responsibility of the head of the Criminal Investigation Department (now CDU). The administrative work is carried out at the Criminal Records Office. There are fees to be paid when the license is obtained and for each renewal every year. It is the responsibility of the holder of the license to present that license to the Firearms Licensing Office by December, 31st. each year to apply for the renewal, which is not automatic as renewals can be refused by the Police.

Should the renewal of your license be refused you will be instructed to turn the gun in to the Police for safekeeping until you can dispose of it. This could be by sale or gift to any other person, who obtains a license. It is very important to note, that firearm licenses in most cases are issued for sports. On the application form the applicant must state the purpose for obtaining the weapon. Security companies that engage armoured vehicles for escorting cash are entitled to hold licenses for shotguns for their trained personnel.

Police Officers receiving information about anyone moving about with any weapon must act promptly to determine
    (a) if the person carrying the weapon has a license
    (b) if the person carrying the weapon is authorized to do so
    (c) if there are reasonable grounds to suspect the likelihood of someone being assaulted or hurt by the person carrying the weapon and
    (d) the security of the weapon being conveyed by the person in possession. License holders are not authorized to carry such weapons for self-protection or business protection.

I recall decades ago when Mr. Salathiel Thompson was Commissioner and I was in charge of CID we decided that all gun license holders must present their guns to the Firearms Licensing Office for inspection before renewal. We had suspected that shotguns had been stolen and not reported to the Police. license holders cooperated. A Member of Parliament ignored the request: Mr. Thompson sent a letter to him demanding, that he bring his four shotguns in for inspection. He did not bring the guns in. We executed a search warrant, collected the guns and the MP's licenses were not renewed.

Leaders and persons in authority in our country must obey the law. It is not the fault of the Police when one does not renew their firearm license and is found to be carrying it around in public places.

Finally, when making an arrest the Police Officer accepts a number of responsibilities, which includes preventing the person arrested from escaping and the safety of himself and the person arrested. The use of handcuffs to be decided by the arresting officer. It is part of Police training. The training demands that Police Officers identify themselves and inform the person of the reason for his/her arrest. Police Officers are expected to be polite but firm. ◨

Police Budget Considerations

REVIEW OF POLICE ESTABLISHMENT AND STRENGTH.

Have manpower needs kept pace with a growing population, expanding residential areas and the continuing growth of a massive industrial and business sector?

- Provide sufficient numbers of vehicles for adequate and effective street patrols. and to maintain the Rapid Response Unit
- Provide for an upgraded Communication System through which every Police Officer on patrol can be in constant contact with the Command Centre and vice versa. (Apart from the traditional two way radios some law enforcement agencies are using cellular telephones, which quite often is more convenient and confidential).
- Discuss with senior Police Officers new technology now available for the prevention and detection of crime. Other agencies abroad can be consulted for advice on the numerous new items on the market that can be used in the war on crime.
- Greater concentration on Police Public Relations Programs to help reduce anti Police sentiments existing in our communities.
- Expansion of Community Policing
- Provide adequate funds for the Police Criminal Investigation fund. (Used to pay informants and for crime information)
- Security of Government Buildings: Arrange for efficient security surveys to be carried out at all Government buildings, in particular those buildings with the most valuable assets. Consider the use of electronic security measures for the protection of such buildings. ◙

Security and Safety Awareness

The most understated or least appreciated phrase in policing today is understated because of the trust. The objective of the Police security and safety programs revolves around the issue of awareness of the Police efforts existence.

"Awareness": *Conscious, realizing one's surroundings, having knowledge of current issues*

The potential criminal :- if security awareness has been established by him, is going to be watchful, he is going to be wary of committing any crime where, if he thinks there is Police presence, even though there is no Police presence, he will most likely move on to another location to engage in any unlawful act.

Awareness of Police presence or possible Police presence is important in discouraging persons from committing crime, but particular effort is required by the Police to sustain such awareness among criminals. They must be made to think that the Police is in the area. Such awareness is a state of mind, recognition of the presence of a Police program aimed at reducing loss and preventing crime in the community. Such Police programs must be perceived to be real and effective.

Prevention is the bottom line of the Police programs and efforts. The programs exist for the prevention of crime and ensuring that the community is safe and secure for the persons, who reside therein. It can be called "Prevention through Deterrence."

There is the term called "Real Presence". It is the quality of the presence that makes Police Awareness function. Seeing a Police Officer on patrol in an area, walking in a parking lot or a Shopping Mall, such existence is real, but if the Police Officer is not alert, not paying attention to his surroundings, not observing the area as he passes through, then his presence loses some value.

The same applies to Mobile Patrol Officers. A person wearing a warm hooded jacket during the summer months ought to be stopped and searched. Any vehicle without number plates or panel trucks moving at nights must receive the attention of the Police Officers on patrol. Officers must be familiar with their powers to stop and search vehicles and persons - reasonable grounds of suspicion authorizes Police Officers to do so.

Quality Police Officers selected for mobile and foot patrols, fitness must be a criteria. Officers must be supported by quality equipment. Efficient and effective communication must be a criterion. The care and effort in the selection process, the care and effort in preparing the officers for their work (inspection and briefing etc.) and recording the daily performance of Officers and recommending commendations when necessary. The latter tends to motivate personnel in their daily performance.

Having the right personnel, adequately trained and properly equipped is required to build Police Awareness. ◙

Aggressive Crime Fighting

30th December, 2016

Our Royal Bahamas Police Force has always worked assiduously and effectively in combating crime in our country. In spite of the criticism by politicians, talk show hosts, media and the public, the Force has stood firm and is gradually winning the battle against the criminals (terrorists), who are trying to destroy our country. I am particularly pleased with the new approach, which I call 'Aggressive Crime Fighting' and the success it is having, not only with the arrests of criminals and the recovery of stolen property, weapons, ammunition and drugs, but what appears to be the support of communities and the expressions of faith and patience displayed by residents. I am proud to have been a member of this Police Force and will continue to support the leadership in the same way as our predecessors.

As a former Police Officer, I am aware of the frustration and disgust as a result of the recent murders, in particular after the successes in the detection of offences and the encouraging decline in crime over the past months. I am aware of the dedication and determination of your executive team and the Force in dealing with this vexing situation to secure the country.

As an outsider looking in I am able to observe the work of the Police on the streets and with my Police experience, comment on performance, which is superb. In particular in the area of major crimes; fair in the area of minor crimes, however, some offences appear to be ignored. It is with the greatest of respect and hope that the contents of this document will be accepted as constructive and will not in any way doubt my devoted loyalty to the Force.

I have observed the practices of Police personnel on patrol, in particular, the Mobile Units, which do not adhere to basic training and instructions and thus cannot effect efficient policing. The population should not only respect the Police, but believe that there is the likelihood of being caught in the act, when committing an offence; this would certainly earn the police further respect and instill fear in the mind of a would be perpetrator. It appears to me that the Force needs to become more aggressive in its methods. Following are recommendations for a more aggressive approach; I am sure that you and your executive team would be familiar with my suggestions:

MOBILE UNITS, INCLUDING MOTORCYCLIST

These officers should drive vehicles with the glass down for better hearing and observation. Officers should search men loitering on streets, sitting on walls, carrying backpacks or exhibiting behavior, that would be considered reasonable grounds for suspicion. The Mobile Units must be the front line of the attack, which must be relentless. Any offence exposed must be prosecuted; arrests made should be followed by a warrant executed on residences.

TRAFFIC DIVISION AND ALL UNIFORM UNITS

There are hundreds of motorcycles on our streets that are not licensed. These unlicensed motorcycles can be seized and held until the appropriate documents are produced, and the rider appears with a helmet. The riders have demonstrated and continue to demonstrate, that they have no respect for the Law; some of them have forged license plates. They ride dangerously on the streets; many without helmets.The noise on West Bay Street and other parts of the Island is disturbing. In fact, I believe many of these persons are involved in gangs and criminal activities as there is no concern about the law. I have seen Police personnel; in particular on Bay Street and Arawak Cay ignore the offences being committed.

STOLEN VEHICLES

We know that persons are stripping most stolen vehicles for their parts. Conduct visits to illicit garages and roadside repair locations and interrogate owners about car parts found on premises. There are those vehicles that are "cloned" and sold to unsuspecting persons and even placed in car lots for sale. I had suggested to a former ACP, that Customs and Police should check all car lots and have the owners produce papers for each vehicle on the lot. We know that there may be stolen vehicles or smuggled vehicles on the lots. In such cases criminal prosecution should occur and their business licenses revoked.

GOLD & COPPER EXPORTS

The Force must lobby to have gold purchases regulated. The vendor must produce proper ID and ownership documents. The purchase must be duly recorded in a ledger, which must be available for inspection by the Police. Copper exports must also be prohibited. Police must lobby for the prohibition; we do not mine copper; we do not manufacture copper materials, but we are exporting copper. The illicit industry encourages thefts, resulting, in significant damage to premises. I have received information that stolen copper is being melted into nuggets for export. It may be a consideration that Police visits are made to all junk dealers with search warrants to search for copper. There must be proper explanations and documentation for copper found on premises. Surveillance at these facilities could prove rewarding. I have also been told that most of the copper thefts are being perpetrated by Haitian and Jamaican nationals.

FOOD VENDORS

All restaurants as well as roadside vendors selling food and drinks must have valid health certificates, including those around our schools. Police Officers at the schools could be instructed to check vendors for the certificates. Health Certificates must be checked, (Sanitary Inspectors should be doing so, but are not) this also applies to staff in restaurants.

DISPLAY OF LICENCES

All shops, restaurants, liquor license premises and stores are required to show licenses in an area where it is visible for inspection. I have visited several of these places and have not seen any license displayed, (Edney Johnson prosecuted many merchants for ignoring this law).

STRIP JOINTS

There are many. I have read of the Police raids and arrests. They must be eliminated. Each divisional officer should be aware of the locations of strip clubs in his division and it should be his responsibility to close them down. Many of our murders are committed outside these clubs. Immigration must be involved in the process as most of the strippers are from overseas and are working on 'visitors' permits; deport and place on a 'Stop List'. Police should consider objecting to licenses being issued to the proprietors of these clubs. Closing down strip clubs should not be difficult. Undercover officers can sit in and observe the shows, and report the contents. Also, observe for the likelihood of prostitution being in progress at the clubs. The pursuit must be relentless.

THE SHANTY TOWNS

The shanty towns are a threat to our health, safety, security, and our environment. I know for a fact that some shanty towns are owned by Bahamians. In fact, I had given the name of an owner of a Fox Hill shanty town to Bahamas Immigration; he collected the rent weekly from Haitian residents. Those who wanted electricity, had to pay extra; buckets are used as the night toilets and contents dumped in bushes nearby. Criminals exist amongst the Haitian population that reside in shanty towns.

We have in our country thousands of persons living in the shanty towns. We do not know their names or have any information about them. They have their shops and transportation system. Most of these persons are working and could afford to rent proper premises, but being here illegally, they prefer to reside in the shanty towns to maintain their secret identity. Pigeon Pea and the Mud in Abaco are the most notorious.

Governments and Politicians have talked about the subject for several years, but no one has displayed the will to do something about the problem. There have been committees and discussions that have been to no avail. This year there was some hope when action was taken to close shanty towns, however it was not sustained for any length of time. We are still faced with the problem; the fact is that in the shanty towns, houses and shops are erected in contravention of the building codes, in addition to not having approval from the Ministry of Works and very often on lands where, they are squatting; again, against Bahamian Law.

I respectfully submit that this is not or should not be a political matter, but the responsibility of Law Enforcement including, Immigration, the Police and Defence Force. These institutions should use their authority to effect a managed, humane depopulation of all shanty towns and have the buildings destroyed. The residents, who are here legally, should be given time to find suitable accommodation; the illegals to be held for deportation. Once again, I am convinced that this is a law enforcement matter and there should be no interference from the politicians and churchs. ◼

The Use of Deadly Force
In Defence of Police Shootings

Dr. Epps, the rector of Christ the King Church in Atlanta wrote the following article (Taken from the internet) entitled:
'WE SHOOT TO LIVE, NOT TO KILL'

A few weeks ago, a rookie police officer from a North Atlanta suburb faced the horror dreaded by all cops and their families. The suspect a 20 year-old alleged deserter from the Army fired his weapon point blank into the chest of the 28 year-old patrolman. The stricken officer, protected from the potentially fatal round by his bullet-resistant vest, fell to the ground and, although suffering injury from the tremendous impact of the bullet, returned fire, along with another officer. In a few violent seconds, it was over. The fugitive from the Army will not have to be concerned about serving out his enlistment. He died at the scene.

Once in a while, someone will ask, Do the Police shoot to kill? The simple answer to that question is 'No'. But on the other hand, the answer is 'not so simple'.

The average citizen cannot possibly imagine how suddenly a routine traffic stop, warrant service, or interrogation can turn sour. In the movies, the bad guys can be seen planning and calculating their next move and, when the action starts, the cops dive for cover, call backup, and a gun battle ensues for the next fifteen minutes. The cops and the bad guys chase each other through the streets of the City, firing scores of rounds, and amazingly, even exchange taunts. In real life, such a scene almost never happens. In real life, the violence explodes without warning, lasts an average of 3 to 5 seconds, with five rounds being exchanged from a distance of three to seven feet. Think about that, one thousand one, one thousand two, one thousand three, and then it's over: Someone is dead or screaming in agony.

A few months ago Police Officers on patrol in a small village in The Bahamas observed a car with four men speeding on the narrow streets of the village. They also observed that there were no rear lights or number plates on the car. Their suspicion aroused, they pursued the car, which eventually crashed into a tree. As the Officers disembarked from the marked Police vehicle, the suspects opened fire with automatic weapons hitting one officer in the chest. The impact of the bullet into the bullet-resistant vest knocked him to the ground. He and his colleagues returned fire, killing one of the suspects and injuring the three others. Had it not been for the vest the Officer hit in the chest would have died instantly.

In another incdent we had a Police Officer shot when called to the scene of a domestic dispute between man and wife. The Officer died on the scene. The public accepts the garbage seen on television where the bad guys are shot in the leg, or the gun shot out of the hand and many other fictitious situations. In real life it is so different.

If the suspect is down, the officer, with hands shaking, will cuff him and call for an ambulance. If the suspect is bleeding profusely, the officer will try to administer first aid and save the life of the man who just tried to kill him. Officers have even been known to pray at such moments, pleading with God to spare the assailant's life. If on the other hand, the officer is on the ground, more likely than not, the suspect will walk over to him point his still smoking pistol at the officer's head, and pull the trigger. He will then steal the officer's own weapon and flee into the night. An hour or two later, the Chief and the Chaplin will pay a dreadful visit to the Officer's wife and children.

There is no time to talk the suspect down, no time to "shoot the weapon out of the bad guy's hand", no opportunity to carefully aim from cover and concealment and fire to wound. Officers are trained to aim for the "center mass" of the suspect's body and continue to fire until the threat is ended. "That cop fired nine bullets!" a civilian might protest. "He shot too many times!" "He was out to kill that guy" You weren't there. You have no idea. It wasn't your life on the line. You just don't have a clue.

If an officer is inclined to make a mistake, he or she is much more likely to hesitate to shoot for that all important split-second, than he is to fire prematurely. Most Officers have strong moral codes, have an aversion to killing; the reason they became cops is to help people. They are also aware that when things go wrong, they are subject to libel.

The hesitation may well result in the Officer's death. Criminals who would fire on a Police Officer have no such moral restraints. They do not hesitate.

Police Officers are not trained to shoot to kill. They are trained to shoot to live. They are not, regardless of how much anti-law enforcement types might whine, trying to take suspect's life. They are simply trying, desperately, in a few terror-filled seconds to somehow survive the encounter and go home to their spouse and family at the end of the shift. "They are shooting to live." If they do shoot a suspect, and the criminal dies, cops are more likely than not to have severe depression, to experience sleepless nights, endure post-traumatic stress, and be overwhelmed with guilt. He or she will be more at risk than other officers to experience a divorce, become an alcoholic, and take their own life. He would have had 3 - 5 seconds to "shoot to live" while the public, the press, and the courts will have years and decades to second-guess the officer and wonder why he didn't "shoot the gun out of the bad guy's hand."

I have two sons who are on the streets as Police Officers. Tonight they will pull over a car on some dark roadside or will investigate an alarm call. If the moment ever comes, which, I pray it does not, I pray that they will respond to their training. I pray that they will not hesitate, no, not for one second. Then, if their life hangs in the balance, I pray that, in that 3 - 5 seconds of heart-stopping, throat choking horror, that they will "shoot to live". I pray that their aim will be true. I pray that they will come home to their families, safe and uninjured. And, then, the next night, and the next. Then they will face it all over again, night after night, year after year.

They and ten thousands of the men and women like them are cops. It's what they do. ◉

The Use of Force

Illustrations given in Sections 98 through 105 (see below) must be known and practiced. It states the grounds for which force or harm may be justified, within prescribed limits.

Section 98 - Force may be justified in the cases and manner, and subject to the conditions, hereafter in this title mentioned, on the ground of any of the following matters, namely;

1. *Express authority given by statute.*
2. *Authority to execute the lawful sentence or order of a Court.*
3. *Authority of an Officer to keep the peace or of a Court to preserve order.*
4. *Authority to arrest and detain for felony.*
5. *Authority to arrest, detain or search a person otherwise than for felony.*
6. *Necessity for prevention of or defence against crime.*
7. *Necessity for defence of property or possession or for overcoming obstruction to the exercise of lawful rights.*
8. *Necessity for preserving order aboard a vessel.*
9. *Authority to correct a child, servant or other similar person, for misconduct.*
10. *The consent of the person against whom force is used. (Save where otherwise expressly provided in this Code)*

General Limits of justifiable force or harm.

Section 99 - Notwithstanding the existence of any matter of justification for force, force cannot be justified as having been used in pursuance of that matter:

1. *Which is in excess of the limits herein after prescribed in the section of this title relating to the matter.*
2. *Which in any case extends beyond the amount and kind of force reasonably necessary for the purpose for which force is permitted to be used.*

Section 100 - *Whoever is authorized by the provisions of this Code or any statute to use force may justify the use of necessary force according to the terms and conditions of his authority.*

Section 101-*Whoever is authorized to execute any lawful sentence or order of a court may justify the use of the force mentioned in the sentence or order.*

Section 102 - *Whoever is authorized as a peace officer, or in any judicial or official capacity, to keep the peace or preserve order at any place, or to remove or exclude a person from any place, or to use force for any similar purpose, may justify the execution of his authority by any necessary force not extending to a blow, wound or grievous harm.*

Section 103(1) - *Any person may, with or without a warrant or legal process, arrest and detain another person who has committed a felony, and may, if the other person, having notice or believing that he is accused of felony, avoids arrest by resistance or flight or escapes or endeavors to escape from custody, use any force which is necessary for their arrest, detention or recapture and may kill him, if he cannot by any means otherwise be arrested, detained or re-taken.*

Section 103 (2) *Whoever is duly authorized by warrant or other legal process to arrest or detain a person for felony may, if that person believes that a warrant or other legal process in in force against him, justify any force which is necessary for his arrest, detention or recapture, and may kill him, if he cannot by any means otherwise be arrested, detained or re-taken, although in fact the felony has not been committed by the other person, or although in fact no felony has been committed.*

Section 104 (1) - *Any peace officer and all persons whom he shall call to his assistance may arrest and take persons into custody without a warrant in the following cases:*

> *(a) Any person whom he finds committing an offence against the person or against property as to which it is provided under this Code that the offender may be punished by imprisonment.*
> *(b) Any intoxicated or idle or disorderly person whom he finds in any way disturbing the peace or committing an offence which may be an outrage to public decency or morality.*
> *(c) Any person whom he finds during the night lying or loitering in*

any highway, yard or other place and whom he shall have good cause to suspect of having committed, or being about to commit, any offence against this Code.

(d) Any person whom any other person positively charges or states, that he suspects of having committed a crime or offence of stealing or obtaining goods by false pretenses, or receiving stolen goods, or the offence of cruelty to or causing injury to an animal, if the charge or suspicion appears to the peace officer to be well-founded and the informant is willing to accompany the peace officer and at the police station is willing to enter into recognizance conditioned to prosecute the charge.

(e) Any person whom any other person charges with having committed an aggravated assault, if the peace officer has good reason to believe, that such as assault has been committed, although not within his view, and that by reason of its recent commission a warrant could not have been obtained for the apprehension of the person charged.

Section 104 (2) Any such person arrested as aforesaid shall be taken, as soon as reasonably may be, before a Magistrate to be dealt with according to law; unless he be released on bail, approved by the Commissioner of Police or other authorized member of the Force.

Section 105 - Whoever has authority, by warrant or other legal process or under the provisions of any statute, to arrest, detain or search another person otherwise than for felony, may justify any necessary force not extending to a blow, wound or grievous harm, if the other person has notice or believes that the force is used by virtue of any such authority."

INDOOR SHOOTING RANGE

28-9-2010

In the decades of the Fifties and Sixties the Police Force had a make-shift shooting range in the Police Barracks where Police Officers practiced to improve their shooting skills. The location now accommodates INTERPOL and the Communications Unit. During those years we had marksmen, such as; the Tynes brothers, Freddie Wilson, Edney Johnson, Errington Watkins, Salathiel Thompson, Anthony Fields Wilfred Jack and others. We had a winning record shooting against crews of visiting U.S.

and British warships, who we entertained.

Several years later Mr. Salathiel Thompson and I investigated the possibility of acquiring a modern indoor shooting range here. We selected Arthur House (old Prison Building) as a location. We obtained pledges from the FBI, DEA and Sir Albert Miller to provide the equipment and furnishings. Mr. Thompson approached Prime Minister Pindling about the project. He was in favor, but we were unable to proceed at the time due to the cost of renovations and special equipment, that was needed to circulate fresh air into the room. There is a greater need now, than ever before for an Indoor Shooting Range. The crime trend mandates, that Police Officers are armed as criminals are armed, many with the most deadly weapons as most violent crimes are perpetrated by criminals using firearms.

The Range would be available to all law enforcement officers. The Firearms Licensing Office would be able to test the capability etc. of persons applying for firearms license, which is not presently the case. Our law enforcement Officers may also qualify for the Olympic Games like Trinidad & Tobago. The latter has won medals at the Games. Most importantly our officers would be able to develop their shooting skill on their time thereby saving the Force man-hours of organized training. The range could be staffed by qualified former law enforcement officers.

Discussions were held with Mr. Garrard Forrester, formerly of the FBI and Mr. Bill Pennypacker of the Broward County Sheriff's Office. The latter introduced me to Mr. Randy Graham V.P. of Actions Target Inc. and Mr. Adam White, range consultant for his firm. I continued communications with the Minister of National Security to whom brochures from Actions Target Inc. were sent.

I indicated in my communications, two locations, namely; the Customs warehouse on East Street opposite Mortimer's Candy Kitchen and the old City Market building on Market Street (first choice). There has been no comments in recent years about the subject, except for a proposal made by a former Police Officer, who offered to provide the range if Government would meet with him to discuss the lease of the selected premises and a fee arrangement for the training of law enforcement officers. There has been no response from Governments.

Case No.684/75.

Five C.I.D. Officers charged with Manslaughter.
**(Officers defended by Messrs Cecil Wallace-Whitfield and former
Prime Minister Perry Christie.)**

**The following paragraphs contain excerpts from the written Ruling
of the Examining Magistrate Wilton Hercules.** *23 April 1975*

The ruling of the Magistrate exemplifies the importance of efficient
diary keeping and the recording of communications with persons in
custody. In reading the ruling of the Magistrate it is evident, that the diary
entries, together with lies told by other criminals in custody caused the
dismissal of the charges during the preliminary inquiry.

The Accused in this matter appeared before me as Examining
Magistrate in a Preliminary Inquiry, on the 17th March 1975. They were
informed of the charges against them in accordance with section 115 of
the Criminal Procedure Code. The matter was then adjourned to the 19th
March 1975. Mr. C. Wallace-Whitfield, of Counsel, appeared for the 5
accused, and with him were associated Mr. P. Christie, Mr. A. Butler, Mr.
A. Allen and Mr. E. Knowles.

Before the commencement of the Inquiry, Mr. Wallace-Whitfield,
leading Counsel, raised a point "in limine" as to the section under which
the accused were charged. This was overruled, and the Inquiry into the
charge of Manslaughter under Section 339 of the -Penal Code began.

The Examining court proceeded almost daily thereafter, to record
depositions from a total of 25 witnesses, concluding on the 11th April
1975. Cross examination of nearly all of these witnesses, was most detailed
and trenchant. Cross examination of some of these witnesses took, in some
instances, as long as three days, and in many instances, examination-in-
chief of some of the prosecutions' witnesses extended: beyond a single
day.

Inspector Hugh Burke, who conducted the prosecution, did, to my
mind, a masterly job, with whatever material he had at his disposal. He
was most courageous in the presentation of the evidence available to him.
Above all, he displayed great impartiality and honesty in his presentation
of the evidence for the Prosecution.

106

All the evidence having been adduced before the Examining Magistrate by Friday, 11th April, the matter was then adjourned to Monday, the 14th April, Mr. Whitfield having indicated to the Court his intention to make a no case submission.

On the 14th April 1975, the Court resumed, and the matter continued. Mr. Whitfield addressed the Court at some length. Briefly summarized, he asked the Examining Court to consider carefully the following:

(a) The inconsistency and unreliability of the testimonies from most of the material witnesses for the prosecution; more especially of the alleged eyewitnesses and three felons with most enviable criminal records.

(b) The irregularity of the identification parade, and

(c) The disagreement between the testimonies of the two medical experts, as to the time of the injury received by the deceased Franklyn Stubbs.

As Examining Magistrate, let me state at the outset that it is not my duty to 'try' the case, and to decide whether these Accused persons are innocent or guilty. My duty is merely to decide whether the Prosecution has made out a case against the Accused. If a case has been made out, from cogent and unimpeachable evidence adduced, then my duty is clear; these men must be committed for trial before the Supreme Court. If I find that no case has been made out, then my duty is equally clear, and these 5 Accused men must be discharged by me at this stage.: But it must be remembered that refusal by an Examining Magistrate to commit Accused persons does not mean that those persons have been acquitted, and may not be put in peril again on the particular charge. It is then a matter for the Attorney General's Department. Section 122 of the Criminal Procedure Code states as follows:

"If, at the close of the case for the prosecution, or after hearing any evidence in defence, the Magistrate considers that the evidence against the accused person is not sufficient to put him on trial, the court shall forthwith order him to be discharged as to the particular charge under inquiry; but such discharge shall not be a bar to any subsequent charge in respect to the same facts:Provided that nothing contained in this section shall prevent the court from proceeding either forthwith, or after such adjournment of the inquiry as may seem expedient in the interest of justice, to investigate any other

charge upon which the accused person may have been summoned or otherwise brought before it, or which, from the evidence given in the course of the hearing of the charge so dismissed as aforesaid, it may appear that the accused person has committed."

This is the, procedure as it obtains here.

You will note that I have underlined 'but such a discharge shall not be a bar to any subsequent charge in respect of the same facts.' Indeed, if the Attorney General's Department disagrees with the refusal of an Examining Magistrate to commit, then, if the English procedure is followed, the case may be represented before another Examining Magistrate; there are three other such in this Commonwealth, or an application may be made to the Supreme Court for a Bill of Indictment, which if granted, would result in the accused person or persons, being taken before a higher court for trial.

I have taken the time, the patience and the industry to go into this matter carefully, so that whatever my findings in this preliminary Inquiry might be, it is my own considered opinion, which is subject to all the errors of human frailty. I can only act in accordance with my own interpretation of the law, as I understand it and the facts as I comprehend them.

The Inquiry commenced with the evidence from members of the family of the deceased, Franklyn Stubbs. They were not eye witnesses to the event, and certainly whatever evidence they gave was in many instances, purely circumstantial, and equally so in a number of other instances, merely figments of their imagination. It was my opinion that they came into the witness box with preconceived notions of what evidence they were bound to give against these 5 accused men, and attempted persistently, albeit unsuccessfully, to have the Court admit inadmissible testimony. In the confusion emanating from their testimony, it was impossible for this court to place reliance upon their word as to time or circumstances as related by them.

They all testified that the deceased was taken away by the Police in the daytime, on the 18th December. He was then in good health. The next time they saw him was between 11:00 and 11:30 that same night. When they saw him again he was being supported by two members of the C.I.D. He had been, at that time, brought back to his home for further investigations by the C.I.D. There was definite confusion as to the circumstances, and the events surrounding the deceased return home by all the witnesses testifying as to his return. The only aspect, upon which there appeared to have been general consensus by them, was that the deceased was being supported by two C.I.D. men. In other words, he appeared, to have been too weak to walk. With their testimony, I compare the evidence as given by the police officers on sentry duty at both the C.I.D. and the Central Police Station. As a result, I found that there was some positive conflict between the testimonies of the two sets of Prosecution witnesses. And as an article of faith, I was inclined,   more to belief in the statements of the police officers.

And then William Lockhart took the stand. Lockhart, at 36 years of age, established himself as a convicted criminal, who had had convictions with prison sentences totaling nearly 22 years of his life. He proudly presented himself as a criminal, at present serving terms of imprisonment of some "21 years and 5 months."

His testimony was significant, both as to the alleged beating of Franklyn Stubbs by the police on the night of the 18th December 1974, and also of himself, on the same night and at the same place. He left the court in no doubt whatsoever, that while he was being beaten, there was no one else except police officers present in the "interrogation Room."

Above all that, when Franklyn Stubbs was being beaten, there was no one else in that room, other than himself (Lockhart) and the aforementioned police officers. The evidence of the two other eye witnesses would most certainly have given the lie to this. It is noteworthy that he said that Franklyn Stubbs was beaten between 4:30 and 5 p.m. on the 18th December. When this testimony is compared with that of Joseph Anderson and Leroy Brown, one is left to wonder at the truthfulness of this statement. So far as he was concerned, the officer holding the piece of 2x4 wood, and inflicting blows upon Stubbs, was the accused, Bullard. When this evidence is compared with that given by the witness, Leroy Brown, we find that Bullard, according to Brown, had nothing whatever to do with the beating of the deceased. As a result, I have concluded that neither of these two witnesses had been honest in their testimonies, and I find that no reliance whatsoever could be placed on their credibility.

The evidence of Joseph Anderson, the 12th witness called for the Prosecution, was to my mind, a saga of vituperation against the Police. He had himself spent most of his adult life in prison, as a convicted criminal. As recently as the 29th January 1971, he had been imprisoned by the Supreme Court for armed robbery. In fact, at the time of giving his testimony, he was on remand in custody, on another similar charge. Just like Lockhart, his demeanor in the witness box did not commend itself to me, and I found it extremely difficult to believe that he was capable of telling the truth.

The 16th witness called was another convicted criminal, Leroy Brown. He gave his testimony between the 7th and 9th April 1975. Like the other two unsavory characters before him, he had also spent most of his adult life in prison. One of his convictions was for making a false statement in order to obtain a passport in 1972. He admitted that when he did this, he knew that he was telling a lie. In addition to this, he admitted to a total of 23 convictions, all for dishonesty.

As a result, I feel that any Examining Magistrate would be hard put, to believe the testimony of these three witnesses. I certainly could not. As Examining Magistrate, it is my duty to decide whether or not I believe the evidence of the more important and material witnesses tendered by the prosecution. In this instant inquiry, I am afraid that I cannot, in all good conscience, believe the testimony as given by these three convicted criminals, brought into court as witnesses for the prosecution. These were the only eyewitnesses tendered by the prosecution, to the alleged beating of the deceased Franklyn Stubbs, whilst he was in police custody. Their evidence was an essential element in this inquiry, and if I do not believe their testimony, then it would appear to me that my duty is clear.

In contrast with the evidence of the felons referred to above, we have the evidence for the prosecution of the policemen on sentry duty both at the Central Police Station and the CID, between the 18th December and the 19th December. Constable Burkie Wright produced the CID diary covering the relevant period, in which mention is made of the name of the deceased Franklyn Stubbs. No complaint was ever made to him about, or by Franklyn Stubbs, of maltreatment. Constable Eric Strachan of the CID produced the said CID diary with entries made, by him on the 18th December 1974. He had seen Stubbs at 10:25 p.m. on this day, and in his own words. "Stubbs appeared alright to me". Again, I have before me, the testimony of Cpl Charlton and Cpl. Bostwick, officers in charge of the Central Police Station, between the 18th December and 19th December 1974. Charlton was in charge from 10 p.m. on the 18th December to 7 a.m. on the 19th December. This officer saw Franklyn Stubbs during his tour of duty at the station, between the hours stated above. At no time was any complaint made to him, by or on behalf of Stubbs in respect of brutality. and certainly not to him. Stubbs appeared to be normal at 11:55 p.m. on the evening of the 18th December, when he was taken out of his custody and up to the CID Cpl. Bostwick testified under oath that his tour of duty began at 2:03 p.m. on the 18th and ended at 10 p.m., when Chariton took over from him. He also saw Franklyn Stubbs at the station during this period, and he appeared to him to be normal. Again, no complaint was ever made to him by anyone concerning Franklyn Stubbs, or by Stubbs himself.

The testimony of all these last named witnesses was evidence tendered by the prosecution. I have already stated that I do not, in fact I cannot, in all good conscience; believe the evidence of the three felons. There is nothing whatever in the testimony of these policemen, and I include in this the evidence of PC Bain, which speaks for itself, and can be considered as being unworthy of belief. In each instance their testimony was backed up by entries made in their station diaries. If these policemen were lying, and I do not believe that they were, then it was not my duty to decide as to who were the greater of the liars tendered by the prosecution, the convicted criminals or the policemen, whose characters up to the present time, were unblemished. My duty as I have said before is to decide, as Examining Magistrate, whether I believe or do not believe the evidence of the more important of the prosecution's witnesses.

I come now to the purported Identification Parade of which Assistant Commissioner Strachan deposed that he was the officer in charge. At the outset, I stated without any trepidation whatever, or hesitation, that this method of identification of suspected persons as used by the police on this occasion, constituted an exercise in futility. It was to my mind, not conducted with the scrupulous regularity of the required fairness of Identification Parades. The evidence is that these three witnesses were brought to Police Headquarters, in an ambulance. They were made to wait in it, outside in an open yard. While there, they must most assuredly have had every opportunity to see the suspected police officers; who also had to pass in this same area. In a situation such as this, it is not too difficult to envisage these three criminals choosing the men who would be their victims, letting their imaginations run riot and concocting between them evidence against men whom they believed that they had every reason to hate. To carry this farcical situation a bit further, each of the 12 suspected persons were put in a room by themselfs along with Assistant Superintendent Ifill and Mr. P. Christie, of counsel. Then one of the three witnesses, who had hitherto sat in the ambulance in the yard at Headquarters, was brought into the room and was asked, pointing to the lone suspect in that room, "Is that the man?"

At this stage I refer to the decision of the Court of Criminal Appeal in the matter of R.V. Chapman of the 20th November 1911, and reported in C.A.R. at page 53, where the Headnote reads as follows:

'The identification of a suspected person must be carefully conducted. It is wrong to point out the suspected person and ask, Is that the man?'

Lord Alverston, L.C.J., in giving the judgment of the court said as follows:

"It is not right to point out and ask questions in this way. The usual and proper way in such cases is to place the suspected man with a sufficient number of others, and to have the identifying person, pick out a man without assistance. Although identification is difficult, this method does strengthen it."

No such procedure was here followed.

Chapman's case was exemplified on the 18th November 1912, in the case of R.V. George Harold Williams reported 1912, 8 C.A.R. at page 84. The Lord Chief justice Alverstone sitting with Justices Channell and Avory, in handing down the decision of the court quashing the conviction, said at page 88:

'The case for the Prosecution at the trial evidently rested on the identification by Fulcher, this identification was not properly carried out. Fulcher saw the Appellant alone in the police station, and did not pick him out from among other men. In the opinion of the court the mode adopted was not a proper one and therefore the identification cannot be said to have been satisfactory'

Again, in the case of R. V. William Chadwick and others, in which the Lord Chief Justice Reading sat with Justice Rudley and Avory, there appears the following Headnote: 'Evidence of identification is weakened if the identifying witness has previously been shown a photograph of the accused for the express purpose.'

His Lordship then went on to set aside the verdict of the jury and to quash the conviction. In this Preliminary Inquiry, it would appear to me that the evidence of the manner in which the Identification Parade was conducted, offends against all the known rules in respect of Identification Parades. Surely, even if the 12 suspected men refused to go on 'a normal and conventional' Identification Parade, there were other methods by which these men could have been identified, which would have been consonant with the high standard of scrupulous fairness, contemplated in the identification of suspects. I am of the very humble opinion that the identification of the 12 suspects, which included the 5 accused here in Court, was a complete nullity. It was most unsatisfactory. The authorities on this subject are so clear, that it makes further comment by me, unnecessary.

Another duty of the Examining Magistrate is to ensure that the time of Juries is not wasted in trying men who will patently be acquitted if committed for trial before a Judge and Jury. (Harrison: The Work of a Magistrate, at page 65 — published May 1964.)

And here, I refer to the case of R. V. Hipson (Court of Criminal Appeal (Criminal Division) 1969 — Criminal Law Reports — 85 — February 1969), where the Court of Appeal held in allowing this appeal that:

'When a submission is made that the case should not be left to the Jury, it is a Judge's duty not only to consider whether there is some scintilla of evidence, which in law could go to the Jury, but also whether it would be safe for a Jury to convict on the evidence as it stands.'

Again, in Ryder v. Wombmell (1869) L.R.4 Exchequer 32, in the course of delivering the judgment of the Court, Willis J., said inter alia, at pages 38 + 39: (subject of course to review) is, as is stated by Maule J. in Jewell v. Parr, not whether there is literally no evidence, but whether there is none that ought reasonably to satisfy the Jury that the fact sought to be proved is established.

In Toome v. London and Brighton Railway Company, Williams J., enunciates the same idea thus:

'It is not enough to say that there was some evidence. A scintilla of evidence... clearly would not justify the Judge in leaving the case to the Jury. There must be some evidence on which they might reasonably and properly conclude that there was negligence — the fact in that case to be established.'

- And in Wheelton v. Hardisty in the considered judgment of the majority of the Court, it was said:

'The question is, whether the proof was such that the jury would reasonably come to the conclusion that the issue was proved. This they say, is now settled to be the real question in such cases by the Exchequer Chamber, which have in our opinion so properly put an end to what had

been treated as a rule, that a case must go to the jury, if there were what had been termed a scintilla of evidence.'

In this instant inquiry, one would have to stretch credulity to far beyond the pale of breaking point in order to feel that on the evidence of Lockhart, Anderson and Brown, self-styled eyewitnesses to this melancholy event, these 5 accused men should be committed for trial before a Judge and Jury.

- And now I turn to the medical evidence given in this Inquiry.

At the outset, I would state that I disagree with the submission of Mr. Whitfield of Counsel that the testimonies of the two pathologists did not agree in a common finding. My perusal of my own notes in the matter shows the contrary to be the case. Both agreed that the deceased died as a result of some external force being applied to his body with a blunt object. The only divergent difference in their testimony is the approximate time of death. Dr. Joan Read, Pathologist of the Rand Laboratory, was convinced that the injuries which she saw on the deceased, when she performed an autopsy on his body some 2-4 hours after his death, had been inflicted a minimum of 3 days before her autopsy on the 19th. She was also present when the exhumed body of Franklyn Stubbs was autopsied on the 17th February 1975, by a Dr. Russell Fisher. She also assisted in this autopsy. On that same day, on which Dr. Read deposed, evidence was taken from the said Dr. Russell Fisher. In addition to his distinguished list of academic qualifications, he is now the Chief Medical Examiner for the state of Maryland in the United States of America. He deposed as to having been invited here at the instance of the Attorney General of the Commonwealth. His testimony was to the effect that he had examined some tissues from the body of the Deceased. He said that there was injury to the body of the Deceased; that it was consistent with the deceased having been struck by a blunt instrument, to wit, a fist or a piece of wood; and that his examination of the tissue led him to the conclusion that the injuries were administered to the body between 18 to 24 hours before death.

This in short, is the testimony of these two medical experts. Again, my duty is not to determine which of them is the better expert", or which one possesses greater proficiency in the practice of his chosen profession. My duty is merely to accept their evidence and try to apply it to the facts of the case and to arrive at a finding, which is fair and reasonable in all the circumstances.

Phipson on Evidence the 10th Edition, Paragraph 1286 treats the value of expert evidence in this manner:

'The testimony of experts is usually considered to be of slight value since they cannot be indicted for perjury, are proverbially, though perhaps unwittingly, biased in favor of the side which called them, as well as over ready, to regard harmless facts as confirmation of preconceived theories; moreover, support or opposition to given hypotheses can generally be multiplied at will. Indeed where the jury accepts the mere untested opinions of experts in preference to direct and positive testimony as to facts, a new trial may be granted. where two medical experts are differing in their opinions as to the exact time of the injury sustained by the deceased'. As a result therefore, can anyone, with any degree of certainty, whatever, find any nexus between the medical testimony and the five accused.

With great respect, I say, that I cannot.

There were three counts against these 5 accused men. I proceeded to inquire into the charges as laid under section 339 of the Criminal Code, that the accused (the 5 herein named), on "19th December 1974, at New Providence, did unlawfully cause the death of Franklyn Stubbs."

This section which appears to me to be the Penal Section is set out in two parts, embracing both offences, envisaged by Section 335, the section creating the offence. It contemplates manslaughter by negligence, or in any other case. 'Manslaughter' is defined in Section 335 of the Penal Code, as causing the death of another person by 'Unlawful Harm'. If the harm was negligently caused, then this is manslaughter by negligence.

I feel that it is incumbent upon me at this stage, to refer to a practice note handed down to magistrates, by Lord Chief Justice Parker and captioned — 'Practice Note — Magistrates — No Case to Answer — Criminal Charge — Considerations for Guidance of Justice.'

This is reported at page 448, A.E.R. 1962. There the Learned Chief Justice, said as follows:

"Those of us who sit in the Divisional Court have the distinct impression that Justices today are being persuaded all too often to uphold a submission of no case. In the result, this Court has had on many occasions to send the case back to the Justices for the hearing to be continued with inevitable delay and expenditure. Without attempting to lay down any principle of law, we think that as a matter of practice, Justices should be guided by the following considerations.

A submission that there is no case to answer, may properly be made and upheld;

(a)   When there has been no evidence to prove an essential element in the alleged offence.

(b)   When the evidence adduced by the prosecution has been so discredited as a result of cross-examination or is so manifestly unreliable that no reasonable tribunal could safely convict on it.

Apart from these two situations a tribunal should not in general be called on to reach a decision as to conviction or acquittal until the whole of the evidence which either side wishes to tender has been placed before it. If, however, a submission is made that there is no case to answer, the decision should depend not so much on whether the adjudicating tribunal (if compelled to do so) would at that stage convict or acquit but on whether the evidence is such that a reasonable tribunal might convict on the evidence so far laid before it. There is a case to answer."

In this Inquiry, there has been testimony that the deceased Franklyn Stubbs, died whilst in police custody, on the 19th December 1974.

The testimony in respect of the circumstances surrounding his death was related to the Court by the 25 witnesses who deposed. I have already referred to the station diaries produced in Court, and tendered in evidence by witnesses for the Prosecution. Of particular significance, are entries Nos. 38 and 40 of the C.I.D. diary, dated 19th December 1974, and written at 11:45 a.m. on the same date.

These entries are as follows—
"No. 38 — 19th December 1974 — 11:45 a.m. Franklyn Stubbs who is being held at C.I.D. Office for questioning ref. to armed robbery and possession of firearms called Sgt. 255 Johnson, requesting him to send someone to purchase something cool to drink as he was not feeling well because of a transmission which had fallen on him while doing mechanical repairs to his car.
Sgd. D/C 645 Pinder"

The cross entry reads as follows—
11:46 a.m.
Sgt. Johnson spoke to Stubbs and asked him if he wish to see a doctor at the hospital, he said no. He requested to lie down after getting a drink of ice water and milk stating that he did not wish to see a doctor as the drink had given him a little relief and that by lying down he would feel

better. He was taken from CID main office to the back section where he was permitted to lie on a mat. D/C Murphy was detailed to be with him to prevent him from escaping.

Sgd. D/C 645 Pinder

Entry No. 40 dated 19th December 1974 at 12:45, and written by the same constable Pinder, states as follows-

'D/C Murphy informed that Franklyn Stubbs started vomiting and then collapsed.'

Sgd. D/ C 645 Pinder

A cross entry to this is in the following terms—
12:46 p.m.
Sgt. Johnson went and checked Franklyn Stubbs heartbeat and pulse and got no response, as a result A/D.S.P. Briggs and Insp. Yearwood were informed of this."

"So that when all the facts and circumstances of this Inquiry are assembled together, we find that Stubbs died at a time when none of these 5 accused was present at the C.I.D. Again, I could not find a link in this chain of circumstances which could connect them with the death of this man. I have already said, and I cannot too strongly repeat, that place no reliance whatever upon the words of the three convicted criminals.

"Their evidence is that they saw him beaten by the 5 accused here in Court. It is upon their evidence chiefly, that the Prosecution relies. But this evidence, to my mind, has been so totally discredited, as a result of cross-examination, that I find it impossible to place any reliance whatever on the credibility of the three alleged eyewitnesses. As a result, I ask myself the pertinent question, could a reasonable tribunal safely convict on the evidence of these three witnesses? The answer is undoubtedly in the negative. Therefore, I conclude that if it would be most unsafe to accept their testimony and to commit on it. Again, I do not have before me any credible evidence upon which I could safely say that these 5 men committed 'Manslaughter':

(a) By negligence, thereby causing the death of Franklyn Stubbs, or
(b) By any other act, that might have caused his death.

I am constrained therefore to feel that essential elements in the alleged offence have not been proven to my satisfaction. I feel that there is no *evidence before me, except the testimony of three felons upon whose credit I place no trust or reliance, that would form any nexus between these 5 Accused men and the death of Franklyn Stubbs.*

As a result, and bearing in mind all that I have said about the powers of the Attorney General, to re-indict these 5 accused, I, as Examining Magistrate, have no hesitation whatever in discharging all of them of 'Manslaughter.' I will myself await directions from the Attorney General, as to whether or not the other charges against these Accused men will be proceeded with.

All the Accused are therefore discharged on this first charge. The other charges are adjourned since he died."

Wilton Hercules
Chief Magistrate
23 April 1975

An Introduction & Guide to First Response
(A lesson from Overseas Training)

The following may be of use in the training of Police officers, in particular those officers involved in the investigation of major crimes.
18th October 2011

YES - A good course of action is appropriate and beneficial to any subsequent inquiries in securing trust and cooperation.

They are also victims and probably not for the first time, victims of minority attacks. We are on their side and must appear to always be. If our actions can be interpreted as not caring then we only add to their sense of isolation, if the police don't care, then who does! You may probably act the same way for all people in similar circumstances, but some members of our society are more vulnerable and need us more, so we must consider their special needs.

NO - why, consider this... you may be damaging or failing to enhance our relationship with the family of the victim. If we act in a way which they interpret as non-caring then not only are we non-caring, but our behavior may be put down to some other more sinister attitudes. If you accept that in our society, there are people who experience others not caring for them based on discrimination, is it not reasonable for them to think that when police behave in a non caring manner, it is for the same reasons?

Experienced officers are aware of the possible outcomes from a situation and their actions are based on what they anticipate. It is not unlike a skilled driver, who looks ahead as far as possible and anticipates hazards and dangers that other less experienced drivers don't even notice!

You have now completed the section on critical incidents in which you would have learnt what a critical incident is: those incidents with the potential to become 'critical'. The Importance of the 'Golden Hour', those actions you must consider at any 'critical incident', and the first response to crime incident; decisive action.

The crime scene must be secured, the safety of victims and witnesses must be assured, and information about the incident must be collected. The first responder has a great deal of responsibility and limited time to accomplish what needs to be done. To add to the pressure, how these initial tasks are accomplished has a tremendous impact on the investigation of the crime incident, the long term safety of victims, and for that matter, the safety of the entire community.

More than anything else; the first response is an opportunity for Police to build a collaborative, problem solving relationship with victims. If done well, the first response can help to make a bad situation better. If done poorly, the first response can alienate victims and reduce the possibility of a successful investigation and/or decrease a victim's willingness to participate in the criminal justice process.

An effective first response should meet the needs of the Police and the victims. Police should be sensitive to victims' emotional response to crime. They should also respect the important role that victims can play in the investigation of the crime and the prevention of future incidents. Victims may have special knowledge about crime and disorder problems. Sometimes they may not be aware of this knowledge. For this reason it is important to discuss with the victim not only the circumstances of the particular crime, but also why this problem is occurring and ways it might be solved. Ultimately, first response is an opportunity to learn the facts of the present, understand the past, and develop strategies to prevent repetitive victimization in the future.

Police Departments have become increasingly concerned with the needs of crime victims. Victims and victim service organizations have urged Police to improve sensitivity, develop services to assist victims, and to guide victims through the intricacies of the criminal justice system. Police services have responded to the call for better victim services by developing a host of programs intended to increase Police sensitivity and provide support.

Incorporating the philosophy of 'community policing' into first response, presents the opportunity to do more. The initial contact between Police and victims could be much more than a chance for Police to provide support and comfort. It could be the beginning of a problem solving partnership. Crime victims have a tremendous stake in the crime that has affected them and they can be powerful partners with Police.

As partners, victims can help;
(a) Solve crime - they are vital to crime solving
(b) Reduce their own risk of re-victimization if they are educated about what they can do to prevent a repeated incident, and then receive help with safety planning and implementation
(c) Prevent community crime by working with the Police to solve and prevent crime and enhance safety in the communities. ◼

What is a 'Critical' Incident?

Broadly speaking a 'Critical Incident' will have certain complicating factors present that will make additional demands. These factors may not be immediately apparent and may not be present as long as the correct course of action is taken. Anyone who encounters the incident at any stage can introduce a factor that could make it a 'critical incident', like a neglect of duty in respect of an investigation.

However, do not depend on this definition to identify every incident that should be treated as critical. Your common sense, experience and training will sometimes tell you that a situation has serious potential and requires careful handling, something we will look at later.

A 'Critical Incident' is any incident where an individual is believed to be seriously endangered; the confidence of that person's family and or community cannot be assumed.

A Police early response is critical to safeguard that person's interests and subsequent enquirers.

The definition covers the majority of potential critical incidents, but you may be thinking of incidents not covered by the definition but should be treated as critical.

That is good, because you are now thinking about potential critical incidents. This list is not the definitive. You must exercise your own judgment at every incident, but if the following elements are present, you should be thinking "should I be treating this as a critical incident?"

Here are some examples of critical incidents and tips on how to identify them: • Life Endangering or Serious injury or assault

- Child or Vulnerable Person at risk or Sexual Offences Potential to damage harmony within Community
- Potential for Adverse media coverage VIP's concerned
- When you go to any incident, ask yourself the question... 'Is this a critical incident or has it the potential to become a critical incident? If the answer is not clear, don't hesitate; treat it as 'critical'.
- How you identify a 'critical incident', whether by definition or

because of your experience, are incidental, your actions in the first hour are the most important matter. What follows next is the idea that the first hour of any incident is the 'Golden Hour', during which anything we do will have a significant effect on the outcome of any subsequent investigation.

- This first hour, described as the 'Golden Hour', is so important in' terms of police action. The prospect of achieving a positive outcome will be greatly enhanced if you remember this concept.
- So, what must you do in this hour?
- In that 'Golden Hour', the potential for a successful conclusion can be secured or lost. In that hour, we must do our best to guarantee the following:
    - **Preserve life**
    - **Identify and Safeguard Victims**
    - **Ensure Public Safety**
    - **Provide information to Duty Officer/Control Room**
    - **Identify the Crime Scene – Preserve Evidence**
    - **Obtain and Deploy Resources**
    - **Secure the family, friends and local community's trust**
    - **Secure witnesses and ensure their co-operation.**

These are all important tasks that you must carry out.
- What you do in that first hour is vitally important
Remember, you are the first in a long chain of professionals, not the first in a procession of incompetent workers.

In the section on Critical Incidents these five guiding principles are introduced. They were identified by officers working in a busy inner London borough who examined what had contributed to success in dealing with many critical or potentially critical incidents.
- Focusing on the task which improves the RESULT
- Reputation
- Be Objective, increase SCRUTINY
- Record Keeping
- Persistence
- The successful investigator is tenacious and persistent, they don't give up and most importantly, they do these things without alienating people!

- Do not assume anything
- Do not stereotype
- Do not take anything at face value
- Challenge everything
- Believe nothing
- Focus on the task
- That means keeping your mind on the job' don't be distracted from what has to be done clearly identify what you are setting out to achieve
- Obtain whatever resources you require, inform whomever needs to be informed, give clear instructions and orders, and ensure everyone knows their role
- Deal with the job in hand and apply 100 percent effort

Reputation

Every officer who represents the R.B.P.F. and everything we do reflects on our reputation, but it is not just the R.B.P.F., it is about everyone involved:

- The Victim
- You
- The Police
- Civil Society

Any incident, which has an adverse effect on anyone, or harms someone's reputation, must be considered from all points of view and the interests of every one involved must be safeguarded.

The first three principles are concerned with getting the job done or to put it another way getting a result. However, it's not good enough that the R.B.P.F. get the result if it means that some sections of the community feel they have been badly treated.

The Result

The first three principles were concerned with obtaining the right results. We must seek a 'Win-Win' situation where all parties feel they have been properly treated, with fairness and professionalism.

- Concentrate the bulk of your efforts on achieving success and do not be distracted by irrelevancies.
- Be objective
- Check out what we're doing, making sure it's for the right reasons.

It follows on from Persistence, but includes reviewing what we have done and examining what we plan to do. Don't wear 'blinkers', holding on to some obstinate belief or idea only to end up going down a false trail and looking foolish. Most importantly, it's about not letting anyone's prejudices get in the way of the right course of action.

Record Keeping

Keeping records is of the utmost importance. Relevant information must be recorded. If what is relevant is not at first apparent, apply the rule, 'not sure whether to record it? Then record it!' Accurate and comprehensive record keeping will provide any subsequent inquiry with the information required to fully investigate the crime or incident. Officers who do their best for the right reasons and keep good records will find their job much easier than those who do not.

These two aspects are concerned with 'surviving scrutiny'. Every profession is becoming more open to scrutiny all the time. Everyone in the police service must accept that scrutiny is a part of their work. Police have considerable power in society, and how we use that power is the concern of all who are subject to it. A liberal democracy safeguards the rights of its citizens. It is every officer's responsibility to ensure that the R.B.P.F. withstands scrutiny with its reputation intact and the continued support of the public.

When handling a critical incident it helps to bear in mind that such incidents are generally characterized by:
1. Limited Time Frame for Action
2. High Stakes
3. Decisions must be made on partial or contradicting information

These characteristics will determine the way you deal with the incident.

Limited Time Frame for action

Some situations demanded almost immediate action; you don't have the luxury of being able to consider every possible option in great detail, such as when injured people require First-Aid at public order events, where immediate crowd control measures are required to prevent danger or disorder. An aspect of this type of situation is that with the benefit of hindsight, other options become apparent and this worry or added concern can intensify the nature of the incident.

High Stakes

This can be in terms of personal consequences or that of others; it can apply to organizations or even society in general.

Consider this. How high were the stakes in the murder of Stephen Lawrence? Personal consequences to any individual must be considered with respect to that person's specific needs. It may mean that you have to treat people differently because that is what is needed.

This can have far reaching effects. Most importantly to family and friends, who indirectly are victims. There are also implications for those who have responsibilities concerning how the incident and any subsequent investigation is handled.

Organizations may stand to lose as a result of the incident. How an organization responds when it is affected by an incident determines the public image it has. The damage to the relationships between different sections of society has far reaching consequences for social harmony and public unrest.

Feelings of inequality, based on unfair treatment, damage every aspect of the lives of those aggrieved and rightly so, cause outrage and protest.

Making the initial Decisions

Decisions must be made on partial or contradicting information, gathering good information is therefore essential. One of the aims of your primary investigation must be to improve the quality of information upon which decisions will have to be made. However, time limits may dictate that decisions must be made without delay and be based on information which at the time may appear inadequate. Thus it is very important that you record the reasons for your actions?

With hindsight, your decisions and actions could appear to be poor, but at the time based on the information available to you, the decision appeared the best option ....So Record It! Whilst dealing with the incident review your decisions in the light of new information and record that as well. Experience helps you to identify 'critical incidents'.

To some officers a situation may not appear critical at the outset, but more experienced officers can recognize the potential of something more serious developing. They have a greater awareness, they anticipate outcomes, they understand consequences, and they see the big picture and don't wear blinkers.

Example 1;

You arrest a drunk in the street, as you are putting the person into the van he trips and gashes his head on the step; the person who called you to the scene witnesses this. Would you ask them to come to the station with you to make a statement now? ..... Yes or No?

YES - A good course of action, you would also seek medical aid for the prisoner.

In addition, it would be wise to secure the evidence of someone who could corroborate your account, in the event the prisoner died; it could happen. You must think about safe guarding your position and the reputation of the R.B.P.F. Any routine incident has the potential to be a 'critical incident'.

NO - Of course not; you will take their details and record details of what they told you but you wouldn't go to all that trouble for a routine drunk.

Example 2;

You are sent to a house to tell the parents of a boy that he has been beaten up and is in hospital with broken ribs and a broken arm. It may be an ethnic attack, the family is Haitian.

Would you offer to take the parents to the hospital? .... Yes or No?

Training for Regional Law Enforcement Agencies at the Police College.

18th April 2006

The Bahamas is well respected regionally for the high level of training that is given to their various law enforcement agencies. This being so, affords us the opportunity to offer our counterprts in the region, the opportunity to receive the same training. The complex at the Police College at Oakes Field can be easily upgraded to facilitate such an academy.

We have many Police Officers who are accredited lecturers in various disciplines and who also have many years of actual field experience.

It is my opinion that consideration should be given to following subject areas:

- **Drug enforcement, Interdiction and Prosecution**
    - Identification of drugs
    - Search for drugs
    - Investigation Techniques
    - Use of Informants
- **Community Policing & Urban Renewal**
    - Neighbourhood Watch and Crime Prevention Education
- **Crime Reporting and Statistics**
    - The professional and informative reporting of crime statistics.
- **Detective Training School**
    - The training of Investigators
    - Interviews and Interrogations
    - Crime Scene Investigations and Techniques.
    - Collecting evidence at Scenes of Crime. (D.N.A.)

The foregoing are the areas in which I think our Force excels and could help Regional Police Forces.

On the home front, I think that the Royal Bahamas Police Force should be involved in is the training and grading of security officers for work in The Bahamas. ◉

Overseas Training
(Beneficial to Police Officers of all ranks)

During the decades of the Fifties, Sixtys and Seventies, many of our Police personnel, of all ranks, received overseas training at Police Colleges. Many of us were trained in the United Kingdom at colleges such as Bramshill, Hendon, West Riding Detective Training College, Yorkshire Fingerprint College and the Scottish Police College for Administration and Management. Officers were also sent to the Royal Canadian Mounted Police Academy, the F.B.I. Academy and to seminars frequently held in the U.S.A. by, the Drug Enforcement Administration, United States Secret Service, U.S. Customs and the U.S. Firearms and Alcohol Unit. Many of our officers excelled in these courses and most importantly, returned with new ideas and an enthusiasm to introduce measures and methods here to enhance our performance.

We requested, through our Commissioners and were successful in getting; Police Women, Police Dogs, improved communications, Civilianization, improved environments, Laboratory (Drugs) and improvements in our working conditions

We learned a lot by touring Police facilities in the U.K. Our Governments have often overlooked many of the recommendations made by Commissioners and senior executive personnel in three notable areas; Prisons facilities, Indoor Shooting Range, and Motorola GPS System for the Rapid Response Unit.

In the U.K. many of us toured Borstal Institutes, a type of prison that is more like a college. Offenders are provided with opportunities to learn trades, such as; motor mechanic, body repairs, welding, pipe-fitting, plumbing, tailoring, carpentry, masonry, and computer training among with other occupations.

The students (as they are called) are frequently used to repairs Government buildings, such as offices, schools, even residences etc. as well as repairs to Government vehicles. Each department using the services pays a fee to the Institute for the work done by the students; most of the funds are placed in the account of the student engaged in the work. These payments are held until the student/prisoner is discharged. Discipline is of a very high standard. Penalties such as, denial of outdoor work privileges, television,sports, denial of family visits and indoor socializing are most feared. There is a committee of prominent citizens, who work with prison administration in finding suitable employment for prisoners prior to their discharge.

The Borstal Institute concept was highly recommended by Police Commissioner Salathiel Thompson in the mid-seventies. He wanted a Maximum Security Prison built on an Island and the Fox Hill Prison to become our Borstal Institute. The choice of Islands were; Inagua where he wanted a Defence Force mini-base to be located, Ragged Island or Andros, where full scale farming could have been introduced.

A maximum security prison on Inagua, with reinforcement from the Defence Force, could also be used as a Detention Centre from where the cost of repatriation to Haiti would be reduced considerably as it could be done by boat.

Thompson was aware, that at one time the prisoners at Fox Hill had a tailor shop and produced uniforms. There was also a concrete block making plant from which the blocks were offered for sale.

He expressed concern about prisoners in the maximum security unit being held in our tourism mecca.

In the early Eighties, former Assistant Commissioners Courtney Stranchan, Lawrence Major and I, were invited by then P.M. Sir Lynden Pindling to discuss crime. The above recommendation for a maximum security prison was presented.

The same recommendation was made by me to other Governments, through letters to the press since then. ■

The Policeman in Court

Public Prosecution is an important component of the justice system. Prosecution of an offender is the duty of the State, which is carried out through Public Prosecutors. The Public Prosecutor in the Supreme Court is appointed by the Director of Public Prosecutions, an officer in the Office of the Attorney General. The Prosecutor in the Magistrate Court is appointed by the Police Force. While it is the responsibility of the Prosecutor to see, that the trial results in conviction, he need not be overwhelmingly concerned with the outcome of the trial

The Prosecutor is an Officer of the Court and is required to present a truthful picture before the Court. Even though he appears on behalf of the State, it is equally his duty to see that the accused does not suffer in an unfair and unethical manner. The Prosecutor is also an Officer of the Court and is duty bound to render assistance to the Court. He represents the State and the State is committed to the Administration of Justice as against advancing the interest of one party at the cost of the other. The Prosecutor has to be truthful and impartial so that even the accused person receives justice.

The Police Officer is supposed to be a professional witness when required to give evidence in any Court. To many it can be a fearful prospect, in particular, when it is the officer's first appearance as a witness. Some have been known to become totally incoherent from fear. The witness who tells the truth and remains calm will have no real cause for concern. I was told during my early training, that "if you don't know, say you don't know. If you don't remember say you don't remember" Do not assume or guess. I have lived by it.

Do not argue with Attorneys. Do not get impatient. Be respectful and calm. Under cross-examination defense attorneys will attempt to create doubt and truthfulness in your evidence. They may even accuse you of fabricating evidence.

The procedure followed in the Magistrate's Courts is similar to that of the Supreme Courts. Witnesses are normally outside the Court until called, and then enter the witness box, take the oath or affirmation administered by the clerk of the Court, to tell the truth. The Court Prosecutor or Defence Attorney, depending on whose side the witness is appearing, leads the witness through the evidence, after obtaining from the witness; full name, address and other information. Following the testimony the legal representative of the opposing side will cross-examine the witness. Following the cross-examination the representative of the party presenting the witness may re-examine the witness. In the initial examination the witness is expected to follow the information documented in a report or statement. In cross-examination the legal representative will try to create doubt on the memory, truthfulness, veracity and credibility of the witness. In re-examination the legal representative will attempt to clear any ambiguity that the cross-examination may have revealed.

Advice on Attending Court
- Dress appropriately.
- The preparation begins hours before attending Court. e.g.; checking and marking the particular pages in the officer's pocket notebook that are relevant to the trial.
- Arrive early and refresh your memory from your previous report or deposition, to be made available to you by the Prosecutor. View exhibits to locate and identify marks you placed on them or identifiable numbers on them.
- In the witness box, relax and speak clearly and loud enough for all to hear.
- Answer questions without undue delay. Just answer the question asked.
- Do not become flustered or lose your temper.

(Police Officers are trained not to lose their tempers in any situation. Remain calm and answer questions truthfully. Defence Attorneys will try any means that would result in unprofessional conduct in the witness box. Any misconduct or indisciplined attitude and demeanor tends to undermine your professionalism and credibility, with the Magistrate, Judge or Jury.)

- Do not attempt to score points. Tell the truth and do not exaggerate. (Judges, Magistrates and Jurors will tend to place a greater degree of confidence in the word of the witness, if he demonstrates that he is telling the truth, knows what he is talking about and is trustworthy.)

The Use of The Police Notebooks in Court

During my twenty-five years in the Criminal Investigation Department, I had the opportunity to attend various training courses and seminars at home and overseas. Officers' use of their notebooks was always emphasized. It became a habit for me to make entries in my notebook. I followed all the rules in keeping the notebook. I was involved in many criminal investigations throughout The Bahamas. I maintained my notebook efficiently, including all relevant entries, such as, departures and arrivals, locations, scenes of crime investigation and observations of persons interviewed, suspects arrested, search warrants executed, identification of exhibits and statements made by suspects, verbal and written.

I found the notebook to be very useful when testifying in any Court. As I entered the witness-box my notebook was out of my pocket. The pages with all entries pertaining to the trail were properly marked for easy reference. I never trusted my memory with regards to dates, times, names, distances, serial numbers and any other relevant information that I would have recorded in my notebook. The notebook was effectively used and it made me feel confident.

The permission of Judges and Magistrates was always forthcoming. With the long adjournments being given in today's criminal trials, I advise Police Officers to use their notebooks and do not trust to memory, those things that could be written and referred to when giving testimony in Court.

My experience in the Courts taught me a lot about local attorneys and what to expect from them during cross-examination. Accusations, that I was telling untruths did not change my attitude or demeanor. I remained respectful to the defence attorneys.

Police Officers working together must always compare notes to avoid giving, defence attorneys any advantage. Detectives arriving at the scene in one vehicle must have arrived at the same time. Items collected at the scene and delivered to the technicians, must be coordinated with regards to the markings, the times and dates of deliveries, the names of the technicians receiving and all the other relevant information. There must never be any doubt as to who collected what and who delivered or received what. It should all be documented and coordinated. All Officers and technicians must be in accord.

Pre-Trial Conferences

It was started by Kendal Isaacs, when he was the Solicitor General and prosecuted criminal cases. A day or two before the trial, Isaacs would meet with the Police witnesses and review the evidence with them. He would ask the hard questions. During these sessions we sometimes discovered ambiguities that had to be corrected before the trial. He also insisted that investigating officers use copies of the depositions from the Magistrate's Court to refresh the memories of civilian witnesses before they enter the court to testify.

We had a very good relationship with Prosecutors, such as Kendal Isaacs, Neville Smith and Langton, Hilton.

There were also other outstanding Police Prosecutors; such as; Salathiel Thompson, John Crawley, Cyril Joseph, Chilean Turner and Summer Bannister.

The importance of Police Officers, the professional witnesses at trials, conducting themselves in a manner that would convince a Magistrate, Judge or Jury of their professional ability and integrity, cannot be overemphasized.

I have occasionally listened to our prosecutors in the Magistrate's Courts. They are consummate professionals. However, there are two areas in which I believe, they could be more forceful; firstly, objecting to bail and secondly objecting to the long adjournments in the 'GUN COURT', in cases of possession of firearms. Possession cases should be very short as there are usually only three witnesses; the officers finding the firearm and the expert from the Police armoury, who identifies it, to be a firearm; in accordance with the act. Such cases should not last longer than 30 minutes. It would also help for shorter adjournments in all of the high profile cases, such as the large seizures of drugs and posession of high powered weapons. ▣

"LET THE ELDERS, THAT RULE WELL BE COUNTED
WORTHY OF DOUBLE HONOR, ESPECIALLY THEY WHO LABOR
IN THE WORD AND DOCTRINE.
1 Timothy: 5-17

Recommendations - Police Promotions
Health & Fitness
June 2018

(a) To discontinue big promotions and promote as vacancies occur. After the big promotions, personnel excluded become despondent, resulting in low performance for a period.

(b) To fight corruption of officers by rewarding those officers who arrest persons for bribery.

(c) To formulate a policy to encourage fitness of personnel. There are too many overweight officers, which is unhealthy and can be a handicap when stamina and physical fitness are needed. The F.B.I has a policy you may wish to consider. In the Eighties, whilst employed at Resorts International, I was able to acquire fitness equipment, which was donated to the Police Gym to encourage fitness.

(d) The system of promotions in the Fifties through the Eighties was fair and consideration should be given to return to that system, with the DCP as chairman and five ACPs. If you are not familiar with the process I can update you. The half yearly reports on performance, work ethics, discipline, and commendations were most important and any supression had to be explained by the senior officers making recommendations. The force had a rank structure that was mandatory.

(e) Former Prime Minister the Hon. Perry Christie stated that he was uncertain if all monies collected by the Courts are reaching the public treasury. Former Chief Justice Barnett in his retirement address stated, that there are about 7,000 warrants that have not been executed in New Providence; mostly non-payments of fines by traffic offenders.

I had discussed a system with a now retired ACP that could effectively eradicate this problem and enrich the Public Treasury. I am available to discuss. The lack of communication between the courts and the Police is what causes persons, who have paid fines to be arrested for non-payment and there are cases pending in the Magistrate's Courts for several years. I suggest an audit.

(f) My training at the Scottish police college in Scotland in 1970 included an extensive course in crime prevention. On my return we started the Force's Crime Prevention Unit. Mrs. Dorothy Davis and Mrs. Sheila Ambrister (deceased) were attached and with my training and assistance lectured in communities. We assisted in the formulation of the first Neighborhood Watch Program in Blair Estate, which still exists. I have retained all of my crime prevention literature that could be made available to the Force's Crime Prevention Unit, if interested.

(g) Finally, there is a need for a Police Indoor Shooting Range. I have written to two previous Ministers on several occasions on the subject. My last letter to the Hon. B.J. Nottage included a businessman (former policeman), who was interested in financing the project. The matter was to be discussed with the Hon. B.J. Nottage, but we never did.
My letters contained the costs and how the projects would enhance efficiency and the effective use of firearms. The Range would make training available within the city during off duty hours and would include training of residents to be certified before obtaining a Firearms License, which is not presently the case.

(h) The Ankle Bracelets - The cost of having the monitoring and tracking appears to me, to be enormous. You may wish to consider having a special unit in the force undertake this important aid, I know that the response to calls and complaints from former contractor (ICS) was an issue.

Recommendation - Recruitment of All Law Enforcement Officers.

Publish Passport Photographs of applicants, with their residential addresses. Request public assistance in answering the following question: If you are aware of any reason why any of the applicants should not be accepted for positions as Law Enforcement Officers, please call us at telephone numbers listed. Please be assured that information disclosed would be dealt with discreetly. The information received will be investigated by the Police for credibility. This process is being used in some Caribbean countries where investigators conducting background checks on applicants for positions in Law Enforcement Agencies are not receiving factual information from many persons interviewed, which resulted in undesirable individuals being recruited. Our Police College investigators encountered the same problem.

Health & Physical Fitness of Police Officers.

Health and physical fitness are assets to Police Officers in the duties they are committed to perform. Most of the officers on leaving the Police College are healthy and fit. Overweight appears to be a serious problem amongst some senior personnel; they should be mandated to frequent the gymnasium at the Police College.

In situations where an officer becomes engaged in the use of deadly force, a fit, agile officer would naturally be more effective in protecting himself as well as his fellow officers.

Many Law enforcement agencies in the United States, deal with overweight officers by having them take vacation leave to address the problem. The same applies to some Caribbean Police Services. ◙

Health and the Environment
30 January 2007

In the early to mid-seventies when Mr. Loftus Roker was Minister of Health, there was national concern about the large number of roadside garages. New Providence residents voiced their concerns in the local media. Their main objections to the roadside garages were; the large number of rodents nesting in the abandoned vehicles on the premises, the danger being caused to the water table by the oil leaking from the vehicles and the reduction of their property value by the presence of the large number of vehicles in a state of disrepair on streets in their area.

Minister Roker appointed a committee consisting of senior personnel from the Ministry of Health & Environment, Town Planning Department and the Police. I was the Assistant Commissioner in charge of New Providence and attended all meetings to represent the Police. The committee's mandate was to make recommendations to the Minister and to provide information in support of the recommendations.

After months of work the committee provided the Minister with a report, which included the following information and recommendations to eliminate the problem of roadside garages and abandoned vehicles.

- The committee with the assistance of the Police in the various Divisions of New Providence provided information pertaining to the number of roadside garages, the locations of each and the names of the operators and their residential addresses. Through the Town Planning Department we were able to establish if any of the operators had permission to conduct such a business in their areas.
- The personnel from the Ministry of Health and Environment and Sanitation Departments confirmed that there was evidence of environmental damage and the communities where these garages are located were being destroyed.

The recommendations made to the Minister were as follows:

- Ask Government to provide the land and construct a huge warehouse type building for use by the garage operators. The floor of the building and the areas around it, paved and fenced for security reasons.
- Provide office space in the building.
- Adequate lighting, toilet facilities, water faucets and garbage disposal bins.
- Write all of the operators informing them that roadside garages will be discontinued with effect from a designated date. Invite them to view the newly built premises where they can continue their operations.
- A small fee to be paid by each operator to eventually cover the cost of the building and to provide maintenance.
- Encourage them to get organized and provide the funds to pay for the personnel needed to staff the office, the telephones, electricity and water. Also security arrangements.
- The committee had suggested that the building be erected at the Industrial Parl.
- The Town Planning Department would prepare letters advising the roadside garage operators that they will not be allowed to continue their operations in these residential areas and they must end their operations by a designated date. Should they fail to comply the Police would serve summonses for Court Action.

As far as I can remember the above recommendations were made to the Minister, the Hon. A. Loftus Roker. Shortly thereafter, Roker was transferred to another Ministry. I heard no more about the work we did and the recommendations made.

During the meetings held it was decided that the old procedures of dealing with abandoned vehicles be effectively implemented by the Police and the Ministry. Police patrols reported abandoned vehicles to their respective Police Stations. At the end of each month a list was submitted to the Deputy Commissioner of Police for the Director of Public Works. The list contained all of the available information on the abandoned vehicles such as location, type of vehicle, license number, name of the owner and the condition of the vehicle. Public works personnel would paint on the vehicle for the information of the owner that the vehicle must be moved by a designated date. If the vehicle was not moved by the stated date the Public Works Department would have the vehicle removed and the owner charged the fee for its removal. This system worked and saved the

Government the cost of having to pay to have vehicles removed.

It was a time when New Providence was one of the cleanest Islands I had ever seen. The Public Service Departments and the Police ensured that our environmental laws were rigidly enforced.

On the 21 January, 2013, I met with the Minister and two senior members of his staff. We discussed the following:

(a) The system of reporting abandoned vehicles in the Fifties and Sixties and the removal of the vehicles.

(b) Garbage collectors who dump garbage on sites other than the dump. A plan and investigation procedures that could be implemented to detect and prosecute the offenders.

(c) Parking building needed for the city. Recommended area southwest of the General Post Office.

(d) Offered to provide training for staff in Investigation Methods .... Gratis.

In recent days I saw an article in a local newspaper recommending that we consider doing what is being done in South Florida and several other States in U.S.A. with old tyres. The writer stated, that the old tyres are being minced and mixed with the asphalt for road paving. The writer suggested, that we have personnel visit South Florida to study what is being done there. The article stated, that the process is saving money, improving the road surface and getting rid of all discarded tyres. It is very well known that discarded old tyres with water in them are places where mosquitoes breed. ■

Illegal Dumping of Garbage
13th September, 2012

I wish to offer my services, gratis, to discuss with the Health Inspectors and others in your department, initiatives, that could assist in the detection and prosecution of person involved in the illegal dumping of garbage in New Providence. Develop through inquiries among merchants and others, a list of those persons and vehicles engaged in the collection of garbage from their establishments and check records at the dump to ascertain if all of these persons/vehicles are in fact arriving at the dump with the garbage. The checks will identify those persons/vehicles, who are not going to the dump. These are the likely culprits. Determine the locations from where they are collecting garbage and use unmarked vehicles to follow them to the site where they are dumping. Inspectors must have powers of arrest and prosecution must be mandatory.

On evenings, in particular vehicles used for collecting garbage can be seen, frequently heading in directions other than the dump. Seek public and police assistance in the identification (description & licence numbers) of all such vehicles and follow-up investigation. Search garbage in illegal dump sites for evidence, that may identify the location from where the garbage was collected e.g. letterheads, invoices and other correspondence and items. Interrogation of person at the source may identify the collector.

Illegal dumping is a problem in many cities worldwide. We must endeavour to deal with it here by prosecution and conviction. Examples must be made of such person even to the extent of discouraging merchants and others from giving them contracts to collect garbage or even banning them from the dump. Residents in New Providence communities can assist in identifying locations where garbage is dumped illegally. Inspectors could be assigned to maintain surveillance at these locations. It may require some personnel assistance from the Police or Government security officer assigned to other departments or even retaining the services of private security. ■

A Practical Guide to Crime Prevention
INTERPOL - F.B.I - UK POLICE - RCMP and others

This is about Crime and what you can do to prevent it. We can all help to bring it down. Most of our crime is against property, not people, and most of these crimes are not carefully planned. Most of the crimes are committed by men on the spur of the moment when they see the chance. Possessions left in a car, or, a door or window to a house left open. You can reduce the risk by securing your car and home. Put property in your car trunk where it is safer.

I am convinced that crime prevention education and action help to reduce the large number of crimes against property being perpetrated. If we can do this, Police Officers would have more time to deal with the serious/violent crimes against the person.

That is good for you, your family and your country. It makes your neighborhood and the country a safer place to live in.

It is said that a man's house is his castle therefore he should live there with little or no fear of crime. J. Edgar Hoover once said that no building could be considered crime proof. However security measures taken to frustrate and reduce opportunity of the criminal could prevent crime.

THE 10 PRINCIPLES OF PREVENTION
1.   Target Hardening
2.   Target Removal
3.   Remove the Means to Commit Crime
4.   Reduce the Payoff
5.   Access Control
6.   Surveillance (natural, formal, employees)
7.   Environmental Design
8.   Rule Setting
9.   Increase the Chance of being caught
10.   Deflecting Offenders

How to stay safe at home?

Trees and objects that offer concealment should be trimmed or removed. Install outside lighting to eliminate dark areas in all possible areas. Neighbors must look after each other and report strange and suspicious persons seen loitering.

- Make sure your house or apartment is secure.
- Always secure outside doors.
- Fit proper locks top and bottom. (Seek locksmith advice) Keep keys handy to get out in the event of fire. Don't give keys to workmen, as they can easily make copies.
- If you wake to hear the sound of an intruder, only you can decide how best to handle the situation. You may want to lie quietly to avoid attracting attention to yourself, in the hope that the intruder will leave, or you may feel more confident if you switch on the lights and make a lot of noise. If you are on your own, call out to an imaginary companion. Most burglars will flee empty-handed rather than risk confrontation. Call the Police 911 or 919 as soon as it is safe to do so (A telephone extension in your bedroom will make you feel more secure as it allows you to call the Police immediately, without alerting the intruder). If there are no children in other bedrooms lock your bedroom door at night.
- Draw your curtains after dark and if you think there is a prowler outside, dial - 911 or 919.

Many of these security measures are affordable and in some instances free. Some measures recommended are:

• Solid core doors • Hinges on the inside • Dead bolts • Peepholes • Pins on sliding doors • Security screens • Panic buttons

Personal Safety

- When you answer the phone, simply say "hello" - don't give out your number.
- Never reveal any information about yourself to a stranger and never say you are alone in the house.
- If you receive an abusive or threatening phone call, put the receiver down beside the phone and walk away. Come back a few minutes later and replace the receiver; don't listen to see if the caller is still there. Don't say anything. An emotional reaction is just what the caller wants. If the calls continue tell the Police and keep a record of the

date, time and content. This may help the authorities trace the caller.

- All threats are to be taken seriously and must be reported to the Police.
- If you see signs of a break-in at your home, like a smashed window or open door, don't go in. Go to a neighbor and call the Police.
- The Crime Prevention Officer in the area must inform the neighborhood watch leaders in their respective area of crime perpetrated in their areas as soon as it is reasonably practicable.
- The Police could advise residents of crime hazards and of the availability of suitable electronic equipment to assist in the security and safety of their residences.
- The Police could arrange for dealers to provide demonstrations of such equipment. that would significantly reduce the 'breaking and entering' offences, as well as assist in the apprehension of offenders.
- Self-defense and safety awareness classes may help you feel more secure.

The Public
- The victims of crime must be motivated to be alert and concerned about incidents, strangers and strange vehicles in their neighborhoods.
- Support neighborhood watch programs.
- Investigate and thoroughly screen job applicants.
- Parents and children must learn how to inform the Police immediately of incidents and suspicions. They must develop their ability to give proper directions on how to locate their residences for quick response.

Out and About
- If you often walk home in the dark, get a personal attack alarm. Carry it in your hand so you can use it immediately to scare off an attacker. Make sure that it is designed to continue sounding if it's dropped or falls to the ground.
- Carry your bag close to you with the clasp facing inwards.
- Carry your house keys in your pocket. If someone grabs your bag let it go. If you hang on you could get hurt. Remember your safety is more important than your property.
- If you think someone is following you, check by crossing the street more than once if necessary to see who follows. If you are still worried, get to the nearest place where there are other people - or any area that is well illuminated. Call the Police 911 or 919.
- If you regularly go jogging or cycling, try to vary your route and time, or do so along with others. Stick to well-lit roads. In parks, keep to

main paths and open spaces where you can see other people and be seen by them - avoid wooded areas. If you wear a personal stereo, remember you can't hear traffic, or someone approaching from behind.
- Don't take shortcuts through dark alleys, parks or across undeveloped land.
- Walk facing traffic so a car cannot pull up behind you unnoticed.
- If a car stops and you are threatened, scream and shout and set off your personal attack alarm. Get away as quickly as you can. This will gain you vital seconds and make it more difficult for the car driver to follow. If you can, make a mental note of the number and description of the car. Write down details as soon as possible afterwards.
- Don't hitchhike or take lifts from strangers. Cover up expensive looking jewelry.

On Public Transport
- Try to stay away from isolated bus stops, especially after dark.
- On an empty bus sit near the driver.

When Driving
- Plan how to get to your destination before leaving and stay on main roads if you can.
- Carry a flashlight.
- Before you leave, tell whoever you are planning to meet, what time you think you will get there, and the route you are taking.
- Do not pick up hitch-hikers.
- Keep doors locked when driving and keep any bag, car phone or valuables out of sight.
- If you have the window open, only wind it down a little.
Don't wind it down far enough to allow someone to reach in while you are stopped in traffic.
- If you think you are being followed, try to alert others by flashing your lights and sounding your horn. Make as much noise as possible. If you can, keep driving until you come to a busy place.
- After dark, park in a well-lit, busy place. Look around before you get out.
- If you are parking in daylight, but coming back for your car at night, think about how things will look in the dark. You may consider parking your car closer to the office when leaving work late.
- Have your key ready when you get into your car. Make sure there is no one in the car. Lock the doors before moving.

- If you frequently have to travel after dark, consider getting a mobile/ cellular phone.

What men can do?

Men can help by taking the issue of women's safety seriously in their everyday lives. Bear these points in mind:

- If you are walking in the same direction as a woman on her own, don't walk behind her - this may worry her. Simply walk pass her. This may assure her that you are not following her.
- If you are thinking of chatting to a woman (waiting for example) at a lonely bus stop, remember that she won't know that you mean her no harm.
- Realize how threatening actions such as staring, whistling, passing comments and jostling can be, particularly when you are one of a group of men.
- Help female friends or family members by giving them a lift or walking them home when you can. If you do, make sure they are safely indoors before you leave.

If the worst happens.

Think what you would do if someone attacked you. Could you fight back, or would you avoid resisting and wait to escape? Only you can decide whether to fight back, but preparing yourself for all possibilities could provide a split-second advantage.

If the attacker is armed, do not resist.

If you have been assaulted or raped

- Call the Police immediately. They need your help to catch the attacker. You can help the Police by:
- Taking the name and address of any witness
- Trying to remember what the attacker looked like
- If a car was involved, try to note the color, model and registration number
- You do not need to go to the Police Station to report an assault. You can be interviewed in your home if you wish. These crimes are dealt with sympathetically, regardless of sex.

Police Stations have specially trained officers who will help support you. There are areas where you can be interviewed privately.
- In the case of rape: although your immediate reaction will be to wash, try not to if you can possibly help it. It will destroy vital evidence

which may help prove the case against the person who raped or assaulted you. Should your case come to trial, by law your anonymity will be guaranteed, if you are female, or less than 18 years old. The law forbids newspapers to publish anything that might identify you. Also, as a general rule, you should not be asked about your previous sexual history in court.

- If the violence is in your family, legal protection is possible under either civil or criminal law.

Domestic Violence

Violent attacks, inside or outside the home, is a criminal offence. Nobody has the right to abuse you physically, sexually or emotionally. Victims may be made to feel responsible and guilty for the abuse. The decision to take action against the abuser may be a difficult one, but it is important to remember that you do not have to suffer in silence.

In the short term, you can plan emergency measures. Talk to a neighbor you trust, maybe arrange a signal, and ask them to contact the Police if they hear a disturbance in your home. You may even feel more comfortable if an overnight bag is packed, with enough money for incidentials, and if possible, a place to go for at least one night's lodging. Consider taking a change of clothing for yourself and your children. If you can, take any legal and financial documents which you might need, along with any treasured possessions and any medicines you may require.

- In the longer term, you have to plan what you will do to alter your situation. Remember that domestic violence is a crime and can be dealt with through the Police and the Courts. You should report any violent attack to the Police; they can help you. Our Police have dedicated domestic violence units, which are staffed by specially trained Officers who will tell you what help is available, and will offer advice and support.
- You can get legal advice from an attorney. If you pursue the case against your attacker, there are a number of possible legal outcomes, ranging from court injunctions, and possible criminal conviction and custodial sentence.
- In addition there are organizations which can offer support and practical advice. Their services are confidential and in many cases, completely free. ◼

Neighbours Watching Out For Neighbours

'NEIGHBOURHOOD WATCH'

The program is a proactive concept to reduce residential breaks and entry and other property crimes within a community. Through increased awareness and crime prevention tips, participating community members are encouraged to develop good security habits and to watch out for each other's property. A Police Officer patrolling your community may not recognize a stranger inside your yard or an unusual vehicle in your neighborhood, but your neighbors would.

HOW IT WORKS

The program works through mutual aid. Neighborhood watch members look out for their neighbor's home and property.

Watch for:
- Suspicious persons or activities.
- Vehicles passing by numerous times, suspiciously parked, or constantly travelling in back alleys.
- Strangers in your neighborhood. Someone may use an unanswered doorbell as an indication that no one is home, and use the opportunity to break into the house.
- The person taking a short cut through a yard.
- Strange vehicles parked at your neighbor's house.
- If you see something suspicious don't assume that that someone else has called the Police. It is your neighborhood, if you see something you feel suspicious take action and do something about it: Note the description of the suspicious person and or vehicle and call the Police.
- Teach your children on how to call the Police and how to give the exact location of your residence.
- Do not confront any suspicious persons yourself or attempt an arrest, as your safety could be jeopardized. Call the Police. 911 or 919.

HOW TO DEVELOP THE PROGRAM.

The most important thing is to get involved.

Crime prevention is everyone's responsibility and the safest communities are those where the residents are committed to crime prevention and the Neighborhood Watch Program.To have an active Neighborhood Watch Block, there must be someone on the block who is designated as Block Captain.

The Block Captain is the backbone of the Neighborhood Watch Program. Block Captains on active blocks receive crime notifications from the Police and 'fan out' this information to other Neighborhood Watch groups. They also attend one or two special Block Captain Meetings each year, arranged by the Divisional Police Commander, where they are given additional information on crime prevention and related topics.

Once a block meets the criteria, information will start flowing from the Police to the block captains for distribution to all Neighborhood Watch members on the block. The Police will pass on information regarding recent crimes that have occurred in the area as well as other special information that will be of interest to members. **Without volunteers this program does not work.**

NEIGHBOURHOOD WATCH TIPS

- Put up Neighborhood Watch window decals.
- Get to know your neighbors and encourage them to attend meetings.
- Conduct a security audit of your home and make every effort to upgrade any weaknesses. Get assistance from an expert.
- Mark and record items of value-for identification.
- Practice personal safety and home security precautions.
- If you see activity that you feel to be suspicious, phone the Police 911 or 919.
- If you are the victim of any type of crime — report it to the Police.

Remember that the Police do not know what crimes are happening in neighborhood unless you tell them.

You should also advise your block captain and neighbors. They may have seen or heard something that could help the Police in their investigation.

Following these simple tips can make your neighborhood a safer place to live in. An active Neighborhood Watch can result in savings on your insurance premium. Remember it takes three: you, your Block Captain and the Police to keep your Neighborhood Watch working.

If there are no Neighborhood Watch groups in your area, speak to the Commander of the Police Division. He is committed to getting the Programs started. You may also contact the Police Community Relations Officer.

Basic Crime Prevention considerations:
- Target Hardening - Understanding that you or your property are the target of the criminal. This means you must make yourself and your property less vulnerable to attack. Implement proper security systems in your home.
- Target Removal - Possibly removing your property from view or access to the criminal and not allowing yourself to be in high risk situations.
- Remove the means to commit crimes.
- Report persons who loiter in your neighborhood.
- Clear vacant lots or bushes near your property.
- Reducing the payoff - Mark all your valuables or record the serial numbers so that in the event they are stolen they may be easily identified and recovered.
- Access Control - Placing fences around your property you create a controlled access thus preventing your property becoming a shortcut and an excuse for persons to be there.
  Installing peep holes so that persons on the outside may be identified before opening the door.
- Entry buzzer, security guard, key pad or swipe card.
- Surveillance cameras (with recording and storing capability)
- Ensure that staff can see who enters and leaves, and that they challenge anyone observed in any unauthorized areas to avoid the opportunity for persons to wonder about the premises.
- Environmental Design.
- Discussing security features with the architect, contractor, landscaper, and developers. E.g. security doors and windows, types of shrubbery etc.
- Rule Setting - Rules for customers and signs restricting movement.

The crime trend in the world today dictates that we be more alert and observant to be able to protect ourselves from becoming victims. ◼

Reasonable Grounds of Suspicion

Reasonable Grounds of Suspicion is a term used by Police Officers and Law enforcement Officers worldwide. It is written in our laws and gives the law enforcement officers wide powers to search and if necessary, arrest offenders. Police Officers are expected to develop a suspicious mind and to follow up on their suspicions.

In New Providence, we must endeavour to motivate residents to become suspicious of persons, vehicles and activities, observed by them and report their observations to the Police immediately. It would be a major contribution in our efforts to eradicate crime. The motivation of the public must come from the politicians and pastors, whose voices are heard most frequently and their statements are more respected.

Reasonable Ground for Suspicion could be considered in any of the following circumstances:

- A person(s) standing in the dark, who appears to be going nowhere in particular dressed in dark clothing and wearing a hooded jacket.
- A person(s) parks a vehicle, including a motorcycle and walkthrough brushes in your residential area. Note the number plate on the vehicle if there is one.
- A vehicle, usually with heavy tint driving slowly in the neighbourhood with multiple persons inside. Note the number of the licence plate, if there is one or if the plate is heavily tinted.
- Strange vehicles parked in your residential area could be a cause for concern.
- Vehicles, in particular trucks unloading items at night to homes in your residental areas.
- Person visiting your residence claiming to be from a utilities company seeking entry to check or conduct repairs or be from a utilities company seeking entry to check or conduct repairs. Do not open your door. Note the number of the vehicle.
- Movement in your yard by strange persons, in particular at night-time.
- Being followed by a vehicle at any time and through any roads you turn into.

The above are just some forms of suspicious activities that we must report to the Police. In reporting such matters to the Police you would be asked your name, which you don't have to give. Just give the information and properly describe the location.

Report activities, such as drug houses, strip joints and any other suspicious activities in houses or shops in your residential area.

To eradicate the crimes of violence taking place in New Providence, we must fully cooperate with the Police and inform them of all suspicious persons, vehicles and activities that we observe.◙

Crime Prevention Programs
A Letter as presented to:

Mr. John Rolle
Deputy Commissioner of Police, Royal Bahamas Police Force
East Street,
Nassau, Bahamas

8th August, 2002

Dear Sir,

The Commissioner of Police requested that upon completion of the inventory of the Police Armory, I assist in reorganizing our Crime Prevention Unit. We did not have a lengthy discussion on the matter, but the impression I got was that he would like to see the Force become proactive in Crime Prevention Education and promoting Crime Prevention action; such as Neighborhood Watch programs etc. We are aware of the Prime Minister's statement concerning the need for greater efforts in the areas of Crime Prevention Education and Neighborhood Watch programs.

I have completed the work I was doing in the armory, with Grand Bahama being the final. I would like to begin some work on the Crime Prevention concept (for which I received training in the United Kingdom and had set up the first Crime Prevention Unit) here. I have already begun doing some research on the subject and have prepared the attached document with my views on the subject and with the hope that the Force's Top Team and all of the Divisional Commanders would be prepared to discuss the crime prevention programs planned.

It is my opinion that the Force would need major support from the media, in particular the electronic media to promote crime prevention education. In addition, The Bahamas Government should sponsor programs on Z.N.S. to educate residents about Crime Prevention and to promote Neighborhood Watch and other programs designed to reduce crime. The crime statistics indicate that 75% of the major crimes reported are crimes against property. Most of these are preventable crimes, but the victims would have to be educated and advised about prevention measures. This could be done by short radio/TV programs, newspaper notices, lectures at schools and to adult groups, such as Clubs and Associationsadult. The whole idea is to get residents to be alert, observant, and to take commonsense measures in protecting themselves from becoming victims; also to unite their communities in protecting themselves from criminals.

- Persons taking cash deposits to night safes at banks not having a second person to drive and observe suspicious persons in the area and not having the keys ready to open the night safe and make the deposit.
- The neglect of householders to report suspicious persons or noises to the Police promptly (such persons have exposed themselves to crime by investigating odd circumstances themselves)
- Persons not paying serious attention to threats made against them and not reporting such threats to the Police,
- Persons employing servants and not first having a background investigation conducted, in many instances the names and addresses of such employees are not known to the employer,
- Persons walking or driving home at night who are unconcerned about what is going on around them or whether there are persons following them.
- Persons who admit individuals into their homes on the pretense that they are from utility companies.
- Shop owners who continually keep large sums of cash on their business premises. ◙

Crime Prevention Programs
12 August, 2002

I refer to my memorandum dated 8th August 2002, on the captioned subject.

In the following paragraphs, I am outlining for your information further thoughts I have on the matter that would help in the planning of a Crime Prevention (education & action) "blitz" in New Providence and Grand Bahama. There are a number of organizations listed below from which the Police must solicit help for this program to be a success. I have also described the kind of assistance that would be required.

Bahamas Government
The Ministry of National Security must lead in convincing the public of the importance of this exercise. The Ministry must solicit assistance from the media, in particular the electronic media to promote crime prevention education and advise residents of simple personal and collective precautions they may take to protect themselves and their property. The Bahamas Broadcasting Corporation must play the leadership role.

The Church
Preach crime prevention education and recommend the 'Neighborhood Watch' concept to its members using the commandment 'Love thy neighbor as thyself' approach, to motivate residents to participate in such programs.

Politicians
Help to organize groups in their constituencies for crime prevention education and action lectures by qualified Police Personnel and encourage their constituents to participate in neighborhood watch programs.

The Media
To publicize more information and details of those preventable crimes that occur daily and give details of commonsense measures that could be

practiced by the public, to protect their property. Provide information on crime daily as often as possible to keep citizens thinking and being alert. Publicizing stolen vehicles; asking residents to call in information if the vehicles are seen. (Insurance Companies should offer rewards for early recovery)

Insurance Companies
Stealing of vehicles is a major crime that is very profitable to criminals. It is well organized and is growing in New Providence. The cost to Insurance Companies each year is massive. Recovery of stolen vehicles is low, just about 10 percent. Vehicles recovered are usually stripped of parts and even the license plate and stickers are being removed by the criminals, making identification difficult. A reward for information leading to recovery of stolen vehicles should be offered by the Insurance Companies.

Shipping Agencies
It is known that some vehicles are refurbished, painted and upholstered and shipped to Family Islands. Police should be informed of all shipments and the identification of all such vehicles checked at the docks.

The Police
- A 100 day challenge to Divisional Commanders to get neighborhood watch programs started in their districts.
- The Commanders to help organize crime prevention lectures in their districts.
- The Police Crime Prevention Unit to prepare crime prevention tips for both Radio and Television. The messages could be done by well known Bahamians, such as our "Golden Girls" and other top sporting individuals, politicians, and clergy.

The Police must designate someone (an Inspector or Sargent) to be the Crime Prevention Officer for each area. The selected officers will be taught about crime prevention and given assignments in their respective areas. (These appointees should be the Station Officers, who can assist their Commanders in organizing the 'Neighborhood Watch' programs.

Crime Prevention - Education & Action
An Overview By Paul Thompson

Educating the Public.

Many Police Officers share my view that if the Police, the Public and the Media were able to corrobarate their efforts to fight crime, there could be a vast reduction in a matter of months, but it must be a joint effort.

The information disclosed herein is just a part of crime prevention and detection education that could be given to the public at regular intervals to help protect themselves and help the Police eradicate crime.

Our talk shows have become very popular. It is known that a large percentage of our population listen to the talk shows daily. If a talk show host or a newspaper could publish or talk about a small portion of what is written here, it would help to educate people on how to fight crime and prevent those preventable crimes from being perpetrated against them.

The City of Nassau and the Island of New Providence, once recognized as a leader in the field of crime prevention education and action, had attained that position by the efforts and commitment of many of its residents. In New Providence there were at least 22 crime watch groups formed to increase citizens' awareness of crime and the methods that should be used to help in preventing it. The Crime Prevention Unit of the Police Force assisted these groups in this regard and has always been available to do so. It appears however that the enthusiasm and dedication of residents to the crime prevention concept has waned. This statement is supported by crime reports that disclose a complete lack of safety and crime prevention concerns by many residents, who have become victims.

The statement is also supported by crime statistics. For example the total number of serious crimes reported for the months January through October 2002 was 9,336; of that number, 1,135 were crime against people, the violent crimes. The remaining 8,201 were crimes against property, which are preventable crimes and can be reduced through crime prevention education, commonsense precautions by property owners, Neighborhood Watch programs and the purchase and installation of technology to protect property.

STATISTICS ON CRIMES AGAINST PROPERTY

(The Preventable Crimes)

Burglary	192
Housebreaking	1718
Shop breaking	1191
Stealing	2785
Stealing from Vehicles	1 344
Stolen Vehicles	683
Attempted Breakings	226
Attempted Stealing	62

This discussion is about crime and what you can do to prevent it. We can all help to bring it down. Most of our crime is against property, not people, and most of these crimes are not carefully planned. Most of the crimes are committed by men on the spur of the moment when they see an opportunity - possessions left in a car or a door or window of a house left unsecured. You can reduce the risk by securing your property. Reducing the crimes against property will give the Police more time and man-hours to tackle serious/violent crimes. This would be good for you and the country. It will make your neighborhood and the country a safer place in which to live.

SAVE THE CHILDREN — PROTECT THEM FROM DANGER

Parents must equip themselves with the skills to keep their children safe. Read and follow these tips:

(a) Teach your children in whose car they must ride. Children should be cautioned never to approach any vehicle, occupied or not, unless accompanied by a parent or trusted adult.

(b) Create an atmosphere in your own home where your children feel safe confiding information about uncomfortable experiences.

(c) Tell your children to always tell an adult where they are going and never to take a ride with someone they don't know.

(d) Discuss with your children whose homes they can visit, and the boundaries where they can and can't go in the neighborhood.

(e) Make sure your children know their address and telephone numbers,

(f) Make sure that they do not tell anyone, who calls that they are home alone.

(g) Don't drop children off alone at malls, movies, video arcades and parks or playgrounds.

(h) Know where your children are and whom they are with.

(i) Don't let them go out alone. There is safety in numbers.

(j) Speak openly with them about their safety.

(k) Practice what you talk about. Go over scenarios and ask your children what they would do.

(l) Don't take candy from strangers.

(m) Children have the right to say no. If a grownup comes to a child asking help to search for a puppy or for directions. The child should refer the person to an adult for help.

(n) Children don't have to be polite. We put a high premium on making sure our children are polite, especially to adults, and that translates into 'do what the man says.

(o) Communicate - If a child feels frightened, he/she should be encouraged to talk with a trusted person; mom, dad, counselor or teacher. Teach children about the menace of being too close with strangers and to advise their parents of persons who may be trying to do so.

The message to parents! .... Listen to your children.

NOTIFY, IDENTIFY & TESTIFY

Large numbers of persons in the 'Over-the-Hill' area are assisting Police with information on crime, in particular violent crimes and armed robberies. It appears that many of these persons have come to realize that 70% of the violent crimes perpetrated are in their districts and the one way to eradicate it, is by working with the Police, either openly or anonymously. The Police on the other hand have been very active in those districts. Several persons have been arrested for firearms possession and drugs. Following are some hints of ways in which the public can help:

Report vehicles seen parked for long periods. They could be stolen or they may have been used to commit crime and abandoned.

Give information on garages where motor vehicle parts could be easily obtained at cheap prices, include road side garages. Cars are being stolen and stripped for parts.

Report suspicious vehicles with persons inside, parked in dark areas, in particular near to areas of entertainment. These could be the drive-by shooters waiting for their victims.

Many crimes on our Island are committed by motorcyclists, in particular the fast trail bike riders. Most of them have no license plates for identification. They are difficult to catch on the busy streets and the track roads through bushes. You can help by reporting any such motorcycles seen parked in yards in your neighborhood, at the food stores, at the beaches, at the movies or anywhere on this Island. The Police would have a better chance in seizing these motorcycles and apprehending the owners for questioning.

Develop neighborhood watches - Report strange and suspicious persons seen in your neighborhoods loitering. Burglaries and housebreakings in areas such as Elizabeth Estates and Yellow Elder where houses are very close to each other, could be eradicated. In New Providence there is an average of two vehicles stolen per day. Many are stolen from parking lots where there are no security patrols. Many are also stolen from outside residences, even from open garages. The theft of vehicles can be reduced by installing proper locking devices or alarms.

Give the Police information on wreckers seen moving vehicles at night and during the early morning hours. Try to get the license number of the wrecker and the color etc.

Do not leave the engine running and the keys in your car while making a quick purchase.

Walking the streets with large sums of cash is unwise.
Resisting an armed bandit(s) is stupid.

Take threats made to you seriously. Discuss with family any threats made by drug dealers, money lenders, or anyone else with whom you had an altercation. Report threats to the Police and do not take them lightly.

If you have information about Police Corruption seek an audience with the Officer in charge of the Police Corruption Unit and discuss the matter. This could be done discreetly and with confidentiality.

Practice vigilance at Home - Many armed robberies are committed in homes where persons are seated enjoying the evening with the doors open. At least lock the doors and pay some attention to the noises on the outside or the movement of persons outside.

In describing bandits apart from clothing etc. look for scars, left handed or right handed and listen for any names or nicknames called. It is good to write these down for the Police.

Record serial numbers - Many items are sold at Police Auctions because people do not record serial numbers and have no identifying marks on property, such as; televisions, video records, stereos etc.

Consider an alarm system, in particular, the panic button that notifies the Police when a robbery is in progress or when the bandits are entering the store. Check Sure Alarms or Migrafill for the installation of these items. In instances where these items have been used the Police arrival at the scene have been fast and successful.

Banking - When going to the bank to make a deposit or withdrawal of a substantial sum, take someone with you. Check out the parking lot before leaving or returning to your car, or have the second person circle in the car until you reappear at the bank's door. Pay wages by cheque.

Home Safes - It is not advisable to keep a safe in your house unless it is well hidden from all persons, who enter as guests or as workers. The safe attracts robbers and could cause you pain. Put the expensive jewelry and the large sums of cash in a bank. ◙

Special to The Tribune
Crime Prevention by
Paul Thompson:
Former Assistant Commissioner of Police was Training Officer at the
Royal Bahamas Police Force.

Over a period of years, the term "Crime Prevention" became synonymous with the philosophy that emphasizes action before a crime is committed.

The definition well-known to Police Officers is
'The anticipation, recognition, and the appraisal of a crime risk, and the initiation of action to eliminate or reduce the risk.'

The crime trend in New Providence dictates the need for crime prevention to be uppermost in our minds, but it is evident from the large number of preventable crimes that this is not the case. The police need help from the media in educating Bahamians about crime prevention.

In the following paragraphs I will describe in brief, crimes committed in New Providence that with some common-sense precautions, alertness and care about security and safety, may have been prevented.

- Two girls in their early teens left school at noon. Instead of going home, they proceeded to walk along Soldier Road. They accepted a ride with two men in a car. Both girls were eventually taken to a secluded area and raped.
- A female, small business owner drives directly to the bank to make a night safe deposit. She has the money pouch in her hand and is searching a large bag for the key to the night safe. She is robbed by a passing youth.

In the first case, the girls should not have accepted the ride, and in the second case the lady should have had the key in her hand ready to make the deposit in a matter of seconds. She should not have gone alone.

In the Police daily reports, many small businesses are robbed of very large sums of money. With regular deposits or removal of the money, the loss would be minimal. Robbers enter shops, make small purchases so as to get a look at what is in the cash register, before robbing the cashier.

- A minister of religion on leaving a fund-raising meeting places several thousands dollars in a briefcase, which he placed in the trunk of his car in the presence of several persons.
  On arrival home, a robber relieves him of the car and drove away. The car is later found just blocks away with the briefcase missing.

- A woman in the food store examines the meat, her back turned to the cart which holds her handbag with wallet and cash inside. The wallet is promptly removed by a thief. She does not even miss it until reaching the cashier.

- The young school girl walking home decides on taking a short cut through an isolated area. She is attacked and brutally raped.

- A woman inside her residence sees a man outside with a knife. The man is about to cut the screen to climb into the house. She panics. Instead of closing the window she runs to the telephone in another room. On the phone she cannot give the police a good description of the location of her residence. The man enters and she is seriously injured. It could have been avoided had she closed the window, locked herself in her bedroom and telephoned the Police.

- A man drives home, opens his gate and drives into his yard, leaving the gate open while he proceeds to move groceries from the trunk of the car. While doing so, the masked armed bandit enters the yard and robs him of valuables and cash. The man has a dog that greets him at the gate every night when he arrives home. The dog was not seen on that night and this did not arouse any suspicion. He later found the dog in the back yard shot.

- Every week a business woman goes to the bank for cash to pay staff. She drives the same route and returns by the same route. She is stopped by bandits on the stop sign of a narrow street and robbed of the cash. So many persons are still using cash to pay employees. Cheques are better.

OBSERVATIONS

There are large number of persons who still go to lonely beaches in the late hours of the night for relaxation and romance. Many are being robbed of valuables, cash and vehicles. There have also been assaults on the men and rapes on the women. Such persons are exposing themselves to the criminal attacks.

Many persons are still leaving packages in their cars in the parking lots. At times the damage done to the car exceeds the value of the items stolen from the car. Put the packages in the trunk.

- A prominent dentist was shot by a bandit as he arrived home in his car. Investigations disclosed that neighbors saw a suspicious car with two men sitting in the dark for a long time. No-one called the Police. Fortunately, the dentist did not succumb to the injuries.

- An elderly man and his wife are in bed. They hear a sound in the house that is unfamiliar. The man leaves his wife in the bedroom to investigate the strange sound himself. He is attacked and beaten by gunmen. His wife is also assaulted. They could have secured themselves in the bedroom, called 919, given proper directions to the Police to find their home, and made a lot of noise to awaken the neighborhood.

- The owner of a 1999 Lexus had his car stolen from his driveway at night. One wonders why a person who can afford a Lexus would not have an alarm installed. Thefts of cars would be reduced immensely if owners would have alarms installed or anti theft devices such as "The Club," which to me is even better than the electronic alarm.
Thieves are known to bypass the car with "The Club." Insurance companies should consider providing "The Club" at a low cost and having a clause making the use mandatory.

- A female occupant of a residence in a wealthy neighbourhood, heard the sound of water running, on the outside from a garden tap. It was about 1 a.m.. She opened her door and proceeded outside to turn off the tap. She was met by bandits, who took her inside and robbed her and other occupants of valuables and cash.

- A female motorist goes to a gas station and leaves a young child in her car. The car is stolen with the baby in it.

Foolishly, drivers often park for just a few minutes and leave keys in their cars.

OBSERVATIONS

- It is amazing how many housebreakings are being perpetrated in the crowded neighborhoods of New Providence, such as Yellow Elder Gardens, Elizabeth Estates, Pinewood Gardens and other similar areas. It is obvious that there are no Crime Watch programs in these areas. The Police must encourage the formation of 'Crime Watch' groups in these areas. Remember that Crime Prevention is 'Watching Out and Helping Out.'

- Gun owners are still leaving guns in vehicles, which are subject to thefts. They should acquire proper gun safes in their homes, which should be positioned in a concealed location. Guns could also be taken apart and the parts kept in separate locations in the house.

- Police investigations quite often reveal that many private individuals and businesses employ persons without considering a background check or any investigation, the cost of which is minimal.

- Surprisingly, there are also those persons who employ maids, yardmen and baby-sitters and only know their first name. They have no other information about such individuals. There are firms here that provide the service of investigating job applicants.

- During the Yuletide Season the 'Neighborhood Watch' would play a very important role in preventing crime. Neighbors must get together and help each other in protecting their properties from intruders. When leaving home, cut off Christmas tree lights, but leave some lights on and inform the neighbor of your intended location.

- The Police Force has been making strides in their objective to respond to calls within three minutes, anywhere in New Providence. They have been very successful with this exercise, which has brought about some good results. Many arrests have been made of persons leaving the scene of a crime due to quick arrival of Police personnel.

- There is another challenge, which the public could help to solve and that is the inability of many persons to give proper directions to find their residences. Approach your representatives in Parliament and insist on proper street signs and numbers on buildings. Those street signs taken down by criminals should be replaced and strengthened. There are those persons who complain about the time it takes for the Police to get to them, which quite often is as a result of poor directions being given.

-   If your building is broken into, have a little patience as the Police teams working on burglary may take a bit longer due to complaints made ahead of your complaint.

-   There is so much technology now in the market place for the protection of buildings. Those persons and firms that can afford such equipment should have it installed.

-   If you hire security personnel, ascertain what their firm is paying them and compare it with what you are paying the firm.

-   Have 'patrol stations' in various locations to ensure that visits are being made to all parts of your property and patrols are conducted. ▣

Prevention Measures from Interpol.
Crime Prevention Supplement - The Tribune - 4 December, 2002

PREVENTING CAR THEFT

A motor-vehicle is a very expensive item, and also one that has become indispensable to many people. That is why you should provide as much protection as possible against theft. There are many steps you can take personally, to prevent your car falling into criminal hands.

- Do not leave your car in a dark or deserted area. When at home always park your car in your garage.
- Close all windows and lock all doors and the boot, even if you only leave your car for a moment.
- Turn the wheels towards the curb and lock the steering. Activate the alarm or anti-theft system if your car is fitted with one. These precautions should be taken even if your car is in your garage. Also close all access to the garage (entry barriers) and the garage door itself.
- When at home do not leave the car keys where they can be seen or easily found.
- Do not leave the registration documents in the car. Check regularly to see if you have left your documents in your car.
- Never leave your spare key in your car.
- Do not leave valuables in your car. (Cellphone, handbag, sunglasses, wallet and camera etc.) Items which you have to leave should be left where they cannot be seen from outside, preferably in the boot. They should be put there discreetly.

CAR-JACKING

Lock your car doors if you feel threatened. Be very careful in the event of a minor accident, which may be simulated to get you out of the car. If you suspect anything is wrong, do not get out; open the window only slightly to speak to the other person.

Remain alert and check that you are not being followed and that there are no suspicious vehicles and/or people following you, or loitering around your home.

Do not resist if you are attacked. Whatever the value of your car it is not worth your life.

MARKING AND REGISTERING PROPERTY. FOILING THE THIEVES.

The Police need good descriptions of stolen property if there is to be a reasonable chance of recovering them. A good description does not merely mean that the item must be identifiable by its make and type, but also by a number or mark.

If you are interested in the reduction of crime in our country, read this document and advance the suggestions to your Parliamentarians. Publish the contents and implore your Government to get started. Town Meeting must be arranged with Politicians, the Media and the Public.

THEFT OF VEHICLES

26th: September, 2012

Please accept this letter and its contents as an attempt to provide you with information and suggestions that would assist in the investigations of vehicle thefts. I wish to applaud the personnel in your section for the efforts they have made in this area of policing and your constructive and admirable leadership over the years.

I know of your concern over the large number of vehicles stolen in New Providence and the low percentage of those recovered. I happened to see a copy of the 2011 crime statistics. I have read a report from INTERPOL indicating that they are getting involved, as vehicle theft is now big business and have attracted organized crime.

Some years ago I accompanied Mr. Marvin Bain, a senior insurance executive at Bahamas First General Insurance Company, to Washington D.C., where we attended a seminar hosted by the U.S. Department of Justice and U.S. Security Organizations. We represented The Bahamas Insurance Industry. I was selected to attend as Paul Thompson & Associates, engaged in the investigation of stolen vehicles for several insurance companies. It was a very enlightening experience for me, in particular disclosure of the large number of stolen vehicles shipped out of the U.S.A. to Europe, Asia and Africa, most of them being top quality vehicles. The seminar was attended by vehicle manufacturers, who were persuaded to consider providing anti-theft devices in vehicles being sold to the public. Many of them indicated they were already doing so. In the following paragraphs there is a summary of the preventative measures suggested at that seminar and even in the report from INTERPOL:

- Encourage vehicle owners to use whatever preventative measures are available in their countries, such as; GPS, Loud Alarms, The Club (highly recommended) and other devices, such as the device with a special key, which completely immobolises the vehicle; a device with a key, that switches off the flow of fuel into the carburettor and a device that cuts off the brakes, making it dangerous for the thief to drive the vehicle.
- Police liaising with shipping companies to form a partnership to get information on vehicles at the docks for shipping. Such vehicles can be checked by the Police to ascertain if any are stolen property.
- Frequent visits to docks by the Police to check vehicles parked for shipping.
- Vehicle Licensing Authorities to conduct more detailed inspections, which must include VIN numbers, Engine Numbers and Chassis numbers.
- Any numbers that appear obliterated or tampered with must be reported promptly to Police Authorities. Bill of Sale and other relevant documentation must be thoroughly checked for authentic signatures. Report suspicions.
- Insurance companies to be encouraged to consider lower insurance premiums for vehicle owners, who install recommended anti-theft devices in their vehicles. These are some of the measures I recall, that were discussed at the seminar.

Upon my return to the Bahamas I wrote to a number of agencies in Nassau, including; the Police, the Road Traffic Department and the Insurance Companies, through Insurance Management (Bahamas) Ltd. and a number of the large insurance companies in The Bahamas. I also wrote letters to the news media in which I discussed the preventative measures.

In Trinidad & Tobago, the insurance companies encourage vehicle owners to install anti-theft devices in their vehicles. Two years ago I was the victim of an armed robbery in Port of Spain, Trinidad. The rented car I was driving was the only thing taken from me by the armed bandits. I immediately reported the crime. The car was equipped with a GPS system. In a matter of 45 minutes the car was recovered.

You may wish to recommend, the promotion of a vehicle theft prevention campaign, that could be sponsored by insurance companies, vehicle retailers and providers of anti theft devices as they all stand to benefit immensely.

Efforts must be made to convince the Road Traffic Authority to have their staff trained for the proper inspection of vehicles which must include the checking of the previously mentioned identification.

Police and Customs must consider conducting an audit of all of the car lots in New Providence at which time checks can be made for stolen vehicles as well as those vehicles smuggled into New Providence. We know, that vehicles stolen in New Providence are either;

- Joyriding, in which case recovery is very likely.
- Removing parts needed for repairs or for sale to unscrupulous garage owners and mechanics.
- Cloning, when the vehicle may be repainted and re-upholstered for sale to Used Car Dealers, unsuspecting members of the public and shipping to Family Islands. Sources have told me that "cloning" is big business and may be led by a number of immigrants in our country.

It is with the greatest of respect for your work that I have decided to address the contents of this letter to you. ◙

How To Detect White Collar Crime

What should an organization look for to determine if employees are committing white collar crime?
- (a) The sudden resignation of managers or head cashiers.
- (b) Sudden change in attitude or in the lifestyle of the individual.
- (c) Increased show of affection to management, which was previously lacking.
- (d) Persons not wanting to take vacation.

How can an organization prevent this from happening?
- (a) Employee education.
- (b) Proper remuneration for work done.
- (c) Reporting programs.
- (d) Proactive policies.
- (e) Mandatory vacations.
- (f) Surprise audits.
- (g) Prosecution policy.
- (h) A zero tolerance approach to dishonesty in the workplace.
- (i) Installation of surveillance cameras, that is effective. This will provide two things in the short term; First - It can act as a deterrent and secondly - It can eliminate the need for witch hunts.

Persons on the inside of an establishment facilitate most white collar crimes. These can be tellers, supervisors, cashiers, or other individuals whose ethical standards are not very high.

(Vetting and background investigations of applicants and potential employees should be an important consideration) ■

Fraud and False Pretense Investigations

(The reader is reminded that all excerpts of any Sections of the Laws of The Bahamas as stated in any page of this book should not be referenced without verification).

SECTION 69 (1) DEFINITION OF FRAUD

Fraud can be defined as an act of deceit, falsehood or other fraudulent means, whether or not it is a false pretense by a person of any property, money or valuable security. However, a real definition of fraud is still a question posed by men who have studied this type of offence for many years.

In a true case of fraud, there must be at least two (2) parties, the representor and the representee. There are seven (7) elements or essential ingredients which must go together to make up a case of fraud.

   i   There must be false representation by the representor.

   ii   There must be knowledge on the part of the representor that his representation is false, or his positive assertion made recklessly without knowledge of its truth.

   iii There must be intent by the representor that the false representation be acted on in a manner reasonably contemplated.

   iv There must be ignorance of the falsity of the representation on the part of the representee.

   v   The representee must have the right to rely on the representation

   vi   The representee must actually rely on the false representation made by the representor.

   vii There must be actual injury to the representee as a result of his or her - relative on the false representation.

If it is found that these seven (7) ingredients are not present, the case is not one of fraud.

PERSONATION

The Penal Code (Section 60) explains-

'Personation means a false pretense or representation by a person that he is a different person whether that different person is living, dead or fictitious'.

Examples of False Pretenses are: -

(a)   A man goes into a shop dressed as an Army Officer (which he is not). If he does this in order to obtain credit which he would not otherwise get, he is guilty of a false pretense, although he does not actually say he is an Army Officer

(b)   Within the meaning of our Penal Code the following would be 'false pretenses':-

    (i)   'A' goes into a store and offers for sale a picture which he says (falsely) belongs to him, or

    (ii)   obtains credit, states (falsely) that he is entitled to inherit property under the will of a relative,

    (iii)   obtains credit, states (falsely) that he has an account at a particular bank, or

    (iv)   offers for sale, pieces of brass pretending that they are gold.

(c)   'False pretenses' can also be committed in various ways by a man falsely representing that he is capable of doing such things as to double money.

FALSE PRETENCES

A FALSE PRETENCE. The Penal Code (Section 59) defines this:
A false pretense is a representation of the existence of a state of facts made by a person, either with the knowledge that such representation is false or without the belief that it is true and made with the purpose to defraud. A representation may be made either by written or spoken words, or by personation, or by other conduct, signs or means, of whatever kind.

Example: A man goes into a shop dressed as an Army Officer. If he did this to obtain credit, even if he didn't say he was an Army Officer. He is guilty of false pretenses.

FRAUD BY FALSE PRETENCES

The Penal Code (Ch. 48) defines this: Section 58) "A person is guilty of defrauding by false pretense if, by means of any false pretense, he obtains the consent of another person to part with or transfer the ownership of anything of which the crime of stealing can be committed". (See section 57 of the Penal Code.)

Note: A False Pretense includes cheating at cards, dice etc. (See section 65(1) of The Lotteries & Gaming Act)

ATTEMPTED FALSE PRETENCES

If the property was not obtained as a result of, or if the injured party was deceived (e.g. as in a Police trap) by the False Pretense but parted with his property, the accused may be convicted of attempting to obtain the money or goods etc. by False Pretenses capabilities of an article offered for sale).

The following are not sufficient to constitute False pretenses although they are false:-
   (a)   stating that a picture is a valuable work of art,
   (b)   stating that the picture in five years will have doubled in value,
   (c)   a person stating that he expects to receive property when a relative dies:

The property obtained in False pretenses must be some definite thing, mere benefit e.g. a ride in a bus or taxi, is not sufficient.

POWERS OF ARREST

Under Section 104 of Chapter 48.

POLICE ACTION IN CASES OF FALSE PRETENCFS.

   (a)   Listen to the complaint very carefully.
   (b)   Obtain complainant's name and address etc. and note time of the complaint.
   (c)   Obtain in Pocket Note Book FULL details of:-
       (i)   The time or times of the offence(s).
       (ii)   The story told or style used to the complainant by the accused (suspect).
       (iii) Its effect on the complainant (usually he was deceived).
       (iv)   What was obtained from the complainant
       (v)   The suspect's name and any 'alias' used. (Probably only 'alias' used)
       (vi)   Full description of the suspect's dress, appearance, marks, habits, peculiarities and speech etc.
       (vii) Full description of the property obtained, as an aid to tracing the offender.
       (viii) If possible, obtain a statement, covering the points to be proved.
       (ix)   Report to superior.

POINTS TO PROVE (EVIDENCE) in cases of False Pretense (Evidence)

(a)   Intent to defraud
- (i)   Not necessary to prove defrauding of a particular person,
- (ii)   Intent usually proved by circumstances, e.g. selling brass for gold.
- (iii)   Evidence can be given of similar acts to prove intention to defraud systematic dishonesty.

(b)   False representation of an existing or past fact by the accused by words, writing, conduct or otherwise.
- (i)   By words - telling the tale.
- (ii)   By writing giving a worthless cheque.
- (iii)   By conduct - collecting debts from customers of previous employers after having been dismissed

Note: Regarding (b) above

Existing Fact.
- i)   The false representation must be of something which exists or has existed.
- ii)   Promise of future conduct not intended to be kept is not by itself a false pretense. (Note the difference between — "This is a 9 carat gold ring" and "I will get you a 9 carat gold ring")

(c)   That accused knew the representation to be false.

(d)   That victim believed the representation (was deceived), and as a consequence parted with his property.

(e)   That property was obtained because of the deceit.
- (i)   Property must have been obtained and parted with on the strength of the false pretense.
- (ii)   It is not false pretenses if the loser of the property states he did not believe the story but parted with the property merely to get rid of the accused.

INTENT TO DEFRAUD

Intent to defraud means intent to cause, by means of forgery, falsification or other unlawful act, any gain capable of being measured in money or the possibility of any such gain to any person at the expense or to the loss of any other person.

To defraud is to deprive by deceit or by deceit to induce a course of action.

To defraud is also to induce a person to believe a thing is true which is false and which the person practicing the deceit, knows, or believes it to be false. (In other words, to induce a state of mind).

CREDIT

Credit is the capacity of being trusted and the obtaining of an item on a promise to do something in the future.

CREDIT BY FALSE PRETENCES

A person obtains credit by false pretenses if he obtains any credit and presents a false means of payment; such as forged credit cards.

7. OBTAINING CREDIT BY FRAUD.

A person obtains credit by fraud if he obtains credit and has no means of payment.

Penal Code - Section 395(a) Credit is an advantage not property, goods etc. therefore does not come under False pretenses.
Essentials in this offence are:-
- (i) Incurring debt or liability.
- (ii) Fraud - known as inability to pay.

Example - Restaurant Fraud
'A' entered a restaurant and ordered food and wine. No question was asked as to his ability to pay and no statement was made by him on that matter. After he had consumed the meal he said that he had no money to pay for it. It was held that there was no evidence of false pretenses and that 'A' could not be convicted of larceny, the restaurant owner having voluntarily parted with possession and property, being the food, but it was held that he was guilty of an offence under section 395(a) - Obtaining credit by Fraud.

POINTS TO PROVE IN CASES OF OBTAINING CREDIT BY FRAUD.

(i) that a debt or liability was incurred;
(ii) that credit was obtained;
(iii) that the credit was obtained by means of a false pretense or some other fraud. *Note:*
- (a) In the above example of restaurant fraud it is not false pretenses because the meal would have been supplied to anyone. The main point is the question of credit, pay when you have had your meal.

OTHER FRAUDS

(a) Fraud as to Insurance - Section 392 of the Penal Code, Chap. 48.

(b) Fraud by Companies, officials of public officers Section 393 of the Penal Code. (Falsification of Accounts etc.)

(c) Fraud in the sale or mortgage of land Section 393 of the Penal Code.

(d) Fraudulent Debtors - Section 395 of the Penal Code (See obtaining credit by fraud above).

(e) Fraud as to boundaries or documents - Section 398 of the Penal Code.

(f) Fraud as to thing pledged or taken in execution - Section 399 of the Penal Code.

(g) Fraud in removing goods to evade legal process. - Section 400 of the Penal Code.

(h) Fraudulent Breach of Trust - Sections 48 and 390 of the Penal Code.

DIFFERENCE BETWEEN FALSE PRETENCES AND LARCENY BY TRICK

These offences are closely allied and it is sometimes difficult to decide which offence has been committed. The following comparison may help to decide.

FALSE PRETENCES

(i) Possession is obtained by means of a false pretense that some fact exists or has existed.

(ii) The owner of the property not only parts with possession, but also parts with ownership, by reason of the false pretense.

LARCENY BY TRICK

(i) Possession is obtained by means of some trick or artifice

(ii) The owner of the article has no intention to part with.

Example: Illustrating the difference between false pretenses and Larceny by Trick.

A man was employed by a company selling radios and he left their employment. He later called on a customer of the company who had a radio on the hire purchase system, and without telling the customer that he had left the company, he collected an installment of BS $1.00. He said the radio required repair and took it away.

Offences: (i) False pretenses of B$1.00.

(ii) Larceny by Trick of the radio

An almost infallible system of finding out whether an offence is False Pretense or Larceny by Trick is to ask: 'Did the person parting with the possession still consider that he was the owner'? If the answer is 'Yes' then the offence is Larceny by Trick. (See Penal Code - Section 53).

DISTINCTION BETWEEN STEALING AND FALSE PRETENSES

If a person is accused of stealing something from the owner thereof or any person who has authority to part with the ownership of it, gave consent to the appropriation of the thing, then although the consent was obtained it was obtained by deceit. The person will not be guilty of stealing, but he is guilty of having defrauded the thing by false pretenses.

Example 1: 'A' is intending fraudulently to appropriate a house belonging to 'B', obtains it from 'B' under the pretenses that he wants it for a day. Here A is guilty of stealing.

Example 2: 'A' is intending to defraud 'B' of a horse without paying for it induces 'B' to sell and deliver it to him without present payment by a false pretense that he has $4,000.00 at his bank. Here, 'A' is guilty of obtaining by false pretenses, but is not guilty of stealing.

FRADULENT BREACH OF TRUST

This is when a person dishonestly appropriates a thing; the ownership of which is vested in him as a trustee for any other person.

Example: A lawyer is given $5,000.00 to invest for his client, uses the money to his own advantage and never carries out the investment. Here, the lawyer is guilty of Fraudulent Breach of Trust.

FORGERY

A person forges a document, if he makes or alters the document, or any material part thereof, with intent to cause it to be believed either:
(a) That the document or part has been so made or altered by any person who did not in fact make or alter it.
(b) That the document or part has been so made or altered with the authority or consent of any person who did not in fact give such authority or consent.
(c) That the document or part has been so made or altered at a time different from that at which it was in fact made or altered.
Every word, letter, figure, mark, seal, or thing expressed on or in a document, or forming part thereof or attached thereto, and any coloring,

shape or device used therein, which purports to indicate the person by whom, or with whose authority or consent a document or part thereof has been made, altered, executed, delivered, attested, verified, certified or issued, or which may affect the purport, operation or the validity of the document in any material particular, is a material part of the document.

UTTERING

The offence of uttering is committed by one whom in any manner deals with or uses any forged document or counterfeit stamp or coin, knowing it to be forged, counterfeited or falsified, with intent to defraud, or with intent to defeat, obstruct or pervert the cause of justice or the due execution of the law.

POSSESSION OF FORGED DOCUMENTS

A person possesses or does any act with respect to a document, knowing it not to be genuine, if he possesses it, or does the act with respect to it, knowing that it was not in fact made or altered at the time, or by the person, or with the authority or consent of the person, at which or by whom, or with whose authority or consent, it purports or is pretended by him to have been made or altered; and it is immaterial whether the act of the person who made or altered it was or was not a crime.

STEALING BY REASON OF EMPLOYMENT OR SERVICE

This is when a person steals a thing which he has custody, control or possession of or to which he has the means of access by reason of any office employment or service.

Example 1: 'A' is a cashier at a supermarket and steals cash from the register which she operates

Example 2: 'A' is given $300.00 by 'B' to purchase items from the Hardware Store. 'A' uses the money to his own advantage and never purchases the items or refunds the money given to him.

FALSIFICATION

A person falsifies a coin of any metal coinage, denomination, date or country, if he removes any such part thereof or if by any means he so alters it, whether permanently or temporarily and whether in substance or appearance, as that it may pass for a coin of a different metal, coinage, denomination, date or country.

FALSIFICATION OF ACCOUNTS

(A)The offence of falsification of accounts is committed by one who is employed as a clerk, servant or Public Officer, or an officer of a partnership, company or corporation, who does or concurs to conceal, injure, destroy, alter or falsify any book, paper or account kept by or belonging or entrusted to his employers, or to the partnership, company or corporation, or entrusted to him, or which he has access, as such clerk, servant, or officer, or omits to make a full and true entry in any account of anything which he is bound to enter therein, with intent to cause or enable any person to be defrauded, or with intent to commit or facilitate the commission by himself or by any other person, of any offence.

(B)The Offence of Falsification of accounts is also committed by one who is employed in the same capacity aforementioned, who publishes any account, statement or prospectus relating to the affairs of the partnership, company or corporation, which he knows to be false in any material particular.

CHEQUE

A cheque is a bill of exchange drawn on a banker, payable on demand.

DOCUMENT

A document includes any part of a document, a bank note, telegram, telegraphic code or cypher and any painting, drawing, or photograph or other visible representation.

BANKING BUSINESS

Banking business means the business of receiving on current savings, deposit or other similar account, money which is repayable by cheque or order or other instructions and which may be invested by way of advances to customers or otherwise.

BANK

Bank, means any body of persons corporate or non-corporate carrying on banking business.

COMPANY

Company means a company incorporated either under the laws of the Bahamas or under the laws of any other country or place.

Any five (5) or more persons associated for any lawful purpose may be subscribing their names to a memorandum of association and otherwise complying with the requisitions of the Companies Act in respect to Registration, form an incorporated company, with or without limited liability.

POST OFFICE

Post office includes any house, building, room, carriage or place used for the purpose of the Post Office and any Post Office letter box.

NOTES ON FRAUD INVESTIGATIONS

CHEQUE

A cheque is a bill of exchange drawn on a banker, payable on demand.

COUNTERFEITING

A person "counterfeits" a stamp, coin or mark, if he makes any imitation thereof, or anything which is intended to pass or which may pass as such stamp, coin or mark.

CURRENCY NOTE

Currency note means a note issued by or on behalf of the Government of the Bahamas under and by virtue of the Central Bank of the Bahamas Act any act amending or repealing that act or note issued by or on behalf of the Government of any country outside the Bahamas.

MAIL

Mail includes, every conveyance by which posted packets are carried, whether it be a carriage, cart, dray, horse, or any other conveyance and also a person employed in conveying or delivering postal packets, and also any vessel or boat employed by or under the post Office for the transmission of postal packets by contract or otherwise in respect of postal packets transmitted by the vessel or boat.

MAIL BAG

Mail bag includes a bag, box, parcel, or any other envelope or covering in which postal packets in course of transmission by post are conveyed, whether it does or does not contain any such packets.

TO DEFRAUD

Is to deprive by deceit or by deceit to induce a course of action.

To defraud is also to induce a person to believe that a thing is true which is false and which the person practicing the deceit, knows, or believes it to be false. (In other words, to induce a state of mind.) e.g. A worthless cheque.

15 August 2012

PENAL CODE CHAPTER 84, STATUTE LAWS OF THE BAHAMAS

'517. For the purpose of any provision of this Code by which any forgery, falsification or other unlawful-act is punishable if used or done with intent to defraud, an intent to defraud means an intent to cause, by means of such forgery, falsification or other unlawful act, any gain capable of being measured in money, or the possibility of any such gain, to any person at the expense or to the loss of any other person.'

'S 140(1)(e) Whoever is convicted of a fraudulent breach of trust... where the value of the property alleged to be stolen, in the opinion of the court, Is not more than $500 shall be liable to imprisonment for 3 months or to a fine of $500 or to both.'

'S 347. Whoever is convicted of fraudulent breach of trust is liable to imprisonment for five years.'

TRUST:

Where a Donor grants the Power (legal authority) to another person(s) (Trustee (s) to legally hold property for the benefit of others (Beneficiary/ Beneficiaries... which may include the Donor). The Trustee is obligated to act in the best interest of the beneficiary and in accord with the terms of the Power granted to him.

FIDUCIARY:

A person who holds a position of trust or confidence with respect to someone else and who is therefore obliged to act solely for that person's benefit.

BREACH OF TRUST:

(a)   Where the Trustee is in a fiduciary relationship to the Beneficiary and the Trustee acts in a manner contrary to the terms of his Power to the detriment of the Beneficiary/Beneficiaries.

(b)   Lawyer - client enter into a fiduciary relationship. Eg. State of land conveyancing

(c)   A vendor contracts with an attorney to do legal work for the sale of his land. Sale is completed but lawyer withholds proceeds due to client and unlawfully fails to disburse proceeds due to client

(d)   This amounts to a breach of trust on the part of the lawyer.

(e)   If lawyer uses the proceeds of the sale for his own benefit and fails to deliver up the same to the vendor/client - this would also amount to Conversion.

Another example would be that of a Director of a Company and his fiduciary relationship to the Shareholders ▣

Policing The Bahamas in the Early Fifties
(A brief history)

The Force was about 200 in strength before our arrival (18) from Trinidad & Tobago as recruits in March, 1951. The Commissioner of Police (acting) was Major Edward Sears, formerly of the West Indian Regiment of World War II. He was Bahamian. Sears Road on Shirley Street was named after him. The two story house on the corner was his residence. Major Spencer Harty was Deputy Commissioner.

He was English, a former Olympian in the long jump. The two story building immediately east of the present headquarters building was Police Headquarters. Apart from the Commissioner and Deputy, that building also housed the human resources and accounts office, with Sergeants Stanley Blair and Gerald Bartlette. Inspector Carlton Price Wentworth, who was seconded here from the Trinidad Police Service as a training instructor was also in office there.

The quarter-guard was downstairs. The gate has since been closed and the entry moved to the south. The building that is now Police Headquarters was the Police Barracks, with rooms, that accommodated single officers. The front of the building was open with verandahs up and downstairs. The Police Training School was in the basement at the north end, Police Canteen in the center and stores on the southern end. The canteen served beverages, including alcohol and there were corn beef and tuna salads available. Personnel played darts, whist and checkers. The large stone building south of the barracks called 'Arthur House' was Her Majesty's Prison. The buildings in the area west of Arthur House were all part of the prison.

The Force had three divisions, namely; 'A', 'B' and 'Traffic'. There was the Criminal Investigation Department headed by an English Officer. The Officers in charge of the divisions were Inspector Augustus Roberts 'A' and Inspector Wenzel Grainger "B", both Bahamians and former British Army Officers. Inspector George Knowles was in charge of the Traffic

Division. There was a very good drill instructor, Inspector Atkinson of the British Army. He was also in charge of the Police Stores.

Constable Cyrill Smith, a renowned bodybuilder was in charge of physical training that included the three mile runs, swimming at Montagu or Junkanoo beaches and physical exercises on the grass at the rear of the barracks. There was a small restaurant across the street contracted to feed recruits at two pounds ten shillings per week. Our wages were two pounds fifteen per week and fifteen pounds per month. A group of officers, nicknamed 'self-boarders anonymous' prepared their own meals. John Chea laundry collected uniforms for cleaning for which we paid. 'A' and 'B' divisions provided personnel for the stations; Central, Southern, Eastern, Fox Hill, Western and Cable Beach. Officers would fall in at headquarters, detailed for their stations to which they walked or travelled in the provided pickup trucks. Some officers had bicycles.

Officers were on duty for 24 hours. Cots were provided for rest periods. Personnel had to be provided for the Magistrate Court and the Supreme Court. The prosecutor in the Magistrate Court was a Sargent. I would describe the Policemen of that era as being loyal, courageous, dedicated, honest and hardworking. Discipline was enforced. The uniform was respected and worn with pride. Education was not of today's standard, but commonsense, determination, good leadership and exceptional knowledge of people and places were assets in their performance.

I welcomed the guidance, and on the job training received, working alongside these Bahamian Officers. ◉

Further Recommendations
Made to The Government
by Paul Rupert Thompson Sr.

Cost Cutting Opportunities

In the area of investigation, we could engage fraud & accounting experts from Scotland Yard and the Royal Canadian Mounted Police, we could have employed a cadre of accountants on contract to be attached to the Audit Department to assist law enforcement as is used by the Trinidad & Tobago police and other island nation police units.

There used to be provisions in our laws for special courts, which could expedite such trials. It was hoped, that the Attorney General's Office would obtain through the Courts, authorization for police investigators to acquire information from local and overseas banks (USA, Panama. Cayman Islands & the Turks). Central Bank should be aware of persons who have such accounts.

Public Information

When can we expect to obtain information regarding the $650K reportedly spent by the Ministry of Tourism on the Caribbean Music Festival that did not occur? The former Minister was placing some responsibility on Mr. Alfred Sears to explain. When can we expect to get an itemized account for those millions of dollars spent on the Carnivals? The latter denied having anything to do with the finances. What services, equipment and labor, for example, were provided and by whom.

The present Minister in a press statement said that it would be costly to attempt to recover any missing money, in particular, for the first and second events. I did not see what could have cost $12M for that first event. I also disagree that the funds cannot be recovered. We have lawyers in the Attorney General's office that could pursue this matter. We need to know who got the money and for what purpose?

I have been informed that 3 stages built by a U.S. firm for the first carnival cost $250K each. We should check the firm's Income Tax Returns to confirm if that amount was received.

Furthermore, what has happened to the Stages and attachments, and the generators, which were purchased?

How can a clerk in the Public Treasury steal $500K before the theft is discovered? What has happened to the financial controls, discipline, accountability, enforcement and punishment in our public sector? How could an employee at the then College of The Bahamas steal close to $250K before being found out. The massive amounts of cash taken from government offices indicate either a lack of financial controls or negligence and compliance of those responsible for the enforcement of such controls.

The Collection of Government Revenue

The Bank of The Bahamas is owed hundreds of millions by millionaires, who have failed to make payments on the millions they borrowed. When visiting the Magistrate Court (civil side), representatives of banks are there for civil cases against several persons, who have failed to pay their loans. Bahamas RESOLVE Ltd. was formed by the Government to collect on these troubled loan accounts. The public is not aware if any collections have been achieved. The public is aware, however, that more public funds are being used to keep the bank in operation. Why have we not taken these millionaires to Court? Is it selective justice?

The Seizure & Forfeiture of the Proceeds of Crime

Absolutely nothing is being done to enforce this law. We don't hear of any seizures except cash seized by the Police during raids. The properties and assets of criminals, in particular, drug dealers, are not in any danger from us, but U.S. Law Enforcement Agencies are active in this area. We have buildings to be seized that could house ministry offices.

Disclosure of Assets

Our politicians have contravened the law relative to disclosure for a decade. The public expected those in contravention be charged; it was talked about during the election campaign. Consideration should be given to having the law amended to authorize the Chairman of the Disclosure Commission to mass complaints directly to the Commissioner of Police for investigation and prosecution.

Interpol Bahamas

Established in the seventies, after independence. I had the good fortune to be sent to Interpol in France (the HQ) for training on two occasions before we established an office here, in the Bahamas. Interpol Bahamas, which is occupied by trained Interpol officers and is in communication with INTERPOL ASSOCIATES internationally is not being used by our governments to conduct due diligence on persons and firms coming to The Bahamas, either to reside or conduct business. Because of this, our Governments have been embarrassed on occasion and have been the victims of fraud and wanted fugitives living in our country.

Decades ago the Immigration Department dealt effectively with undesirable persons residing in the country, by asking them to leave or having them deported and placed on a 'Stop List'. Any foreigner found to be committing a major crime in our country was deported. There are cases where persons were not charged or convicted, but the Immigration Department would take action if there was sufficient evidence to convince them that the parties were undesirable.

Public Transportation

It is well known that New Providence needs an efficient bus service. I have suggested in the past that such a service could not be provided here without a Government administrated Public Transport Corporation, such as that which exists in most cities worldwide.

It might be warranted that authorities from the Road Traffic Department and the Ministry of Transport visit Bermuda, Barbados or London to witness examples of efficient public transport. The efficiency of these locations' transportation starts with timely buses to all parts of the city, and bus stops with shelter and seating. The drivers are in uniform, and there are multiple ticketing options.

Immediately stop the rental of bus and taxi plates! Imagine the chosen persons who own the franchise, not having the vehicles, but being able to rent the plates to the owners of vehicles, who have to hustle to acquire the revenue necessary to pay the rental fees. Hence the prevalence of dangerous driving among bus drivers. Can you imagine how lucrative it is for a person having a dozen such franchises along with the plates?

Government Vehicles

A large number of government vehicles allocated to Public Servants are in use in New Providence. Do persons to whom these vehicles are allocated need to have the vehicles for their assignments; could we as a cost-cutting measure investigate and reassign such vehicles to government departments in need of vehicles, such as the police? Ministries could have carpools with drivers and vehicles to take staff out on assignments, the number of vehicles assigned would depend on the size of each ministry, and the drivers would be responsible for the care and maintenance of the vehicles.

Government Rentals vs. Government Ownership

We are aware that the money spent by the Government on the rental of offices is very high. Over the decades we have not done much to remedy this situation, and we surely would have been able to buy the Immigration building, several times over. The Post Office building would be relocated to Gladstone Road, out of the city. Between Elizabeth Avenue and Deveaux Street, in what has been called the 'Dead City', the old abandoned buildings and unused spaces could become a thriving part of the city, if the Government would acquire these properties and with public financing develop a Government Complex to accommodate Ministries, Government offices, post office, and accommodation for entertainment centers, restaurants, shops, and parking. It would be a costly undertaking, but effective in the long-term.

Public shares should cover most of the cost and the rent from the Government would contribute towards the overall cost. Millions spent in rent could go towards such a complex, and that area of the City of Nassau would become alive again.

Rewards

There used to be cash rewards to the Police personnel making an arrest and recovering guns many years ago. I recommended that the law enforcement officers who arrest persons for bribery, be given a percentage of the bribe as a reward. Arrests for bribery and corruption would increase and the attempts to bribe and corrupt would decrease. Merchants, through The Bahamas Chamber of Commerce, could start a reward fund for information leading to the arrest and conviction of those involved in crimes against merchants, e.g. break-ins, armed robberies and stealing. Decades ago there was a massive increase in bank robberies, the Bankers got together and provided cash rewards for information. In one year, we were able to eradicate bank robberies. Information received resulted in several arrests and the recovery of stolen money.

Rent Assessment & Control Board

It was first proposed by Dr. Clarence Bain, but never went anywhere as it would have reduced the income of some landlords who were politicians or political cronies. The Board would have been responsible for the inspection of properties being rented, to ascertain suitability, ensure availability of electricity and sewage systems for bathrooms, along with providing adequate water supply. Outdoor toilets and street faucets would have been eliminated.

Rebuilding the Inner City

Sir Stafford Sands of the United Bahamian Party had secured the services of a University (namely Columbia University) in the United States of America, and carried out a survey of the inner city and presented a plan. The plan included the demolition and rebuilding of homes, the building and resurfacing of roads and sidewalks, and most importantly there was to be a proper sewage system running through the center or New Providence, eliminating the need for outdoor toilets, which exist still to this day. The Edmund Moxey family and Cable Bahamas have copies of the plan, as it was discussed in a subsequent program about "Edmund Moxey". Had we started our low-cost housing projects in the inner city, we would have seen a change by now.

Bahamas Correctional Services (Fox Hill or Fox Hill Prison)

The conditions for the inmates and even the guards are a human rights disaster and a health disaster waiting to happen. The stories coming from that place are shocking. The Government, the Bar Association and the Christian Council are all aware, though we only hear about those conditions when international bodies publish the details. A recommendation by former Commissioner of Police, Salathiel Thompson, in the early seventies was to build a maximum security prison on a Family Island. He had recommended Inagua or Ragged Island because of their proximity to the Royal Bahamas Defence Force Base. The prison in New Providence was to become a

Borstal Institute, like that found in the United Kingdom where inmates upon leaving become tradesmen/women. While in prison they would be taught the trades, for example, plumbing, electrical, carpentry, masonry, auto mechanics, bodywork, and welders.

The inmates would work in the maintenance of Government buildings and vehicles. They were also instructed in tailoring, with earnings deposited into accounts which would be available to them upon discharge, along with access to jobs. Inmate training and work release programs are being done with great success in the U K, and many of us who visited on Police training courses were taken on visits to Borstal Institutes.

The Ankle Bracelets

The use of ankle bracelets should be handled by Police and Prison officers. The monitoring of users would also be done by the police and prison offices making the process more efficient and effective. The Minister should compare the cost of private monitoring, with the cost of having the work done in the police control room, there would also be the added advantage of immediate response by officers.

Overseas Training for Police Officers

Most of the Commissioners and senior officers on our force have received overseas training mostly in the U.K. and the U.S. with the F.B.I. There appears to be a stop to such training opportunities, as far back as Commissioner Salathiel Thompson. Those of us who had the opportunity to be trained overseas returned to The Bahamas with a sense of pride in our occupation, and aware of the importance of implementing new knowledge and systems and training to aid our subordinates in more efficient and effective techniques. The overseas training should be reinstated.

Sexual Offenders

So much is being said about marital rape and amendments to relevant laws are being debated. In all of this, we have forgotten the promise of The Hon: Bernard Nottage to introduce, "Marco's Law" and a sexual offender's register (a Bishop and two Pastors would likely be on the register) which would assist the Police in the investigation of sex crimes and act as a crime prevention measure. It is very noticeable that none of the women's organizations has pursued this, and The Bahamas Christian Council has been silent.

Entertainment for Visitors

We used to be the entertainment and nightlife capital of the Caribbean, with nightclubs such as the Cat and Fiddle, Zanzibar, Junkanoo Club and the Drum Beat, to name a few. Native and foreign entertainment was expected and welcomed by our visitors and locals. Now we have nothing to offer. Visitors who visit Arawak Cay ask for something other than food, but there is nothing consistent offered. There is space there for massive events and space to house nightclubs and theatres, bars, and lounges.

Foreign Investors

The first big investor we had on Paradise Island sold shares to Bahamians. These holders in time, sold those shares to the investors that followed. Government negotiations with such investors should follow the same template and include the sale of limited shares to Bahamians.

Law Enforcement

Our law enforcement agencies have done a commendable job in dealing with major crime such as murder, drug trafficking, human trafficking and corruption. To restore and maintain the order we once had, there must be an organized effort to eradicate minor offences including traffic violations that are so prevalent on our streets.

Examples include:

1. The large number of unlicensed motorcycles being driven by persons without helmets, dangerously and without insurance. Apart from the loss of revenue these persons ignor our laws and are poor examples to our youth. They also pose a threat to our safety on the streets. They do not have any form of insurance and manyof those with license plates are forgeries.
   Apart from the loss of revenue these persons ignore our laws and are poor examples to our youth. They also pose a threat to our safety on the streets. Many do not have any form of insurance, and some of the license plates are forgeries.

2. Parking on pedestrian sidewalks is dangerous for pedestrians using them. In our busy thoroughfares pedestrians having to walk past a vehicle parked on the sidewalk would have to step on the street, which poses a danger.

3. The Police need the breathalyzer and the authority to test drivers believed to be driving while intoxicated. Breathalyzers would help to reduce the number of severe accidents on our streets.

4. Street vendors, in particular, those around our schools, not having the required current health certificates, should be fined. Sanitary Inspectors have the authority to visit and inspect the kitchens where food is prepared.

Social Networking vs. Public Mischief

A letter was sent to the Attorney General's Office on the subject after a former employee of Bahamas Air accused the airline on social media, of purchasing a plane with a cracked fuselage and a guest on a talk show stated that 30 persons were killed in Long Island following a hurricane. Both stories were proven to be false. The Penal Code has a section that related to Public Mischief. It is my opinion that persons making such false statements that would cause a public reaction of fear should be liable to prosecution under this law.

Gaming in the Bahamas

When the legalization of the Web Shops was being debated, I met with a Trinidadian who was a member of the Gaming Corporation of Trinidad & Tobago. He told me that Dr. Eric Williams (Prime Minister of Trinidad and Tobago) took over the managing of the gaming industry, which is wholly Government owned. Play Whe (numbers racket), offshore betting, and horse racing.

Williams and his administration approved agents contracted them for ticket sales on a percentage basis. All revenue derived belongs to the Government. The Government holds the drawings in the corporation office and pay out the winnings through the sales agents. Revenue from gaming is deposited into a special account and funds are used for education, sports and health. Churches and Schools receive financial support from these funds as well. The information was discussed on Mr. Jeff Lloyd's show, and I wrote in to the Tribune. The Bahamas Government should have owned the Web Shop and Lottery business and contract agents for ticket sales. This advice came from a person married to a Bahamian who had lived in the Bahamas for several years. His advice would have cost much less than the New Zealanders.

The Shanty Towns

The Government's committee should have been Law Enforcement Heads (Police, Immigration and Defence) with instructions to deal with the occupants humanely. The following are alternative steps, which could have been taken:

1. Identify and prosecute the landlords for the contravention of all laws.
2. Ask the court to take a serious view of the offences and apart from heavy penalties order the demolition of each shanty town, at the expense of the landlords.
3. Identify and prosecute persons responsible for the illegal supply of utilities

The above suggestions would have avoided the challenge, which now exists because the Courts made an order to demolish the Shanty Towns.

Hurricane Relief for Ragged Island

Consider the purchase of modular homes from the U.S.A. or Canada. They are storm proof, attractive, reasonably priced and can be constructed in just a few days. The private sector and charitable organizations may contribute houses. Consideration should also be given to the construction of homes which are more hurricane resistant. ◙

Parliamentary Elections Act, 1992
(EXTRACTS FOR A POLICE SEMINAR)

1. (i) This Act may be cited as the Parliamentary Elections Act, 1992.
   (ii) This Act shall come into force on such date as the Minister may appoint by notice published in the Gazette.

2. In this Act, unless the context otherwise requires:

"candidate" means any person who stands nominated as a candidate for election for any constituency, and

"intending candidate" means person seeking such nomination for election; *"constituency"* has the meaning assigned thereto in Article 68 of the Constitution;

"Corrupt practice," means any offence against the provisions of Section 96 or Section 98;

"current register" means the register in force for the time being in accordance with the provisions of Section 13 or 14;

"day" includes every day other than Sunday or a public holiday:

"election" means the election in accordance with the provisions of this Act of a Member of Parliament;

"Election Court" means a court constituted in a manner, and having the powers and jurisdiction, mentioned in subsections (2) to (6) of Section 80;

"election agent" means an election agent appointed under the provisions of subsection (1) of Section 46;

"election petition" means a petition to an Election Court under Part VII;

"full age" means the age of eighteen years and upwards;

"general election" means the election of members to a new House of Assembly after any House of Assembly has been dissolved;

"Illegal practice" means any offence against this Act which is not a corrupt practice or an offense by reason of Section 16 (1), 17 (3) or Section 99;

"Minister" means the Minister responsible for Parliamentary Registration and Elections;

"nomination day" means, in relation to any constituency. the day appointed under Section 35 for the delivery of nomination papers by intending candidates;

"Parliamentary Commissioner" means the Parliamentary Commissioner appointed under Section 12, and includes any person who is duly authorized in accordance with the provisions of that section to act on his behalf;

"polling day" means, in relation to any constituency, the day appointed under Section 35 for the taking of the poll;

"polling division" means any of the polling divisions described in any order for the time being in force made by the Governor-General under the provisions of Section 11;

"polling place" means, in relation to any polling division in any constituency, a place appointed under Section 49 as a place where the poll shall be taken in that polling division;

"prescribed" means prescribed by regulations made under the provisions of this Act;

"presiding officer" means in relation to the taking of a poll at any polling place, the person appointed under Section 48 to be in charge of the place:

"protest vote" means a vote which may be cast upon a colored ballot paper under the provisions of Section 58:

"register" or "register of voters" means the register of persons entitled to vote at an election which is to be prepared and kept under the provisions of this Act, and includes any part of the register;

"registered vote" means any persons whose name is included in the register as being entitled to vote at an election: *"regular vote"* means a vote properly cast under the provisions of this Act upon a white ballot paper;

"Member of Parliament" means, a candidate who has been elected -and returned to represent a constituency in the House of Assembly:

"returning officer" means, in relation to any constituency, any person exercising or performing any of the functions of the returning officer under this Act, being the Parliamentary Commissioner or any person who is duly authorized in accordance with the provisions of Section 12 to act as a returning officer;

"revising officer" means any person exercising or performing any of the functions of the revising officer under this Act in relation to any constituency, being the Parliamentary Commissioner or any person who is duly authorized in accordance with the provisions of Section 12 to act as a revising officer;

"Speaker" means the person who holds the office of Speaker and includes any other person who, for the time being, is empowered under the Constitution to exercise the powers of Speaker;

"subscribe" means to sign, or in the case of a person who is unable to sign his name, to make his mark, and the words *"sign" and "signature"* shall be constructed similarly;

"voter's card" means a card issued to a person registered as a voter in accordance with the provisions of this Act;

"writ of election" or *"writ"* means a writ issued in accordance with the provisions of this Act for the election of a Member of Parliament to represent a constituency in the House of Assembly;

ELECTION AGENTS

46 - (1) A candidate may, by appointments in writing, authorize any number of persons to act as his election agent who shall on polling day present their respective appointments to the presiding officer and thereafter only those persons whose appointments have been so notified to the presiding officer shall be entitled to act as election agents for that candidate, subject to the right of the returning officer or the presiding officer to demand from any agent during the course of the polling day the production of his written authority.

(2) Any reference in this Act to election agents shall be taken as a reference to election agents, who are entitled to act as such and, where the number of such agents is restricted, who are within the permitted number.

(3) Where by this Act or any act or thing, is required or authorized to be done in the presence of a candidate or, of his election agent, it may be

done in the presence of the candidate or any one of his election agents who is present at the time and place appointed for the purpose, and the non-attendance of a candidate or of any of his agents at that time and place, shall not, if the act or thing is otherwise duly done, invalidate the act or thing done.

(4) Any person who represents himself to be or acts as an election agent on polling day and whose appointment as such was not presented to the presiding officer in accordance with subsection (1) shall be guilty of an offence under this Act.

DURATION OF THE POLL
53 - (1) Subject to subsection (2) then poll shall be taken on the appointed day for the taking of the poll and between the hours of eight o'clock in the morning and six o'clock in the evening.
(2) If for any reason, voting at a polling place does not commence at the designated time or is interrupted during the polling hours, the Parliamentary Commissioner shall be advised by the respective returning officer and at his direction, the Parliamentary Commissioner shall extend the closing time designated in subsection (1) to such time as is necessary to ensure that the poll has been open with free access to the electors for ten hours in total.

ADVANCED POLL
54 - (1) Where any police officer or member of the Royal Bahamas Defense Force is or is likely to be on the day appointed for the taking of the poll, assigned, sent or employed in the discharge of his duty in some other polling division, so as to prevent his voting at the polling station at which he would otherwise be entitled by law to vote. Such Police officer or member of the Royal Bahamas Defense Force may vote at an advanced poll to be held for this purpose at such place as the Parliamentary Commissioner shall determine upon a date prior to the said day appointed for the taking of the poll as shall be appointed by the Governor-General.

(2) The Commissioner of Police and the Commodore of the Royal Bahamas Defense Force, as the case may be, shall not less than fourteen days prior to the date appointed for the taking of an advance poll submit to the Parliamentary Commissioner a list of the members of the Royal Bahamas

Police Force and of The Royal Bahamas Defense Force, respectively, and which lists the Parliamentary Commissioner shall, not later than seven days before the aforementioned appointed date, make available for inspection and the taking of extracts at the office of the Parliamentary Commissioner.

(3) The provisions of this Act as they apply to voters voting and elections shall apply *mutatis mutandis*, to an advanced poll.

(4) At any advanced poll held as above, a separate ballot box shall be provided for each constituency, and at the close of such poll the ballot papers in each box shall, without any examination, be placed in separate packets and sealed by the presiding officer, each packet clearly designating the number of ballot papers it contains and the constituency to which it relates, and the presiding officer shall also prepare a statement in writing showing the number of regular and protest votes cast in each constituency.

(5) Each sealed packet of ballot papers shall be immediately returned to the Parliamentary Commissioner to be kept intact in his office or in a safe place until delivery by him on the day appointed for the taking of the poll, to one of the presiding officers for the same constituency to which such packet relates.

(6) The presiding officer shall open such packet immediately before the commencement of the poll in the presence of all persons who are lawfully in the polling place and without examining the ballot papers shall place them in the ballot box at his poll, before he locks it up and places his seal on it as hereinafter provided.

ADMISSION TO POLLING PLACE

55 - (1)The presiding officer shall not permit the number of persons who are in the polling place at the time for the purpose of voting to exceed the number of compartments in that polling place, and shall exclude all other persons except: -

- (a) the returning officer and the polling clerks appointed to attend at the polling place;
- (b) the candidates;
- (c) the permitted number of election agents for each candidate, being a number not exceeding three persons at any time:
- (d) the police officers on duty;
- (f) the friend of an incapacitated voter;

7. Subject to subsection (1) a candidate shall not be permitted to have at any time in the day of the poll at the polling place election agents in excess of six.

8. For the purpose of subsection (2) and of section 64 the expression "polling place" includes the area within one hundred yards of any building in which a poll is being taken.

SEALING OF BALLOT BOXES

56 - (1) Immediately before the commencement of the poll, the presiding officer shall, in the presence of all persons who are lawfully in the polling place, unlock the ballot box, remove the ballot papers there from and show the ballot box empty to such persons so that they may see that it is empty, and shall after placing therein any ballot papers which may be delivered to him in respect of an advanced poll. Then lock it up and place his seal on it in such a manner as to prevent its being opened without breaking the seal, and shall place it in his view for the receipt of ballot papers and shall keep it locked and sealed.

FORM 'M' - SECOND SCHEDULE

The presiding officer shall arrive at the polling place on polling day in sufficient time as would facilitate the commencement by him at 7:30 in the morning of the discharge of the duties mentioned in subsection (1), including that of the completion in form 'M' in the Second Schedule of a pre-poll ballot paper account of the ballot papers intended for use at the poll which pre-poll ballot paper account shall be delivered by the presiding officer to the returning officer at the time of the delivery to him of the ballot box.

VOTER TO BE IDENTIFIED BEFORE VOTING

57 - (1) No person shall be permitted to vote in any polling division at any election unless:-

(g) he produces his voter's card or other sufficient means of identification and it is apparent that he has not already voted at the same election in the same constituency or in any other constituency; and

(h) his name is on the part of the register for that polling division, and the presiding officer has scrutinized the voter's card or other means of identification produced by him and is satisfied as to his identity and his right to vote. The name of every voter who is permitted to vote upon production of sufficient means of identification other than his voter's card, and the means of identification produced, shall be entered on a list to be kept by the presiding officer.

(i) In any case where the voter's card bears the date of registration on page two of such card but is defective only because it does not bear a date or stamp on the face of page one of such card then such card shall be accepted as valid.

PROTEST VOTES

58 - (1) If during the course of identifying any person before voting in any polling division at any election under the provisions of paragraphs (*b*) of subsection (1) of section 57, the presiding officer is not satisfied as to the identity of such person or as to his right to vote because: -

- such person's voter's card has any defects;
- the entry relating to such person in the register is incorrect;
- such person has a voter's card but his name does not appear in the register for the relevant constituency or polling division, then the presiding officer shall permit such person to cast a vote upon a colored ballot paper and such vote shall be known as a protest vote

(2) In any other case in which the presiding officer permits any person to vote, such vote shall be cast upon a white ballot paper.

VOTING PROCEDURE

59 - (1)The presiding officer shall give one ballot paper, and no more, to any person whom he permits to vote, but before doing so he shall:

- sign his own name on the back of the ballot paper
- call out the number, full name and description on the counterfoil
- put a mark against the name of that person in the polling place, so as to indicate that person has voted in that polling division; and mark the thumb of the person by dipping the thumb of his right hand up to at least the first joint in such indelible ink or by such other mark as designated by the Parliamentary Commissioner by notice in the Gazette, after approval by the Prime Minister in consultation with the Leader of the Opposition, save that if the person has no right hand thumb or if for any other reason it is, in the opinion of the presiding officer, not practical to mark that thumb of the left hand or such other finger as the presiding officer shall direct shall be marked or if in the opinion of the presiding officer it is not practicable to mark any finger of the person, that person shall be marked in such a way as the presiding officer considers sufficient to indicate that a

ballot has been issued to that person; and stamp that person's voter's card with a stamp which shall indicate that the holder of that card has voted in that election in that polling division.

(2) Subject to any exceptions contained in paragraph (d) of subsection (1), a presiding officer shall refuse to give a ballot paper to a voter unless the officer is satisfied that there does not appear: -

- upon the appropriate finger of the voters;
- or in the case of a voter who the presiding officer is satisfied is suffering from an injury to the appropriate finger, upon any of the fingers of such voters, any mark of the indelible ink, (in this section referred to as 'electoral ink')

(3) For the purpose of satisfying himself in the manner required by subsection (2), the presiding officer shall in the presence of the poll clerk and of the election agents of the candidates inspect the appropriate finger of each voter, as the case may require and for that purpose shall use any equipment designed for the purpose of detecting any mark of indelible ink as may be prescribed.Provided that if the prescribed equipment fails to function or is illegally removed from, or is for any reason not available for use at, any polling place, the presiding officer, in lieu of using that equipment, shall require to vote: -

    i.   to take an oath in the prescribed form to the effect that he has not previously voted in that election;

    ii   and to make one or more impressions in ink on the form of the oath as follows: -
    (a) with his right thumb;
    (b) with the left thumb, should he not have a right thumb;
    or with any other finger should he not have any thumb.

(4) Where the appropriate finger or any other finger which any voter may be required to immerse in electoral ink is concealed or covered with any bandage or other material, the presiding officer shall refuse to give to the voter any ballot paper unless the voter either: -

    (a) removes such bandage or other material and wholly uncovers the appropriate or other finger aforesaid;
    (b) or satisfies the presiding officer that he is suffering from injury to such appropriate or other finger takes an oath to that effect in the prescribed form and makes one or more impressions in

ink on that form as follows: -
(i) with his right thumb;
(ii) with the left thumb, should he not have a right thumb

(5) Where the presiding officer delivers a ballot paper to a voter pursuant to subsection (4), he shall record in the copy of the register in use in the polling place, against the entry of the name of that voter, the facts in relation to the delivery of the ballot paper.

(6) Any presiding officer who refuses to deliver a ballot paper to any voter under the provisions of subsection (2) to (4) shall record in the copy of the register in use in the polling place, against the entry of the name of that voter the facts in relation to such refusal.

(7) Every person who applies for any ballot paper at a time when there is upon any of his fingers or elsewhere upon him pursuant to subsection (1) (d) any mark of electoral ink shall be guilty of an offence against this Act.

(8) The presiding officer shall before giving the ballot paper to the voter satisfy himself, if the voter has an appropriate finger that there does not appear upon such finger any substance which in his opinion is likely to prevent the adhesion of electoral ink and cause the voter to immerse such finger in the electoral ink.

Provided that where the presiding officer is satisfied that the voter is suffering from some injury to his appropriate finger which is of such nature as to render it undesirable for him to immerse such finger in the electoral ink, the presiding officer may require him to immerse in such ink any other finger upon which the presiding officer so satisfied that there is no substance which is likely to prevent the adhesion of electoral ink.

(9) Each voter shall vote without undue delay and, on receiving the ballot paper, shall forthwith go into one of the compartments in the polling place and there secretly with the indelible pencil provided place one cross only on the space opposite the name of the candidate for whom he votes, and shall then fold up the ballot paper so as to conceal his vote, and shall then show the back of the paper to the presiding officer so that that officer can see his own signature thereon, and then drop the ballot paper so folded up into the ballot

box in the presence of the presiding officer without showing the front of the ballot paper to any person, and the voter shall then retire from the polling place without delay.

SPOILT AND VOID BALLOT PAPERS

60 - (1) A voter who has inadvertently dealt with his ballot paper in such a manner that it cannot be conveniently used as a ballot paper may, on returning it to the presiding officer and providing to the satisfaction of that officer the fact of the misadventure, obtain another ballot paper in the place of the ballot paper so returned and the presiding officer shall forthwith endorse the word "spoilt" on the ballot paper so returned.

(2) Any ballot paper: -
(a) which does not bear the signature of the presiding officer;
(b) on which votes are given for more than one candidate;
(c) on which anything is written or marked by which the voter can be identified except for the printed number on the back;
(d) or which is unmarked or void for uncertainty shall be subject to the provisions of subsection (3), (4) and (5), be entirely void and not counted.

(3) A ballot paper on which a vote is marked: -
(a) elsewhere than in the proper place;
(b) otherwise than by means of a cross;
(c) or by more than one mark
shall not by reason thereof be deemed to be void if an intention that the vote shall be for one of the candidates clearly appears, and the way the paper is marked does not of itself identify the voter and it is not shown that he can be identified thereby;
Provided no ballot paper shall be deemed to be void in part and good in part:
   i. At the count of the presiding officer shall in the presence of the candidates of their election agents endorse the word "rejected" on any ballot paper which under subsection (2) and (3) is not counted.
   ii. The decision of the presiding officer on any question arising in respect of a ballot paper shall be final, but shall be subject to review by the returning officer at the recount.

DECLARATION AS TO QUALIFICATIONS BY REGISTERED VOTER FORM 'N' SECOND SCHEDULE

61.- The presiding officer may, and, if required so to do by any candidate or his election agent, shall, require any person applying for a ballot paper at the time of his application, but not afterwards, to take and subscribe an oath before the presiding officer (which shall be certified by the officer) in Form 'N' in the Second Schedule and if such person does not comply with the foregoing provision, he shall not be permitted to vote, and his name shall be marked on the register accordingly.

CHALLENGE AND ARREST OF VOTER

62- (1) If at the time a person applies for a ballot paper for the purpose of voting, or after he has applied for the ballot paper for that purpose and before he has left the polling place, a candidate or his election agent declares to the presiding officer that he has reasonable cause to believe that person has committed an offence or impersonation, and undertakes to substantiate the charge in a court of law, the presiding officer may order a Police Officer to arrest that person and the order of the presiding officer shall be sufficient for the police officer or constable so to do:

    14. elsewhere than in the proper place;

    15. otherwise than by means of a cross;

    16. or by more than one mark

shall not by reason thereof be deemed to be void if an intention that the vote shall be for one of the candidates clearly appears, and the way the paper is marked does not of itself identify the voter and it is not shown that he can be identify thereby:

Provided no ballot paper shall be deemed to be void in part and good in part.

    i.   At the count of the presiding officer shall in the presence of the candidates or their election agents endorse the word "rejected" on any ballot paper which under subsection (2) and (3) is not counted.

    ii. The decision of the presiding officer on any question arising in respect of a ballot paper shall be final, but shall be subject to review by the returning officer at the recount. ◼

The Diary in the Polling Place

It is perhaps the most important book in the polling place. It must be properly and carefully kept and the Police Officer assigned to this duty must be of marked ability. The Polling Place Diary is the hub around which the Police Officers assigned to the Polling Station revolves. The diary shall contain information of all briefings and debriefings that occur and include the deployment of officers. It shall contain a complete history of everything that occurs in and around the Polling Place. It must be a minute-by-minute, hour-by- hour record of everything that happens in the Polling Place. It is the most important book of reference to the day's events, when they occurred and who were the people involved, in chronological order. It must supply the exact times of persons reporting for work at the Polling Place, the names of the persons, the time of opening of the Polling Place, the arrival of the ballot boxes and the names of the persons conveying the same.

Where a person makes a complaint, it is to be recorded in the exact wording of the complaint. The comings and goings of all members of the Force and other staff must be entered. Where an incident occurred that required specific police action, the officer's pocket notebook must be cross-referenced with the diary entry numbers. Senior Officers visiting Polling Places should read and sign the diary on each visit. A t the end of the day's voting the diarist must record an account of the events taking place, the locking down of the Polling Place and accompany the team with the ballot boxes and record the names of the persons escorting the ballot boxes, the route, the arrival and the final deposit and lock down of the same.

THE POLICE POCKET NOTEBOOK

It must be an official Police notebook. It is the most important item of a Police Officer's equipment and must always be carried. Its purpose is to enable Police Officers to record accurate notes and particulars of all matters of which they are bound by law to take official cognizance, or on which they are likely to be called to make a report or testify in a court of law at a later date. The notes are to be recorded at the time of the occurrence or as soon as possible afterwards. The notes made of incidents at the Polling Places should be similar in content to the notes made in the diaries. This could be useful when produced in evidence at any future hearing.

The value of original notes cannot be overemphasized. Although the notes may be brief, no essential details should be omitted. Please be reminded of the ELBOW RULE taught at the Police College.

- NO ERASURES
- NO LEAVES TO BE TORN OUT
- NO BLANK SPACES TO BE LEFT
- NO OVERWRITING
- NO WRITING BETWEEN THE LINES.
- STATEMENTS TO BE IN THE EXACT WORDS USED.

It is important that diaries from Polling Places be properly secured and that Police Officers ensure the security of their notebooks for use as evidence in an Election Court or criminal proceedings in a criminal court. The period for which these records are held could be determined by consulting the Parliamentary Commissioner. Supervisors must inspect all notebooks at the end of the tour of duty and apprise the officer in charge. Any information contained in the notebook that was not previously disclosed must be brought to the attention of the officer in charge immediately in order that any necessary action may be taken.

SUBMISSION OF REPORTS

The officer-in-charge of the polling station has to ensure that all reports are collected at the end of the tour of duty or as soon as practicable for submission to the appropriate Assistant Commissioner. Therefore, where possible, officers should be afforded the opportunity to complete their reports during their tour of duty.

Tension Indicators

The term 'Tension Indicator' means exactly what it suggests, something that indicates tension. In a policing context the term is used to describe circumstances where emotions or behavior of an individual or group are such that it tends to indicate that conditions may escalate into some serious misbehavior or public disorder.

Tension Indicators are useful in assisting police identify potential problems in advance and thus allow time to devise and implement strategies to reduce or eliminate the tension before it develops into a Critical Incident. Critical Incidents will be an issue later in this seminar.

Example:

A trade union intended to hold a protest outside a Government building to emphasize its demands for higher pay. The week preceding the demonstration members of the union engaged in disruption of the corporation's business. There had been reports of scuffles between striking workers and those refusing to strike. The incidents indicate that emotions may be high and the protestors are prone to violence. This would suggest that the possibility exists for disorder at the demonstration.

Attack on Police in Inagua

In the mid 1980's, the Police Station in Inagua was burnt down by an angry mob. Before the incident, there had been a number of confrontations and complaints concerning the policing methods and attitude of the police. These were possibly indications that a physical confrontation between the Police and the populous was imminent.

Within the context of an election, political rallies are one the best measures of mood of the electorate. Other sources are the media, party supporters and general discussion groups.

It is imperative that close and objective scrutiny, is made of the size and mood of the crowd attending political rallies. An accurate assessment should be made and the appropriate Assistant Commissioner informed, in order that the Commissioner may assess what resources would be needed and where best to deploy those resources on Election Day. This is particularly important in the Family Islands where, in the event of disorder, additional support may be delayed.

During the 1987 election campaign emotions were running high in North Andros with political rallies reportedly being emotional. Anticipating public disorder, additional officers were sent to North Andros. However, during the course of the day tension escalated and eventually led to major public disorder. Reinforcements had to be brought from New Providence. Could this incident have been avoided or the police better prepared?

It is possible to defuse tension through the use of church and community leaders. However, care should be taken to ensure that such leaders actually do have influence. Self-appointed leaders can inflame the situation by their mere presence.

Consolidated force order 'c18' outlines the force policy on public order. Below are extracts from the policy that relate to public meetings and elections.

1. The specific responsibilities of the Royal Bahamas Police Force under the Police Act include the maintenance of law and order and the preservation of the peace. The majority of law-abiding citizens recognize their obligations to society but many incidents have the potential to cause public disorder including the following: -
   (a)   public meetings;
   (b)   public demonstrations:
   (c)   public processions:
   (d)   industrial disputes, and
   (e)   elections and political meetings.

2. Force policy is intended to ensure that any incident involving disorder is dealt with in a manner which commands public support. The police should be seen to act impartially, firmly and using only such force as is necessary. Excessive use of force by the police will invariably incite the public to further disorder.

3. Public disorder may arise spontaneously but in most of the situations summarized in paragraph 1 above, some disorder can be anticipated. Police response to disorder, therefore, can either be mobilization at short notice or pre-planned.

4. The procedures associated with mobilization of officers to deal with spontaneous disorder are outlined in Section D2 under 'Police Support Unit'. Where the police are able to plan ahead, details of measures to deal with possible disorder will be included in the operation order for the event.

5. It is essential for pre-planning that all information and intelligence concerning the event is available to the Operational Support Department. The officer in charge of any event will liaise with the organizers at an early stage to ensure that the 'ground rules' are agreed.

6. Freedom of speech is guaranteed under the Constitution and the public can protest and make representations on any issue provided they remain within the law. It follows that opportunities must exist for the public to offer legitimate views and the police should not intervene merely because the views expressed are controversial. This applies particularly to political meetings and it is essential that the police are not seen to be supporting one side or the other.

7. Where the police are obliged to intervene because of an actual or threatened breach of the peace, officers should attempt to resolve the situation by an informal approach where the persons concerned should be warned as to the consequences of further disorder. Where this proves insufficient, a more forceful approach may need to be adopted. If arrests are necessary, they should be carried out as quietly as possible and strictly in accordance with the lawful use of force.

8. The real test of police efficiency is their ability to prevent disorder rather than the visible signs of extreme measures to deal with it.

Police Attitudes

9. Experience has shown that the attitude of the police will often determine the outcome and extent of disorder. All police officers will act with professional detachment and discharge their duties impartially. It should be borne in mind that a large number of police officers can often be the second largest group present in a public order situation that they can be subject to group influences and group behavior as much as the demonstrators.

10. In adopting a professional attitude in public order situations, police officers should: -

(a) be impartial;

(b) ignore abuse directed at the police:

(c) be polite, friendly but act firmly and fairly when necessary;

(d) not make threats or behave aggressively;

(e) not think in terms of 'them' and 'us'

(f) follow orders

(g) bear in mind that police action is in full public view;

(h) calm down and assist colleagues acting improperly

(i) avoid panicking if

(j) colleagues are injured

(k) the crowd does something unexpected

(l) left without specific orders.

Public Meetings

11. Police have no authority to give permission to any person to hold a public meeting, either on premises or in the open air. If such permission is sought and there appears to be no reason for the police to object, the person should be advised that no objection will be raised provided that no other meeting is in progress or planned for that place and that the meeting does not give rise to obstruction, breach of the peace or other offence.

12. Where a meeting has already been arranged and it is proposed to hold another meeting on the same occasion, the organizers should be advised that another meeting is not practicable and they should consider postponing the meeting or selecting an alternative venue.

13. Where a meeting is being held in a public place, including premises to which the public are invited, the OIC of the area will assess the likelihood of disorder and discuss arrangements with the organizers. An appropriate number of officers will be deployed as necessary but it is no part of the police officer's duties to act as steward to secure an uninterrupted hearing for the speakers. Their primary duty is to ensure that no person prevents the transaction of the business for which the meeting was called.

14. Section 442 of the Penal Code (Chapter 77) makes it an offence for a person to unlawfully and with violence obstruct the assembly of any persons for any lawful purpose or disturbs any assembly, or with violence disperses or attempts to disperse any such assembly.

The general power to arrest under Section 33 of the Police Act can be used if a person, on requests, fails to give his name and address but the request should normally come from the Chairman of the meeting.

15. Occasions may arise when the speaker at a meeting deliberately attempts to incite the persons present. Where, having regard to the nature of a meeting, inflammatory speeches or remarks are anticipated, two or more officers will place themselves as near as possible to the speaker so that, even though there may be considerable heckling and interruption, they can hear what the speaker says. Any abusive or insulting comments should be recorded.

16. Section 208 of the Penal Code creates the offences of using violent, scurrilous or highly abusive words or any obscene language with intent to provoke any other person to commit a breach of the peace or in any public place makes use of any threatening or abusive language.

17. When a public meeting is held on private premises, police may be deployed to prevent obstruction near the entrances but they will not normally enter the building unless invited by the Chairman to obtain details of persons disturbing the meeting or to deal with an actual or threatened breach of the peace. The latter is a common law right of entry which the police can exercise independently.

18. The responsibility for the control of a public meeting rests with the Chairman and authorized stewards. The Police should always suggest that stewards be appointed to deal with persons who interrupt the meeting and need to be ejected. Stewards should be readily identifiable to persons at the meeting and the police. They have no delegated police powers or immunity from the law. Their actions in dealing with interruptions and ejecting individuals must only be with such force as is reasonable and necessary. The police have a duty whether they are called upon to do so or not to enter any meeting if those stewards are using more force than is necessary."

19. Where Police officers are present at a meeting, discretion must be exercised when speakers ventilate views which are unpopular. The senior Police officer present should only intervene if he thinks that remarks are grossly offensive or provocative. He should not wait for disorder to break out but should bear in mind that when reasonable criticism and political controversy degenerate into insult and abuse action should be taken even though there may be no

resentment shown by the audience. In many cases, it is sufficient to warn the speaker that the meeting may have to be closed if he persists in making such remarks. This should be done through or by the Chairman.

20. It is not the function of the police at a meeting to secure a hearing for the speaker other than taking action at the request of the Chairman but members of the audience who use violent, abusive or obscene language with intent to provoke a breach of the peace should be dealt with in the same way as speakers and warned. Where warnings have no effect, then more positive action should be taken.

Riotous Assemblies

21. Where any meeting, procession, demonstration or other public event is accompanied by serious disorder, the senior officer or the Assistant Commissioner (District), if not already present, can call for reinforcements as necessary. Any police officers called to assist in a serious disturbance must realize that speed of response is essential and that officers, irrespective of the work they are engaged in, have a duty to respond. Where time permits, reinforcements should be sent to specific rendezvous points so that they can be briefed and deployed to the best advantage. A senior officer requesting assistance must specify the location to which officers should be sent.

22. The Penal Code (Chapter 77) defines the serious public order offences of riot (Section 77) and unlawful assembly (Section 78). Section 79 gives a Magistrate the power to cause a proclamation to be read in the Queen's name when a riot is being committed or is about to take place. Persons, numbering twelve or more, who have not dispersed within one hour of such proclamation can be overpowered by force and arrested. Section 430¬435 of the Penal Code provide for the punishments for rioting, rioting with weapons and for unlawful assembly. Other offences include provoking a riot, committing certain felonies in the course of a riot or unlawful assembly, rioting after a proclamation, preventing or obstructing the making of a proclamation and assaulting a Magistrate during a riot.

23. It is essential that the police regain control of a disorderly or riotous situation at the earliest opportunity and Section 80(2) of the Penal Code places a duty on all citizens to assist in dispersing or arresting

persons who are rioting after a proclamation has been made.

24. The Police are empowered to close all licensed premises which sell intoxicating liquor in the event of any riot and are required to serve written notices on the licensees concerned. Section 34 of the Liquor Licenses Act (Chapter 336) also empowers a Magistrate to order the closure of licensed premises where any riot or tumult happens or is expected to happen in the vicinity of such premises. The Police, in enforcing the order, may use such force as is necessary for the purpose of closing such licensed premises.

Spontaneous Disorder

25. The control of spontaneous disorder is one of the most difficult tasks facing the Police since there is always a time delay in the initial stages before reinforcements can be mobilized. Contingency plans exist within the Force for officers to be mobilized at short notice and the OIC Operational Support Department is responsible for keeping these arrangements under review.

26. An immediate response to spontaneous disorder can be achieved by the deployment of Police Support Units (PSUs) as outlined in Section D2 of these orders. Firm and decisive action in the early stages can often prevent the escalation of disorder and the primary function of the Police is to diffuse the situation and allow for a return to normality.

27. The OIC Operational Support is responsible to the Commissioner of Police for providing a Tactical Options and Training Manual for use in connection with spontaneous order and for the training of officers in the control of public disorder generally (See paragraphs 62-67 below).

28. Police officers should bear in mind that spontaneous disorder is often caused through oppressive, provocative or insensitive police actions even when carrying out their lawful duties. Executing search or arrest warrants and similar Police activities can often provoke hostility in areas where there is anti-police sentiment. Supervisory officers, in charge of any operations which are likely or anticipated to cause a hostile reaction, will inform the OIC Control Room beforehand in order that support units are readily available in the area, for deployment if necessary. ■

Complaints Against Police Presence at Protests

The violent attack on the capital city and the House of Parliament in Washington D.C. in January 2020 must be of concern to law enforcement agencies and democracies around the world, in particular, this region. Media reports disclosed that the Chief of Police received information from the FBI and the New York Police Department of the likelyhood of violent conduct from a so-called peaceful crowd of demonstrators, that intended to march to the Capitol City. The Chief of Police and his executives would have observed the gross misconduct of some groups at a number of demonstrations. e.g. 'Black Lives Matter' and the pro Trump supporters, that protested against the election result. The violence and looting by groups infiltrating the ' Black Lives Matter' protesters and the violent moods of those protesting against the election result, would have been signs of what could have been expected.

The Chief of Police claimed, that he applied to a political office to get approval for reinforcements, days prior to the march. He claims, that he made six applications for resources from the National Guard to supplement his Police unit. His applications were denied.

The National Guard was activated in the middle of the attack, in which one Policeman was killed and several others injured.

The protection of International and National events, Parlimentarians, Judicial Officials and High Profile visitors is the responsibility of the Commissioner of Police and The Royal Bahamas Police Force. We have been well trained by United Kingdom Police Officers, who were effective Police Administrators in our Colonial past. Those of us who attended Police Colleges in the UK were exposed to an extensive amount of this training, which included, crowd control and Police preparation for major events.

The risk involved with the socalled peaceful protest and marches may be heightened by one or more of the following: the size of the crowd, the sensitivity of the issues, the level of rhetoric being used by those opposed, the manner in which the media (Talk Shows, in particular, present the issues) and the demeanour of the leaders and the public.

Most important are awarness of and alertness to pre-incident indicators as important means to prevent problems from developing. Pre-incident indicators are any signals, that an attack is being planned, about to or likely to occur. A surveilance detection program may be the most important security precaution that can be taken, as it could provide information on criminal elements involved, whose agenda is, to create mischief and aid and abet violence and disorder. Nothing to do with the issues. Our Security and Intelligence Branch has been effective over the decades. The Branch was started by the British and continues to be an important Unit of our Ploice Service: We also have the National Intelligence Unit.

The Royal Bahamas Police Force has been excellent in providing, security and safety services to; Royalty, Presidents, Prime Ministers, Movie Stars and many other high profile visitors. The Force has been commended and awarded by Her Majesty the Queen for the administrative and security services provided during her visits. Prime Ministers of CHOGM, have made commendable remarks about us. We have had our share of high profile visitors, who were targets for death in their own countries. Most notable amohg them was the Shah of Iran, who resided in a house at the Ocean Club for a few months. He hired security personnel from both, the USA and The Bahamas.

There was also the leader of an African nation , who could not return to his country after a coup-de-tat.

Politicians, union leaders, media personnel and others who criticize the Police for their presence at protest marches and demonstrations, should learn from the Washington incident. Even though our Constitution provides for freedom of speech, protest, demonstrations and marches, it is more important that the security, safety, comfort and freedom of movement of those of us not involved in the protest, be protected.

In order to hold a protest march etc., there is a requirement that approval be sought from the Police. The Police is then able to avert traffic congestion, prevent clashes of opposing groups, and overall, to preserve good order.

We had our share of socalled peaceful demonstration: Taxi drivers closed our airport by parking vehicles, blocking all entrances and exits. The Police was unprepared. During a general strike involving hotels and supported by BEC and other unions, Police officers holding barricades were hit on their fingers and sprayed with mace. Arrest were made. A group of the protesters proceded to Central Station, but were met by armed Police . Bottles were thrown at a tour bus at a Cable Beach hotel. injuring a boy. Paradise island bridge was blocked and a man, who was mistaken to be a hotel executive was pulled from his car and assaulted. A group of church leaders on a march to ZNS studio were stopped at the gate. Their demonstration was to take place outside the gate, which was locked by security personnel. They took the gate off the hinges and entered.

Another event, perhaps the most frightening of all: I was sent to the airport for crowd control. The Commissioner had permitted a group of Senators, Bishops and other high profile Bahamians to protest peacefully in an area where the Cuban delegation would exit the airport for their visit to the Attorney General's Office, to discuss the settlement for the loss of lives and the destruction of a Defence Force boat. On my arrival at the airport, I met with the group of about 20 high profile Bahamians, led by a Government Senator. I was given the assurance, that they would stand at the side of the street with their placards. I trusted them.

Superintendent Grafton Ifill of the Security and Intelligence Branch warned me, that there would be misconduct and advised that we use another exit, bypassing the protesters. I did not agree.

As the limo with the delegation from Cuba reached the area with the protesters, they blocked the road and used their placards to bang on the vehicle. In the limo were two Cuban military personnel with the delegates. They were armed. Had they panicked there could have been gunshots and injuries. I was spoken to very harshly by the AG, Paul Adderly for not heeding the advice of Special Branch. He understood my reason; trusting that the calibre of the protesters would act sensibly.

Crimes committed against political leaders, judicial executives and other high profile persons will continue to be a fact of life. Similar attacks on institutions, such that on the US Senate in Washington D.C. and the house of Parliament in Port of Spain, Trinidad may invariably be attempted.

No protective measure will ever entirely eliminate the threat. However, proactive planning and intelligence gathering may be effective in early detection of a threat and maintaining control. ▣

The United States - Comments on Corruption in The Bahamas

The United States continues to highlight the inadequacy of local legislation and enforcement efforts to combat corruption and conflicts of interest in public office. (Tribune, dated 6/8/21, page 3)

In its latest investment report the United States said that the political system of the Bahamas remains 'plagued by reports, of corruption, including reports of widespread patronage, etc. The headline of the Tribune's article reads: 'U.S. says efforts to tackle corruption are not enough.' I fully agree with the statement made in the U.S. investment report.

I have lived in my beloved country, The Bahamas for 70 years and have served in the regular Police Force for 30 years, 25 of which were in the Criminal Investigation Department. I retired at the rank of Assistant Commissioner and continue to be in the Police Reserves (inactive). In the following paragraphs I intend to provide information and comments in support of my agreement with the statement of the United States Government.

In the mid-sixties, when I ascended to the gazetted ranks of the Police service, I was privy to a lot of information involving corrupt practices of people residing in The Bahamas. The Commissioner of Police held an Annual General Meeting, which was opened by the address of the Premier and attended by all gazetted Police Officers. At these meetings, we presented information about crime offences and the peace and good order in the country. We also presented intelligence on criminal activities and advised how persons involved, should be dealt with. Reports about criminal activity and criminal backgrounds of foreign nationals were submitted to Governments with our recommendations. Working closely with the F.B.I we received information of undesirable persons residing in The Bahamas, evading criminal persecution abroad while continuing their criminal activities in The Bahamas.

In the mid-sixties I was posted to Grand Bahama where I started the CID Branch. We concentrated our efforts on activities of criminals from the United States, who were involved in the organised prostitution and the importation and sales of stolen vehicles. Our reports to the Immigration Board in New Providence resulted in scores of U.S. Citizens being told to leave Grand Bahama. I recall one of them being a high-ranking Mafia figure. The night clubs, restaurants and other businesses were taken over by affluent Bahamians. I recall three specific recommendations made by the Police Service to Government, that did not receive the deserved consideration. We asked for the deportation of the Columbian drug baron, who owned Norman's Cay.

The Drug Enforcement Administration of the U.S.A. provided evidence of drug trafficking. An American, who was wanted in the U.S.A. for stealing millions of dollars, started a bank here on Shirley Street. The bank became a favourite for politicians and their cronies to acquire large loans. He eventually relocated to Cuba where he was imprisoned. He died in prison. I was involved in his arrest there for extradition proceedings, that failed.

Finally, we planned to destroy landing strips made by drug traffickers to land light aircrafts in transit with cocaine to the U.S.A. The U.S. Drug Enforcement Agency knew the locations of all the strips and required our authority and presence in the destruction of the airstrips. I was told that the plan was not approved as these uncharted airstrips could be used by aircrafts in distress. Corruption existed in the war on drug trafficking. We were called "A Nation for Sale"

There was a Commission of Inquiry into Drug Trafficking, that confirmed our involvement. Since my retirement from the service, I have written scores of letters to the press, politicians and the Police on the following subjects. My comments would be very brief. THE FREEDOM OF INFORMATION ACT.

The failure by governments to enact this law is a massive setback in the fight against corruption. The public needs to know how our money is being spent, with whom and for what services, e.g. the JUNKANOO CARNIVALS $21M, the INTERNATIONAL MUSIC FESTIVAL $650K (that did not happen), The COST OF THE BASEBALL STADIUM and THE MINISITRY OF NATIONAL SECURITY BUILDING (JFK). How much above budget?

When will those projects be completed? Thefts, misappropriations and breaches of financial protocols have been very costly. An employee of the public treasury was able to steal nearly $300K before being caught.

A female employee of the College of The Bahamas was able to steal $250K before being caught. Several other thefts in the public institutions involving thousands of dollars and the latest news of misappropriations in the Bahamas Embassy, Miami, Florida. There appears to be no financial supervision and accountability. The efficiency and competence in some areas of the public service are no longer there, resulting in massive losses in Government revenue.

SIR LYNDEN PINDLING'S PUBLIC DISCLOSURE LAW AND SEIZURE & FORFEITURE OF THE PROCEEDS OF CRIME are not being enforced. Many of our officials and others required by law to disclose, have not complied. It is a criminal offence punishable by a fine of $10K or one year imprisonment or both. There is a commission, that receives the disclosures, but complaints of the crime must be made to the Police by the Prime Minister, not the commission. It is not known if the disclosures made are investigated or just accepted.

We have a Financial Intelligence Unit if the public service, who should be responsible for investigating the information submitted in the disclosures. It is notable, that no disclosures have been published in recent years. In the case of seizures and forfeitures, there has been no action taken against our convicted drug magnates, who own valuable properties throughout The Bahamas. Cash has been seized by the Police and Courts. There were about a score of vehicles seized from Ninety Knowles Car Rental firm. The vehicles were parked on the grounds of the Police College and left there to rot.

I have been told that the U.S. government seized asset Knowles had in Canada and Jamaica. We seized nothing other than the cars. The law is not being enforced. There are many cases of assets of criminals needing investigation and possible seizure under this law. If we intend to tackle corruption there must be discipline, supervision, accountability and enforcement.

There must be no interference from persons in authority. Prosecute criminal offenders and punish other offenders for incompetence, neglect and failure to discharge their duties and responsibilities. I would like to suggest the following for consideration:

INTERGRITY COMMISSION, headed by a person of the calibre and proven record of Bishop Gomez and consisting of very qualified former public servants, who are familiar with financial systems etc. The commission must have at their disposal, the Auditors, the Financial Intelligence Unit and the Commercial Crime Unit of the Police Force. Complaints of suspected corruption and corrupt practices must be made to the commission, who will ensure thorough investigation, without interference.

AN OMBUDSMAN, who should be from the legal profession, with interrogation and investigation skills.

The DIRECTOR OF PUBLIC PROSECUTIONS AND STAFF MUST BE INDEPENDENT OF ANY POLITICAL OFFICE.

Our country is in need of money. We continue to borrow each year to fulfil our obligations. I recall a media report stating, that indebtedness to government is about $1.5B. The reported stated that about 3000 persons had not paid real property taxes in five years. Add to that the millions owed to the Bank of The Bahamas, The Bahamas Development Bank and the Ministry of Education, to name a few; is there anything being done to collect? The offer by the Prime Minister to write-off 50% of delinquent taxes if those persons who are delinquent paid 50% by the end of May. The media report indicates, that the offer yielded $27M, which means, that we lost $27M. Delinquency in paying taxes had its reward. No reward for those of us who pay regularly. It would be good to be delinquent and gain $50%.

We are losing a lot of money in civil actions for unlawful imprisonment and will continue to do so until something is done to ensure that laws, protocols and procedures in place, are not contravened due to negligence and incompetence. Persons responsible must be held accountable.◙

Libel

(Extracts from Deformation Laws of the Bahamas: the LIBEL Act. The abbreviated selections cannot be assumed to be accurate.)

Section 336 (1) - Whoe ver is convicted of negligent libel shall be liable to imprisonment for six months.

Section 336 (2) - Whoever is convicted of intentional libel shall be liable to imprisonment for two years.

Section 337 - A person is guilty of libel, who by print, writing, painting, effigy or by any means otherwise than solely by gestures, spoken words, or other sounds, unlawfully publishes any defamatory matter concerning another person, either negligently or with intent to defame the other person..

Section 338(1) - Matter is defamatory which imputes to a person any crime, or misconduct in any public office, or which is likely to injure him to general hatred, contempt or ridicule.

Section 338(2) - in this section crime includes any act , wheresoever committed, which if committed by a person within the jurisdiction of the court, would be punishable on indictment under the law.

Section 339 (1) - A Person publishes a libel if he causes the print, writing, painting effigy or other means by which the defamatory matter is conveyed, to be so dealt with either by exhibition, reading, recitation, description, delivery or otherwise as that defamatory meaning thereof becomes known or is likely to become known to either the person defamed or any other person.

Section 339 (2) - it is not necessary for libel that a defamatory meaning should be directly or completely expressed; and if it suffices if such meaning and its application to the person alleged to be defamed, can be collected either from the alleged itself or from any extrinsic circumstances, or partly by one and partly by the other means.

Section 340. - Any publication of defamatory matter concerning a person is unlawful, within the meaning of this Title, unless it is privileged on one of the grounds hereafter mentioned in this Title.

Section 341 (1) - The publication of defamatory matter is absolutely privileged, and no person shall under any circumstances be liable to punishment under this code in respect thereof, in any of the following cases, namely;

   a) If the matter is published by the Governor General or by the Senate or the House of Assembly of The Bahamas in any official document or proceeding;

   b) If the matter is published in the: 1011, a0 or in the House of Assembly of The Bahamas by the Governor General or by a member of either house;

   c) If the matter is published by order of the Governor General;

   d) If the matter is published concerning a person subject to military discipline (naval) for the time being, and relates to his conduct as a person subject to such discipline, and is published by some person having authority over him in respect of such conduct, and to some person having authority over him in respect of such conduct;

   e) If the matter is published by a person acting in any judicial proceeding within the meaning of Section 444, whether as a Judge or Magistrate, or as Attorney

   f) If the matter published is in fact a fair report of anything said, done or published in the Senate or the House or Assembly of The Bahamas.

   g) If the person publishing the matter is legally bound to publish it; or

   h) If the matter is true, and if it is found by the jury that it was for the public benefit that it should be published.

Section 341 (2) - Where a publication is absolutely privileged, it is immaterial for the purposes of this Title whether the 2. matter to be true or false, and whether it be or be not known or believed to be false, and whether it be or be not published in good faith.

Section 342 - Publication of a defamatory matter is privileged, on condition that it is published in good faith, in any of the following cases;

1. A fair report of anything done or said, or shown in civil/criminal inquiry
2. If the matter is a copy or reproduction, or in fact a fair abstract, of any matter previously published, and was privileged under section 341.
3. Published by counsel or advocate in the course of, or preparation for, any legal proceeding.
4. An expression of opinion in good faith as to the conduct of a person in a judicial, official or other public capacity, or as to his personal character.
5. An expression in good faith as to the conduct of a person in relation to any public question or matter, or as to his personal character so far as it appears in such conduct,
6. Expression of opinion in good faith re; conduct of a person as disclosed by evidence given in a public proceedings;
7. Expression in good faith as to the merit of any book, or other works submitted by a person for judgement by the public;
8. If the matter is a censure passed by a person in good faith on the conduct of another person in any matter in respect of which he has authority, by contact or otherwise, over the other person, or on the character of the other person so far as it appears in such conduct;
9. If the matter is a complaint or accusation made by a person in good faith against another person ;
10. If the matter published in good faith for the protection of rights or interests of the person who publishes it;

Section 343

1) A publication of defamatory matter shall not be deemed to have been made in good faith by a person, within the meaning of section 342, if it is made to appear either;
    a) That the matter was untrue, and that he did not believe it to be true;
    b) That matter was untrue, and that he published it without having taken reasonable care to ascertain whether it was true or false, or
    c) That, in publishing the matter he acted with intent to injure the person defamed in a substantially greater degree or substantially otherwise, than was reasonably necessary for the interest of the

public or for the protection of the private right or interest in respect of which be claims in be privileged.

2) If it is proved, on behalf of the accused person, that the defamatory matter was published under such circumstances that the publication would have been justified if made in good faith, the publication shall be presumed to have been made in good faith until the contrary is made to appear, either by the libel itself, or from the evidence given on behalf of the accused person, or from evidence given on the part of the prosecution.

(Portions of the above have been abbreviated)

f) Criminal Libels and Related Offences (Smith & Hogan Criminal Law Seventh Edition.)

g) The common law recognised four forms of criminal Libel blasphemous, defamatory, obscene and seditious. Lord Scarman regarded them as

h) part of a group of criminal offences designed to safeguard the internal tranquillity of the kingdom; and thought that there was force in the 'lawyer's conceptual argument' that the requirements of mens rea should be the same for all of them. Regrettably the courts have not approached the offences consistently. If the purpose of the offences is the protection of internal tranquillity, that object has not always been kept clearly in view and the requirements of mens rea differ very significantly. Though all four offences still exist at common law, obscene libels are now in practice, governed by the obscene Publications Act 1959.

i) A Libel is traditionally described as a writing which tend to vilify a man and bring him into hatred, contempt and ridicule. This definition has been thought to be inadequate in the law of tort where it is more likely that the test to be applied today would be that proposed by Lord Atkin;

j) 'Would the words tend to lower the plaintiff in the estimation of right thinking members of society?"

k) generally'

l) The traditional definition has, however, been accepted as representing the law criminal libel in recent cases.

(m) The publication of a libel is a common law misdemeanour but by s.5 of the Libel Act 1843, it is now punishable by no more than one year's imprisonment. It is also short, and the tortuous aspect of libel is much more important. Criminal proceedings for libel are rare and are not encouraged by the courts. It was at one time thought that libel amounted to a criminal offence only if it was likely to result in a breach of the peace. It is now clear that this is not so except perhaps where the libel is published only to the person defamed, or where the person defamed is dead. If criminal libel does require some additional constituent, it is that the libel must be "serious". If it is likely to provoke a breach of the peace or to disturb the peace of the community, then it is certainly serious, but it may be serious although it has no such tendency. "Deliberate character assassination and the wild dissemination of defamatory matter by

(n) 'Cranks' are – and it is said, ought to be – offences, whether or not the person is defamed, or anyone else is likely to resort to unlawful violence. It seems that seriousness is now part of the definition of the offence. An examining magistrate should not commit for trial unless he is satisfied that the alleged libel is so serious as to justify prosecution in the public interest. Evidence of the truth of the statements complained of, or the general bad reputation of P, is not relevant at this stage: Gleaves v Deakin, where the House did not find it necessary to decide whether the examining magistrate had acted rightly in admitting evidence of P's convictions. As evidence of the truth aired, general reputation were inadmissible, it seems that in principle convictions ought also to have been excluded. The House thought that the consent of the Attorney General to the bringing of a prosecution should be required but there are at present no general restrictions.

Where the prosecution is of any person responsible for the publication of a newspaper for any alleged libel therein, the leave of a judge is required by s.8 of the law of Libel Amendment Act 1888. The judge should not exercise his discretion in favour of an applicant unless he is satisfied that (i) there is a clear prima facie case, (ii) the libel is so serious that it is proper for the criminal law to be involved and (iii) that the public interest requires the institution of criminal proceedings. Wein J found these conditions to be satisfied in a case where the applicant occupied important public positions, where his integrity had been impugned and a criminal offence alleged against him and where a campaign of vilification had been carried out for months.

Defamatory libel is best studied as a branch of the Law of tort but it is necessary here to note the differences which exist between the crime and the tort. In the first place libel is the crime. The crime of libel is wider than the tort in at least two and possibly five respects.

(o) (i) Publication to the person defamed is sufficient in crime but not in tort . In tort, the gist of the matter is the loss of the plaintiff's reputation, and this only occurs through publication to a third party; but a principal reason why libel is indictable is the danger to the public peace and this may obviously be even greater where the publication is to the prosecutor himself than where it is to another.

(p) (ii) The truth of the defamatory statement affords a complete defence (justification) in tort but in crime the defendant must prove not only that the statement is true but that it is for the public benefit that it be published. This is the effect of a.6 of the Libel Act 1843, modifying the common law under which it is probable that truth was not a defence to an indictment.

(q) (iii) It is clear that the common law defence of privilege applies equally in crime as in tort, but it is not certain that the defence of fair comment on a matter of public interest is available. Wein J left the matter open in Goldsmith v Pressdram Ltd. and leading works say that the defence may be relied on.

(r) (iv) A libel on a class of persons is not actionable unless the class is so small. Like a body of trustees or directors, that it might be taken to refer to each member individually, or that it is otherwise so worded as to appear to refer to an individual. It is possible , however, that a libel intended to excite public hatred a class, such as the clergy of Durham of the Justices of the Peace of Middle-sex is indictable, though no individual's reputation is harmed.

(s) (v) It is not actionable to defame a dead person, but according to Coke it is indictable, again because of a tendency to cause strife. Later decisions, however ,suggest that this is so only if the designed to bring the surviving relations of the deceased person into hatred or contempt- in which case it seems to be a libel on them – or was actually intended to provoke or annoy the surviving relatives.◙

The Criminal Investigation Department (CID)

It is where I spent 25 years of my service. It is here, that I was exposed to many individuals who were courageous, dedicated, committed, loyal, recognising their role in maintaining law and order in our Country, and most important the prevention and detection of crime. With the training and dedication, I was exposed to, I made a commitment to become one of the top detectives in the department. In the years that followed, I was able to achieve this with my record of detections, that resulted in the recognition, commendations and promotions. Stanley Moir came to the Bahamas as an Assistant Superintendent from the Bermuda Police. He experienced problems working with senior personnel in the uniform branches here. He was moved to CID as second in command. We very soon recognised, that he had immense knowledge and experience in investigations and was a good teacher. He eventually became the Superintendent in charge of CID. He immediately began training sessions on mornings during the shift changes.

By virtue of my rank as Detective Inspector I was his deputy, with responsibility for implementing his directions and instructions. His morning lectures would include subjects, such as; the importance of efficient record keeping (diary & pocket note book), prompt attention to complaints and information, crime scene investigations, collecting, marking and securing exhibits, search of suspects and premises, follow up inquiries, preparation of case files, discipline and conduct when testifying in Courts. The sessions were educational and informative. All detectives attended.

Moir introduced the CRIME BOOK which was the BRAIN & MEMORY of the CID. The book was 30" by 24", with specified sections for the entry of all complaints of crime and all arrests. Directions and instructions were written in the book for investigators to follow. Brief notations were made in the book by investigators. Arrests and convictions were also recorded. The book was perused daily by senior personnel. The Royal Bahamas Police Force has been my alma mater, my college and university. The Force has a proud history and a legacy, that must be maintained by those in the service. Discipline must be maintained and enforced and performance must be efficient, effective, consistent, fair and lawful.

Over the decades the Force has ignored the destructive criticism by many and continued to perform with distinction. Complaints against officers are adequately investigated by a Complaints Unit and the offending officers may be dealt with by a Tribunal or the Courts. It would be advisable that Government appoint a Review Board to peruse the files presented by the Complaints Unit before any final process. There must be communication with the complainant on the outcome of investigations.

The Police Service Commission may be considered to be the review body responsible for examining files and reports submitted by the Police Complaints Unit. In Trinidad & Tobago the Police Complaints Unit is headed by an Attorney, with civilian staff and an office away from Police Headquarters. The Unit is funded within the budget for the Police. ◙

Allegations of Police Corruption
13th July 2006

The subject has been with us for decades and will continue for generations. The occupational opportunities of tradesman, taxi drivers, waiters and general workers to make money illegally are far below those of law enforcement officers. Codes of ethical conduct are important, but only if they in fact become an operational reality 'out on the streets'. Unfortunately, they too often become well-polished, embossed wall decorations. Corruption is defined as the abuse or illegal use of office for the direct or indirect pecuniary gain of the individual law enforcement officer.

This definition covers a variety of clear corrupt behaviour and practices by law enforcement officers. Obviously, under this definition, shaking down traffic violators for money or anything else of monetary value would be corruption. Taking money to facilitate the escape of persons in custody, working privately during off duty hours without the approval of the Commissioner of Police (very common among Policemen in The Bahamas) very often protecting the 'numbers' man's premises and the selling of contraband. The rewards are not always money. There are paid vacations, approval of bank loans and other forms of inducements.

Corruption is certainly not limited to Policemen and they, resent being singled out as it is merely a slice of the larger problem of official corruption in society. The nature of Police work exposes the Policeman, by affinity and affiliation, to opportunities and to characters whose self-interest lay in the corruption of the Police. To such persons, paying off the Police is just one more business expense.

To eradicate corruption we must encourage public participation. The Police Staff Association (P.S.A) must lend itself to fully support the Commissioner of Police and the Complaints Unit to expose those officers involved.

I still feel, however, that the idea of rewarding Policemen, who arrest persons for bribery and corruption would be successful in our efforts to deal with this scourge. ◼

Abetment and Conspiracy

The reader is reminded that all excerpts of any Sections of the Laws of The Bahamas as stated on any page of this book should not be referenced without verification.

Section 85.

1) Whoever directly or indirectly, instigates, commands, counsels, procures, solicits or in any manner purposely aids, facilitates, encourages or promotes, whether by his act or presence or otherwise and every person who does any act for the purpose of aiding facilitating, encouraging or promoting the commission of an offence by any other person whether known or unknown, certain or uncertain, is guilty of abetting the offence and of abetting the other person in respect of that offence.

2) Whoever abets a crime or offence shall, if the same is actually committed in pursuance or during continuance of the abetment, be deemed guilty of that crime or offence.

3) Whoever abets a crime shall, if the crime is not actually committed, be punishable as follows, that is to say. –

   a) If the commission of the crime is prevented by reason only of accident, or of circumstances or events independent of the will of the abettor, the abettor shall, where the crime abetted was murder, be liable to imprisonment for life, or shall where the crime abetted was any crime other than murder, be punishable in the same manner as if the crime had been committed in pursuance of the abetment.

   b) In any other case the abettor shall, if the crime which he abetted was a felony, be deemed guilty of felony or shall be if such a crime was a misdemeanour then it shall be deemed guilty of a misdemeanour.

4) Whoever abets a crime or an offence shall be punishable on indictment or on summary conviction according, as he would be punishable for committing that crime or offence.

5) An abettor may be tried before, with or after a person abetted and

although the person abetted is dead or is otherwise not amenable to justice and any number of abettors at different times to an offence may likewise be tried together.

6) An abettor may be tried before with or after any other abettor, whether he and such other abettor abetted each other in respect of the offence or not and whether they abetted the same or different parts of the offence.

7) An abettor shall have the benefits of any matter of exemption, justification or extenuation to which he is entitled under this Code, notwithstanding that the person abetted, or any other abettor is not entitled to the like benefit.

8) Whoever within the jurisdiction of the courts, abets the doing beyond the jurisdiction of an act which, if done within the jurisdiction, would be an offence and shall be Punishable as if he had abetted that offence.

Illustrations

Subs. (1) (a) 'A' encourages 'B' to commit murder. Here' A' is guilty of abetting murder.

(b) 'A' offers 'B.' five pounds to abetting an assault on 'C.' Here 'A' is guilty of assault on 'C'.

(c) 'A' and 'B' are fighting unlawfully. 'C' and others hinder a peace officer from stopping the fight. Here 'C' and the others are guilty of abetting the fighting.

Subs. (3) (a)' A' encourages 'B' to commit a burglary, 'B' attempts to commit the burglary, but is discovered and arrested. Here 'A' is punishable as if he had committed the burglary.

(b) 'A' employs 'B' to commit a burglary, but before any attempt has been made by 'B', 'A' and 'B' agree to abandon the design. Here 'A' is punishable as for a simple felony, and not with the increased punishment provided for burglary.

Subs. (7) (a) 'A' unlawfully strikes 'B', and 'B' and others immediately set upon 'A' and beat him so that he dies. Here, if the blow struck by 'A' was such as to be a provocation to 'B' (Section 321), 'B' may be guilty of manslaughter, although the others may be guilty of murder.

(b) 'A' unlawfully incites 'B' to assault a person 'B' knows, but 'A' does not know, that the person assaulted is a peace officer acting in the execution of his duty. Here 'B' is but 'A' is not, liable to the increased punishment provided by section 258 with respect to assault on peace officers

Subs (8)   'A' being in The Bahamas, incites 'B' to carry a ship to sea and scuttle her, with intent to defraud the underwriters.

'A' is liable under this provision.

86.(1) Where a person abets a particular offence, or abets an offence against or in respect of a particular, person or thing and the person abetted actually commits a different offence, or commits the offence against or in respect of a different person or thing or in a manner different from that which was intended by the abettor. The following provisions shall have effect, that is to say: -

a)   if it appears that the offence committed was not a probable consequence of the endeavour to commit, nor was substantially the same as the offence which the abettor intended to abet, nor was within the scope of the abetment. The abettor shall be punishable for his abetment of the offence which he intended to abet in the manner provided by this title with respect to the abetment of offences which are not actually committed.

b)   In any other case the abettor shall be deemed to have abetted the offence which was committed and shall be liable to punishment accordingly.

86.(2) If a person abets a riot or unlawful assembly with the knowledge that unlawful violence is intended or is likely to be used, he is guilty of abetting violence of any kind or degree which is committed by any other person in executing the purposes of the riot or assembly, although he did not expressly intend to abet violence of that kind or degree.

Illustrations

Subs. (1) (a) 'A' incites 'B' to commit a robbery by threats without violence on 'C'. 'B', in attempting to commit the robbery by threats without violence on 'C' and 'B' in attempting to commit the robbery, is resisted and murders 'C'; here 'A' is guilty of abetting robbery and not of abetting murder.

(1) (b) 'A' incites 'B', to steal a horse; 'B' in pursuance of the incitement, gets the horse by false pretences. Here 'A' is guilty of abetting the crime which 'B' has committed.

Subs (2) Person assemble for the purpose of breaking open a prison and releasing a prisoner by force. Some of them are armed. If murder is committed by one of these in breaking open the prison, all persons, whether armed or not, who took part in, or otherwise abetted the breaking open the prison, are guilty of abetting murder. If they knew that arms were carried and were intended or likely to be used.

87.   Whoever knowing that a person decides to commit or is committing a felony, fails to use all reasonable means to prevent the commission or completion thereof is guilty of a misdemeanour.

88.   (1)If two or more persons agree or act together with a common purpose in committing or abetting an offence, whether with or without any previous concert or deliberation, each of them is guilty of conspiracy to commit or abet that offence as the case may be.

(2)A person within the jurisdiction of the courts can be guilty of conspiracy by agreeing with another person who is beyond the jurisdiction for the commission or abetment of any offence to be committed by them or either of them or by any other person, either within or beyond the jurisdiction and for the purposes of this subsection as to an offence to be committed beyond the jurisdiction, "offence" means any act which if done within the jurisdiction, would be an offence under this Code or an offence punishable on conviction under any other law.

Illustrations

Subs. (1) (a) if a lawful assembly is violently disturbed (section 442), any persons who take part in the disturbance are guilty of conspiracy to disturb it, although they may not have personally committed any violence and although they do not act in pursuance of any previous concert or deliberation.

(1) (b) 'A' and 'B' agree together to procure 'C' to commit a crime, here 'A' and 'B' are both guilty of conspiracy to abet that crime.

Subs. (2) 'A' in the Bahamas and 'B' in Jamaica, agree and arrange by letter for the scuttling of a ship on the high seas, with intent to defraud the underwriters. Here 'A' is guilty of a conspiracy punishable under this Code.

89.(1)If two or more persons are guilty of conspiracy for the commission or abetment of any offence, each of them shall, in case the offence is committed be punished as for that offence according to the provisions of this Code, or shall in case the offence is not committed, be punished as if he had abetted the offence.

89.(2) Any court having jurisdiction to try a person for an offence shall have jurisdiction to try a person or persons charged with conspiracy to commit or abet the offence.

321   The following matters may amount to extreme provocation to one person to cause the death of another person namely –

(1) An unlawful assault and battery committed upon the accused person by the other person, either in an unlawful fight or otherwise, which is of such a kind, either in respect of its violence or by reason of accompanying words, gestures or other circumstances of insult or aggravation, as to be likely to deprive a person, being of ordinary character and being in the circumstances in which the accused person is, of the power of self-control.

(2) The assumption by the other person, at the commencement of an unlawful fight, of an attitude manifesting an intention of instantly attacking the accused person with deadly or dangerous means or in a deadly manner.

(.3) An act of adultery committed in the view of the accused person with or by his life or her husband, or the crime of unnatural carnal knowledge committed in his or her view upon his or her wife or child and.

(4) A violent assault and battery committed in the view or presence of the accused person upon his or her wife, husband, child or parent or upon any other person being in the presence and in the care or charge of the accused person.

328. The general provisions of Book 1 of this Code with respect to abetment are, in their application for the purposes of this subject to the following special provision namely where a person commands the killing of another person, knowing that the killing will be unlawful then although the offence of the person so commanded be reduced to manslaughter or to an attempt to commit manslaughter by his belief that he was under a legal duty to obey the command the person giving the command is guilty of the same offence as if the person commanded had not believed himself to be under a legal duty to obey the command.

442. Whoever unlawfully and with the violence obstructs the assembly of any persons for any lawful purpose or disturbs any such assembly or with violence disperses to attempts to disperse any such assembly, is guilty of a misdemeanour.

469. Whoever, knowing ot having reason to believe that any person has committed or has been convicted of any crime, aids, conceals or harbours the person with the purpose of enabling him to avoid lawful arrest or the execution of his sentence shall, if the crime is punishable with death or with the imprisonment for ten years or upwards, be liable to imprisonment for five years or shall if the crime is a felony other than aforesaid, be liable to imprisonment for two years, or shall, if the crime is a misdemeanour be liable to imprisonment for six months.

The Search Warrant
Effective Results

It is a very effective weapon available for use by officers in the investigation of crime. To be successful, the administrative process must be very discreet and the search conducted by experienced personnel.

A drug raid conducted on Bimini, provides information, that officers should follow when planning to execute search warrants. It was well known that Bimini had become a transit point for narcotic drugs entering the U.S.A. Commissioner Salathiel Thompson posted an undercover Police Officer to reside on the island on a vacation. Police officers on Bimini were not aware of the reason for his presence there. His ability to obtain information was made easy by the fact, that the drug trafficking enterprise was normal activity. He did a remarkable job obtaining names and addresses of the principals involved in the activity.

The Commissioner of Police discussed a raid on Bimini with me. He provided me with the names and addresses of the suspected drug dealers. We agreed that the utmost secrecy was needed and we discussed a plan. Firstly, I prepared search warrants assisted by a senior detective. The search warrants were signed by a Magistrate, who allowed us to retain his copy, which is normally left with his clerk. I selected the search team and armed officers for the visit to Bimini. It was decided that the team fly to Grand Bahama. During that period any plane with Policemen leaving Nassau was communicated to persons involved in crime on the Island destination. Flying to Bimini would have alerted the criminal element there. A.C.P. Dudley Hanna, the officer in charge of Grand Bahama prepared for our arrival and the few hours stay on his Island. He was not told of the operation.

The Commander of the Defence Force arranged for a boat to collect us in Freeport at midnight. I told the captain of the boat that Bimini was our destination. On the way to Bimini, I informed the team of our destination and we delegated three detectives for the search and one armed uniform officer. Each search team was given the search warrant for their target premises. We arrived in Bimini at about 5:00 a.m. in darkness. The undercover officer left with the teams to direct them to the homes of the suspects. I went to the Bimini Police Station. Officers in Bimini were unaware of our visit. The main drug dealer in Bimini was not at home. His wife told detectives, that he was out to sea and refused to open the door. The search warrant authorised the officers to force open the door and enter in his absence. An axe arrived from the Fire Station. She opened the door. The search revealed huge amounts of marijuana, neatly packed in plastic bags and large quantities of cocaine similarly packaged. We also found thousands of U.S. dollars and a revolver in a desk drawer.

The husband later arrived at the Police Station. He exonerated his wife. Several persons were arrested and brought to New Providence where they appeared in the Magistrates Court. Huge fines were imposed. Our team was commended by the Commissioner of Police.

We were not selected for the raid on Joe Lehder's Norman's Cay, that flopped. I was reliably informed, that some cocaine left the Island before the Police arrived and that Lehder's son, who was arrested with cocaine was released.

Officers must be discreet when planning to execute search warrants as any leak of information could compromise it. Also, it is important to have experienced personnel in the search team. Officers must also be aware, that in addition to the items stated in a search warrant, any other items reasonably suspected of being stolen or involved in criminal activity can be seized from the premises for investigation. It is important that notes be made in the Police Notebook of the items found and the exact location. Also, that the householder is present thourghout the search. Officers must also mark items for future identification.

In a kidnapping case in Freeport, the parents of a child received a note demanding cash and the arrangements for delivery. The note was prepared by cutting words from a newspaper or magazine and sticking a sheet to compile the sentences. The criminals for some reason abandoned their scheme and we found the child unharmed on the road in an isolated area. We received information about a rented vehicle seen in the area. Investigations disclosed, that the vehicle was rented by a young U.S. couple residing in an apartment building in Freeport. We executed a search warrant, but found nothing incriminating. On leaving the premises a detective constable on the team reminded us, that we did not search the garbage. We immediately did so and found the incriminating evidence – a magazine from which the words were cut to prepare the ransom. They were arrested and convicted.

In a murder case involving an American Pastor, who killed his wife and tired to make it appear, that she was killed by a burglar, Police Women on the search team found the weapon, a heavy metal reading lamp with blood and hairs on the base in the garbage bin on the outside of the residence. He was arrested and convicted of the murder, it is important, that senior personnel listen to members of the search team.

Officers must familiarise themselves with following provisions of the Firearms Act: Any Peace Officer, or any officer of Customs authorised in that behalf, by the Commissioner may if necessary by force, enter and search at any time, all premises of persons suspected of possessing, making or selling any firearms without a licence or certificate of authority, as in this Act provided and place, vessel, boat or conveyance, which he reasonable suspects to contain firearms or ammunition for which there is no licence or certificate or authority and every person therein and then and there to take charge and remove any firearm or ammunition, which he reasonable suspects to be without a licence, certificate, or authority as aforesaid. All firearms and ammunition so seized and removed shall be delivered to the Commissioner or to the office in charge of the nearest Police Station.

If the premises or place searched under the provisions of subsection (1) of this section are those of a registered firearms dealer then the officer may examine any books relating to the business. The officer making the search may arrest without warrant any persons found on the premises or place so searched under the provisions of subsection (1) of this section whom he has reason to believe is guilty of an offence under this Act.

A magistrate may, on application made to him in that behalf by or on behalf of the Commissioner, order any firearm or ammunition seized and detained under the provisions of this act to be forfeited to the crown A peace officer may require any person whom he has reasonable cause to suspect of having a firearm, with or without ammunition, with him and to be committing or about to commit and offence under part VI of this act, to head over the firearm and ammunition for examination by the peace officer and any person having a firearm or ammunition with him who fails to hand over the same when required to do so under this sub-section shall be liable on summary conviction to imprisonment for a term of three months or a fine of three hundred dollars or both such imprisonment and fine.

If a peace officer has reasonable cause to suspect any person of having a firearm with him and to be committing or about to commit an offence under part VI of this act, the peace office may search that person and detain him for the purpose of searching him.

If a peace office has reasonable cause to suspect that there is a firearm in a vehicle in a public place or that a vehicle is being or about to be used in connection with the commission of an offence under part VI of this act in any place, he may search the vehicle and for that purpose may require the person driving or in control of it to stop it.

A peace officer may arrest without warrant any person whom he has reasonable grounds for suspecting an offence under part VI of this act.

Without prejudice to the powers otherwise vested in him by law to enter any place, a peace officer shall for the purpose of exercising the powers conferred upon him by this section be entitled to enter any place without a warrant.

The Commissioner of Police after considering the circumstances can authorise the search of premises for firearms or ammunition without a warrant. It is advisable, when possible, to obtain a warrant. Anything found during a search, that is reasonably suspected to have been stolen or unlawfully obtained or may be evidence needed in any other criminal matter.

Officers conducting the search of premises must endeavour to leave the premises in an orderly state.◼

The Evidence Act
chapter 65

Police Officers must read and be conversant with the contents of this ACT, in particular with those section relating to; Domestic Violence, Sexual Abuse of Children, Child Abuse, Bigamy and any other allied offences.

Evidence by Persons charged with Offences and their husbands & wives
Section 171

(a) Every person so charged shall not be called as a witness except upon his own application.

(b) Failure of any person charged with an offence, or the wife or husband as the case maybe, or the person so charged, to give evidence shall not be made the subject by the prosecution.

(c)Subject to Section 175, the wife or husband of the person charged shall not be called as a witness, except upon application of the person charged.

(d) Nothing in this section shall make a husband compellable to disclose any communication made to him by his wife during the marriage, or a wife compellable to disclose any communication made to her by her husband during the marriage

(e) A person charged and being a witness in pursuance of this section maybe compelled to answer any question in cross-examination notwithstanding, that it would tend to incriminate him as to the offence charged.

(f) A person charged and called as a witness in pursuance of this section shall not be asked, and if asked shall not be required to answer, any questions tending to show, that he was committed or been convicted or been charged with any offence other than that where within, he is then charged or is of bad character, unless –

   1) The proof he has committed or been convicted of such other offence is admissible in evidence to show that he is guilty of the offence where with he is then charged.

   2) He has personally or by his counsel and attorney asked questions of the witnesses for the prosecution with view to establish his own good character, or the nature or conduct of the defence is such as to involve

imputations on the character of the prosecutor or the witness for the prosecution.

3) He has given evidence against any other person charged with the same offence.

4) Every person called as a witness in pursuance of this section shall, unless otherwise ordered by the court, give his evidence from the witness box or other place from which other witnesses give their evidence.

Section 175 –

a) A husband is charged with an offence against his wife or a wife charged with an offence against her husband

b) A husband or wife is charged with an offence against any member of their family living with them at the time of commission of the offence; or if the husband and wife are living apart, against any member of their of their Family living with either of them at the time of the commission of the offence.

c) A husband or wife is charged with the offence of bigamy, the husband or wife as the case maybe, of the person accused may be called as a witness without the application of such person and a husband or wife called as a witness in any such case shall not be entitled to refuse to answer questions on the ground that the answer to the question would disclose a communication made during the marriage or that it would intend to incriminate the husband or wife of the witness as to the offence charged.

It is recommended, that officers, who intend to make policing a career, obtain copies of the Evidence Act, the Criminal Procedure Code and the Police Act. The laws can be purchased from the Government Printery for a small fee. The law as it relates to the testimony of spouses must not deter officers from interrogating them during an investigation. The information disclosed may not be admissible in Court but could be very useful in the outcome of the investigation.

Officers are to be aware, that bigamy is an offence against the State. Sexual attacks or abuse of children are crimes against the victims and not either spouse.

Parents, Doctors, Nurses and others, who are aware of sexual attacks on children under the age of 18 years, are required to report such incidents to the Police, Failure to do so make them liable to be charged with a criminal offence. ◙

Identification Procedures

General Guidelines
1. The process of identification of suspected persons plays an important part in the investigation process and identification evidence is usually crucial to the prosecution. Because of its importance it is an aspect of evidence which is often challenged by the defence, and it is necessary for special attention to be given to the manner in which identification is made by a witness in the presence of police officers.
2. In R -v- Turnbull 1976 (2 AER 549), the court of appeal (UK) issued the following guidelines with regard to evidence of identification. These guidelines are important to investigating officers since they emphasise the need to test the quality of identification by each witness and the need to conduct identification parades or other methods of identification in strict accordance with established procedures.
3. The guidelines in R -v- Turnbull suggest that investigating officers should test the quality of identification when a witness makes a statement and pose the following questions :-
   a) How long did the witness have the accused under observation?
   b) At what distance?
   c) In what light?
   d) Was the observation impeded in any way, e.g. by passing traffic or groups of people?
   e) Had the witness ever seen the accused before?
   f) If only occasionally, did he have any special reason for remembering the accused?
   g) How much time elapsed between the original observation and the subsequent identification to the police?
   h) Was there any material discrepancy between the description of the accused given to the police by the witness when first seen by them and his actual appearance?
4. The guidelines also stress that recognition may be more reliable than identification of a stranger but even where the witness is purporting to

recognise someone whom he knows, mistakes in recognition of close relatives and friends were sometimes made. The value of identifying evidence was greater when the identification is made after a long period of observation, or in satisfactory conditions by a relative a neighbour, a close friend, a work mate or other person having previous acquaintance with the suspect.

5. For the purposes of these orders, identification procedures can be categorised as follows:-
a) Identification parades;
b) Street identification;
c) Identification by fingerprints;
d) Identification by photographs;
e) Identification by body samples, swabs and impressions.

IDENTIFICATION PARADES

6. In a case which involves disputed identification evidence, a parade must be held if the suspect asks for one and it is practicable to hold one. A parade may also be held if the officer in charge of the investigation considers that it would be useful. It should be borne in mind that an identification of a suspect, even if masked at the time of the offence, may still be made by a witness since facial recognition is only one aspect of identification. The eyes, special features or characteristics, including the manner of walking or speech, may all be used in order to assist with identification.

7. Arrangements for the parade and its conduct shall be the responsibility of an officer not below the rank of Inspector who is not involved with the investigation ("the identification officer"). No officer involved with the investigation of the case against the suspect may take any part in the arrangements for, or the conduct of, the parade

8. A parade need not be held if the identification officer considers that, whether by reason of the unusual appearance of the suspect or for some other reason, it would not be practicable to assemble sufficient people who resemble him to make a parade fair.

9. If a suspect refuses or, having agreed, fails to attend an identification parade or the holding of a parade is impracticable, arrangements if practicable must be made to allow the witness an opportunity of seeing him in a group of people. Such a group identification may also be

arranged if the officer in charge of the investigation considers, whether because of fear on the part of the witness or for some other reason, that it is, in circumstances, more satisfactory than a parade. Where a witness is afraid of being seen by the suspect, the use of a one-way screen will be considered. (see below)

10. If neither a parade nor a group identification procedure is arranged, the suspect maybe confronted by the witness. Such a confrontation does not require the suspect's consent but may not take place unless neither a parade nor a group identification is practicable, whether because the suspect has withheld his consent to them or his co-operation, or for some other reason.

11. A witness must not be shown photographs or similar pictures for identification purposes if there is a suspect already available to be asked to stand on a parade or participate in a group identification.

12. Before a parade takes place or a group identification is arranged, the identification officer shall explain to the suspect:-
   a) The purpose of the parade or group identification
   b) The procedures for holding it (including his right to have a lawyer or friend present)
   c) Where appropriate the special arrangements for juveniles
   d) where appropriate the special arrangements for mentally ill and mentally handicapped persons;
   e) The fact that he does not have to take apart in either procedure and if it is proposed to hold a group identification, his entitlement to a parade, if this cant practicably be arranged.
   f) The fact that, if he does not consent to take part in a parade or other group identification, he may be confronted by a witness and his refusal may be given in evidence in any subsequent trial, where a witness might be given an opportunity of identifying him in court.

13. This information must also be contained in a written notice which must be handed to the suspect. The identification officer shall give the suspect a reasonable opportunity to read the notice, after which he shall be asked to sign a second copy of the notice to indicate whether or not he is willing to attend the parade or participate in the group identification. The signed copy shall be retained by the identification officer.

14. Immediately before the parade, the identification officer must remind the suspect of the procedures governing its conduct, and caution him under the Judges' Rules

15. All unauthorised person must be strictly excluded from the place where the parade is held.

16. Once the parade has been formed, everything afterwards in respect of it shall take place in the presence and hearing of the suspect and of any interpreter, lawyer, friend or appropriate adult who is present.

17. The parade shall consist of at least eight persons (in addition to the suspect) who so far as possible resemble the suspect in age, height, general appearance, and position in life. One suspect only shall be included in a parade unless there are two suspects of roughly similar appearance in which case they may be paraded together with at least twelve other persons. In no circumstances shall more than two suspects be included in one parade and where there are separate parades, they shall be made up of different persons.

18. Where all members of a similar group are possible suspects, separate parades shall be held for each member of the group unless there are two suspects of similar appearance when they may appear on the same parade with at least twelve other members of the group who are not suspects. Where police officers in uniform form an identification parade, any numerals or identifying badges shall be concealed

19. When the suspect is brought to the place where the parade is to be held, he shall be asked by the identification officer whether he has any objections to the arrangements for the parade or to any of the other participants in it. The suspect may obtain advice from his lawyer or friend, if present, before the parade proceeds. Where practicable, steps shall be taken to remove the grounds for objection. Where it is not practicable to do so, the officer shall explain to the suspect why his objections cannot be met.

20. The suspect may select his own position in the line. Where there is more than one witness, the identification officer must tell the suspect, after each witness has left the room, that he can if he wishes change position in the line. Each position in the line must be clearly numbered, whether by means of a numeral laid on the floor in front of each parade member or by other means.

21. The identification officer is responsible for ensuring that before they attend the parade, witnesses are not able to :
    a) Communicate with each other about the case or overhear a witness who has already seen the parade.
    b) See any member of the parade.
    c) On that occasion see or be reminded of any photograph or

description of the suspect or be given any other indication of his identity.

d)   See the suspect either before (or after) the parade.

22. The officer conducting a witness to a parade must not discuss with him the composition of the parade and in particular he must not disclose whether a previous witness has made any identification.

23. Witnesses shall be brought in one at a time. Immediately before the witness inspects the parade, the identification officer shall tell him that the person he saw may not be on the parade and if he cannot make a positive identification he should say so. The officer shall then ask him to walk along the parade at least twice, taking as much care and time as he wishes. When he has done so the officer shall ask him whether the person he saw in person on an earlier relevant occasion is on the parade.

24. The witness should make an identification by indicating the 'number' of the person concerned.

25. If the witness makes an identification after the parade has ended the suspect and if present his interpreter or friend shall be informed. Where this occurs, consideration should be given to allowing the witness a second opportunity to identify the suspect.

26. If a witness wishes to hear any parade member speak, adopt any specified posture or see him move, the identification officer shall first ask whether he can identify any persons on the parade on the basis or appearance only. When the request is to hear members of the parade speak, the witness shall be reminded that the participants in the parade have been chosen on the basis of physical appearance only. Members of the parade may then be asked to comply with the witness's request to hear them speak to see them move or to adopt any specified posture.

27.   When the last witness has left, the suspect shall be asked by the identification officer whether he wishes to make any comments on the conduct of the parade.

28. If the identification officer asks any person to leave a parade because he is interfering with its conduct, the circumstances shall be recorded. A record must be made of all those present at a parade or group identification whose names are known to the police. A record of the conduct of any parade or group identification must be made on the special forms provided. The record should be signed by both the suspect and his lawyer or representative at the end of the parade after comments as at paragraph 27 above have been invited.

USE OF ONE-WAY SCREENS

29. Great reliance is placed on victims and witnesses in assisting in the investigation of crime and the likelihood of correct identification is enhanced when their anxiety is minimised and their anonymity protected. The use of a one-way screen alleviates the stress experienced by witnesses, particularly where they have been the victims of distasteful, violent or other serious crimes.

30. The use of one-way screen will be considered in such cases by the senior officer who conducts an identification parade. The effect of a one-way screen is achieved by the control of lighting levels on both sides of the glass and it is important that these lighting levels are maintained during the identification process.

31. The tendency for a witness to receive a "wide angle lens" view of the identification parade when viewing through a limited aperture can be overcome by deploying the parade in an arc. Each member of the parade will hold a numbered card. The parade will be conducted in accordance with the procedures at paragraphs 6-28 above except that the witness is screened from the view of the suspect.

32. The suspect will take his normal place in the parade in accordance with procedure but the suspect's lawyer or representative will remain with the identification officer and the witness on the viewing side of the screen. This is to ensure that no allegation can be made that the identification officer used undue influence with the witness and that any identification was fair and proper.

33. The aperture in the screen should be covered until such time as the witness is ready for viewing the parade. The suspect's lawyer or representative should be asked if he is satisfied with the arrangements and he should be invited to view the parade through the screen. Any objections should be considered and recorded.

34. The witness will then be asked in the normal way to attempt an identification and the lawyer or representative asked to take a final look at the parade. Instructions can be given to members of the parade (see paragraph 26 above) in the presence and hearing of the suspect's lawyer or representative and the police officer, standing on the parade side of the screen for security purposes, can repeat the instruction to the members of the parade. (Care should be taken that this officer does not obscure the screen aperture whilst viewing the parade). The aperture should be covered again after each witness and at the ned of the parade.

STREET IDENTIFICATION

35. A police officer may take a witness to a particular neighbourhood or place to observe the persons there to see whether he can identity the person whom he said he saw on the relevant occasion. Care should be taken however not to direct the witness's attention to any individual. Where the suspect is at a police station, the provisions of paragraphs 6 to 28 above apply.

36. The above procedure refers to a witness being taken to a particular location in order to identify a suspect. On no account will a suspect be taken to a witness or group of witnesses to be identified in this way. Once a person has been arrested, he must be taken to the nearest police station in accordance with procedure and any subsequent identification will be in the form of a formal parade or confrontation on police premises.

IDENTIFICATION BY FINGERPRINTS

37. The legal authority for taking the fingerprints of accused persons and the manner in which an identification by fingerprints will be carried out is set out in Section F6, paragraphs 4-5 and 15-17.

IDENTIFICATION BY PHOTOGRAPHS

38. The legal authority for taking a photograph of an accused person is the same as that for fingerprinting (see Section F6, paragraphs 4-5).

39. An officer of the rank or Sergeant or above shall be responsible for supervising and directing the showing of photographs. The actual showing may be done by a Constable.

40. Only one witness shall be shown photographs at any one time. He shall be given as much privacy as practicable and shall not be allowed to communicate with or overhear any other witness in the case.

41. The witness shall be shown not less than twelve photographs at a time. These photographs shall either be in an album or loose photographs mounted in a frame and shall, as far as possible, all be of a similar type. If the photographs include that of a person suspected by the police of the offence concerned, the other photographs shall resemble the suspect as closely as possible.

42. When the witness is shown the photographs, he shall be told that the

photograph of the person he saw may or may not be amongst them. He shall not be prompted or guided in any way but shall be left to make any selection without help.

43. If a witness makes a positive identification from photographs then unless the person identified is otherwise eliminated from the enquiries, other witnesses shall not be shown photographs. But both they and the witness who has made the identification shall be asked to attend an identification parade of groups identification, if practicable, unless there is no dispute about the identification of the suspect.

44. Where a witness attending an identification parade has previously been shown photographs or similar pictures then the suspect and his lawyer must be informed of this fact before any committal proceedings or summary trial.

45. Any photographs used shall be retained for production in court if necessary, whether or not an identification is made, a record shall be kept of the showing of photographs and any comment made by the witness.

IDENTIFICATION BY
BODY SAMPLES SWABS AND IMPRESSIONS

46. The procedures for taking impressions and intimate body samples from a person in custody are set out in Section C4, paragraphs 91-97.

47. Before the impression, sample or swab is taken, the person must be informed of the grounds on which the required authority has been given, including the nature of the suspected offence.

48. Identification by body samples, swabs and impressions. ◉

CRIMINAL DESCRIPTION SHEET

PHYSICAL DESCRIPTION

MALE_____ FEMALE _____

COLOUR ________________
(White Black Brown)

AGE ________________

HEIGHT ________________

WEIGHT ________________

COMPLEXION ________________
(Light/Dark Acne)

VOICE ________________
(High/Low Accent)

MARKS or SCARS ________________

UNUSUAL FEATURES ________________
(Deformities Limp)

METHOD OF ESCAPE

DIRECTION ________________

LICENCE ________________

VEHICLE DESCRIPTION ________________

____

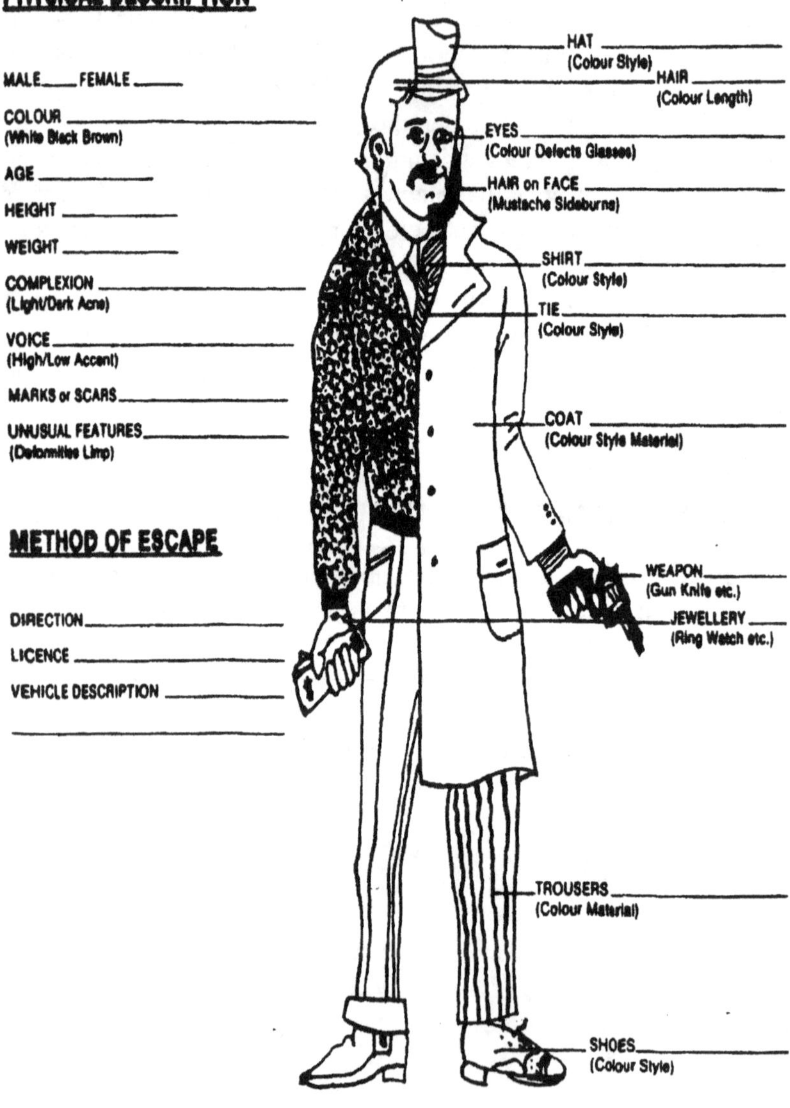

Statements of Deceased Persons
Privy Council Ruling

During the term of Mr. B.K. Bonaby as Commissioner of Police I wrote to him and copied the then Attorney General about a law that exist in Trinidad & Tobago, which helps to protect witnesses, In the following paragraphs I will provide information of a case in that country in which the provisions of the act were correctly used by the Police and help to get a guilty verdict, which resulted in the hanging of eight dangerous and vicious criminals.

Mr. Dole Chadee one of Trinidad's most infamous criminals, a wealthy man, who was the leader in drug trafficking in that country. He had a gang of men and women working for him. A large shipment of cocaine was seized by the Police on a coastline. Mr. Chadee believed that a resident in the area of the coastline, tipped off the Police about the landing of the drugs. Chadee ordered his gang members to kill the man and his family, a wife and child. The gang of eight men, which included a teenage boy proceeded to carry out Chadee's instructions. The manner in which the killings were perpetrated was very upsetting to the teenager. He saw the man gutted with a knife before being shot. The man's intestines were placed in his mouth after he was gutted and for days the teenager could not get over what he had seen. He eventually revealed what he saw and heard, to an adult, who communicated with the Police. The Police recorded what is called in Trinidad & Tobago a 'Notarised Statement' in the presence of and under oath by a Justice of the Peace.

Chadee and his seven conspirators were arrested and subsequently charged with the triple murder. The teenager was placed in protective custody at the Regiment Base at Chaguaramas in North Trinidad. It was known that if left unprotected, Mr. Chadee's gang would assassinate him. On a night before the trial the teenage boy sneaked out of the base. He had done so before to vist a female. On this occasion Mr. Chadee's gang captured him. His head was blown off with a shotgun and his body burnt in a car. He could no longer be a witness at the trial as he was dead.
At the trial the defence challenged the reading of his statement to the Court and Jury. ◉

Murder and Capital Punishment

Murder, it is not a preventable crime and in most cases requires extensive investigations. This statement is confirmed in writings by J. Edgar Hoover, founder and Director of the Federal Bureau of Investigations (F.B.I) and other heads of large Police Forces and Law Enforcement Organisations in democracies around the world.

Mr. Hoover further stated, that the murderer, knows his target/victim, he selects the time and place and the weapon of choice. Mr. Hoover also stated, that if murder was a preventable crime so many political leaders and other protected persons would not have been assassinated. These person are usually escorted and protected, but the killers look for the opportunity to take the shot.

Mr. Hoover and many other leaders of Law Enforcement Agencies have been supportive of Capital Punishment, which was carried out in the U.S.A., during his decades as director of the F.B.I.; it continues today in some States. The punishment is not being carried out in many countries around the world.

In 1958 I was sent by the Bahamas Government to study at the Westriding Detective Training School in Yorkshire, England. At that time the British still had Capital punishment in their laws as the punishment for capital murder. As student detectives we had to memorize and discuss the murders that constituted capital murders. As I recall the killing.
   a)   In the course of furtherance of a crime, e.g. rape, armed robbery, kidnapping and burglary etc.
   b)   A law enforcement Officer in the execution of his duty or while trying to escape Lawful Custody.
   c)   By the use of the explosives; bombs etc.
   d)   By the use of poison (premeditated and planned)
   e)   After being previously convicted of murder (a second murder conviction)

I think treason was also on the list.

Decades later Capitol Punishment was abolished in the United Kingdom and Europe.

In the decades of Fifties through Seventies, Capitol Punishment was carried out as the punishment for murder in The Bahamas. A person convicted of murder in the Supreme Court could appeal to the Privy Counsel in London. If the appeal was denied the case was then reviewed by a Prerogative of a Mercy Committee appointed by the Government to make the final decision. In those years most murderers were hanged. The Committee had the authority to recommend, that the sentence be changed to incarceration and not death. The process was very quick.

Capitol Punishment remains in our Laws, but is not applied. Murder continues to be a very prevalent crime. Many of the victims, about 90% are unarmed when they are killed. The motives are mainly; rival gangs, drug trafficking, armed robberies and domestic violence. The Police have done well in the detection of these murderers. There are many persons in custody, who were convicted and those awaiting trial.

There will be no hangings. The problem is the Privy Counsel in England where Capitol Punishment has been abolished.

The Bahamas are yet to be persuaded hangings will significantly reduce the spiral of crime in the country. Many argue that they are yet to see any empirical evidence that executions significantly reduce murder and crime rates generally, and should not be seen as a universal remedy.

Police Officers discern hanging as being similar to a lighthouse, which if not there several ships may be wrecked. Police records will reveal that several persons convicted for murder and not put to death have returned and killed again. Police Officers cannot be blamed for their views as they are the ones who are exposed to the blood, gore and often death, at the scene. They are the ones who become engaged in the tedious investigation required to bring the murderer to justice.

I am a supporter of hanging for murder, but would recommend changes in the law to have two degrees of murder, namely capital murder and murder with the death penalty for capital murder. It is also recommended, that the Director of Public Prosecutions consider using conspiracy to murder as an additional charge where applicable.

There are those murder cases to be retried for which jurors may have convicted for conspiracy where a unanimous verdict is not the requirement.

It is my humble view, which is shared by many that the Privy Council will continue to obstruct hangings in the former colonies of Britain. They are likely to support the British and European efforts to abolish capital punishment.

Serial Killings In New Providence

In 1964 a man went to his wife's house in Grant's Town. She was not at home. He became very angry when he left the house. An ice-cream vendor was on the street outside, the man shot him dead. He then went on a rampage killing at least six other persons.

Police Officers were on the streets of New Providence hunting for him. Calls were being received in the Police Control Room about the shooting and his whereabouts. It was observed that the English Officers in charge of the Force at the time, remained in the safety of the Control Room, except for Supt. Jim Bryan. We eventually located a residence where he was presumed to be residing. Supt. Wensel Grainger, who was in charge of the Police Operations on the street, summoned us to the location. Keith Mason, Deputy Commissioner of Police (Ret.), Constable Sacko Turnquest and I, were chosen by Mr. Grainger to enter the house. We were accompanied by Supt. Bryan. We went into the house, armed with pistols, banged the door open and listened. We heard nothing. We crawled on our stomachs with our guns ready. The front room was checked as well as his bathroom, he was not there. We moved very quietly and cautiously to a back bedroom where we saw the man lying on the bed with a shot gun pointed towards his head. He had shot himself dead. He obviously used his toe to discharge the weapon. ■

Private Security as a Business in The Bahamas

Introduction

The purpose of security in its widest sense is to protect a way of life and for this reason, much time and effort has been devoted throughout the ages to its achievement. It is agreed that the best deterrent against crime and disorder is an efficient Police Service. In the case of private security, customers and clients require an efficient, effective and disciplined security force, that is honest, reliable and responsible. In any approach to providing private security, it must be understood that the objective to be attained, is the prevention of crime, and the preservation of good order in the places assigned. Every effort must be directed towards the security and safety of persons and properties, the preservation of tranquillity and the protection of assets. Every member of the security unit must endeavour to distinguish themselves by such vigilance and activity, which would render it impossible for anyone to commit a crime within the confines of the property assigned to be protected.

Security Companies & Firms in The Bahamas

Over the years the security business in The Bahamas has blossomed and has become a flourishing industry. The number of security companies has grown from mere dozens to several hundreds. The competition for business is intensive. Research the Yellow Pages of the Telephone Directory and locate the listings of security firms from page 750 to 762. Included among the listings are the large security companies, such as; Wemco, I.C.S., Maximum International, Executive, Atcun, Trace and numerous others.

We are aware of other security firms in operation, that are not licensed or registered at the Ministry of National Security. They can provide security services at a much lower rate than the established firms, which has resulted in an ongoing price war. One will find, that the established security firms or most of them obey the laws governing the industry: Licensing, National

Insurance and minimum wage etc., the overhead expenses of the unlicensed and unregistered firms are much lower. They pose a threat to the industry.

Available Security Assignments

Hotel Resorts recruit and train their personnel, in particular those resorts with casinos where specialist training is required. Private Security would obtain assignments and contracts to work; in Banks, Corporate Offices, Shopping Centres, Industrial Plants, Construction Sites, Marinas, Restaurants, Places of Entertainment, Medical Facilities, Residential Complexes (The Gated Communities), Sports Facilities and Government Departments. In most cases the assignments are to provide guard service. In addition to the foregoing, there are the Armoured Car Services, Alarms System and the Monitoring of such systems and private Investigations. Canine (K9) Services are frequently used for the protection of constructions sites and large car parks.

There have been three major setbacks in the progress of private security as an industry and business;

1) The price war, which would have been eradicated if efforts to organize and maintain a Private Security Association had materialized. The efforts by former Police Commissioner Paul Farquharson failed because of the lack of cooperation from the owners of security firms. The objective was to have the police conduct training and have the rates for providing security services regulated.

2) The price war is damaging to the industry as there is no criteria, standard or qualification of personnel introduced to customers and clients as security officers.

3) The Police policy to be engaged privately has reduced the security assignments available to private security firms. It is common practise to find the off-duty Police Officers providing security services in banks, web shops, food stores. places of entertainment and private functions. Politics also play a major role in the selection of the security provider, in particular at Government facilities.

The crime threat in our Bahamas today is of grave concern to all of us law abiding citizens and residents. It is very fortunate that in most instances visitors to our shores have not been victims. It would be very damaging to our tourism industry and our economy. Many investments have been announced for our Islands, mostly in hotel resorts. The law enforcement agencies have a tremendous responsibility to protect our citizens, residents and visitors. It is a massive burden, that demands efficient/effective performance, discipline, hard work, loyalty and integrity. I have every reason to believe, that they have those qualities.

For decades the security business in The Bahamas has thrived and is a growing industry. The number of security companies have increased considerably. The competition is intensive. Customers are able to demand low paying contracts, while requiring effective and efficient security. To most customers security is a non-profit expenditure. In the U.S.A. resorts have paid millions in civil actions when Courts rule, that security was "Inadequate."

Wemco Security & Co. Ltd. has been able to remain at the top as a security provider because of their tailored uniforms, performance, conduct, discipline and loyalty of its employees. The company's dedication to; training, supervision, discipline, employee relations and most importantly most reasonable conditions of service contribute immensely to performance and success.

All persons involved in security work as an occupation must take their positions seriously. Their future is assured. Training must be engaging and continuous. Rewards and benefits could be derived by those who excel.

Several investment proposal have been signed by the Government of The Bahamas, for hotel resorts, tourists playgrounds, beaches and other ventures where trained security personnel would be required from the start of construction and onwards after completion. Security firms must be prepared for the influx of these opportunities.

Security firms must provide classroom training as well as on- the-job training for officers. It is my hope, that our Police Service will eventually take over the training of security officers for a fee charged to the firms and

that successful candidates would be sworn in as District Constables, which would enhance the strength of the Force. ■

Oil Drilling in The Bahamas

Issue: Oil Spills of huge proportions, causing major damage to fisheries and the environment.

In the midst of the massive protests and objections to drilling for oil in Bahamian waters by environmentalist groups from both The Bahamas and the United States. I wish to make a contribution of my experience living and working in a oil town in Trinidad. It was in the mid-forties, just after the second world war, I left elementary school in Cunupia Village and joined my mother in the small-town of Point Fortin, in the heart of the oil industry. She was the housekeeper for the general manager of United British Oil Trinidad (U.B.O.T) the largest oil producer in the country. I was employed in the Material Accounts office as an office boy/messenger and later filing clerk.

Trinidad was still a British Colony at the time. Point Fortin, with the largest oil refinery in the world and the center of oil exploration in Trinidad, thrived, and very soon became the wealthiest town in the country. Unemployment and poverty did not exist in the oil belt of South Trinidad. Communities compared favourably or even better than many in the city of Port of Spain, sixty miles to the north . People in north Trinidad regarded the southerners as being wealthy. Excursions by hundreds of southerners accompanying sports teams to the City encountered increased prices for retail services. The huge pipes with oil flowing from the wells to the refinery and the smell of oil in the air, were a part of the environment.

The sand in the water at Point Fortin beaches contained residue of crude oil, which covered your feet when you stood in the sand. Residents visiting the beaches took bottles containing kerosene or coconut oil to clean their feet after the beach visits. The oil residue in the sand was caused by leakage from pipes and drilling overflows. We learned to live with it. To the south of Point Fortin, a distance of about 10 miles is the village of Cedros. It is Trinidad's major fishing area. Cedros could supply the entire country with its fish needs, undamaged by oil residue. A visit to Cedros when the fishing boats were arriving would disclose the massive size of the industry there, unaffected by the oil industry. Residents in the oil towns of South Trinidad have accepted the environment they have lived in for the decades. The rewards from oil production have been massive; schools, health care and social services, Sports and recreation and a good standard of living. I have visited Trinidad annually for many years from the 1970s, during the carnival period. South Trinidad continues to boom.

In addition to the oil industry, there is natural gas, exported to the world, new industries such as clothing manufacture, flour mills, steel mills and chemicals. Exports to Caribbean Countries and parts of the world. During my visits there, I travel between Port of Spain, San Fernando and Tobago on the government's ferry boats in the Gulf of Paria, that separates Trinidad from Venezuela.

Drilling for oil and natural gas is now also at sea. The rigs and wells can be seen from the shore in many ares. I have not seen any oil spills. Venezuela, a large oil producing country is just 7 miles across the Gulf of Paria from Cedros Village. Trinidad is now experiencing major problems with illegal immigrants from Venezuela.

Barbados, is an Island whose economy thrives on tourism, is a very very limited oil producer. Production there has not been hazardous to their beaches and fisheries.

Oil has been found in Guyana. I am told, that there are negotiations between Guyana and Trinidad for exploration and production.

Naturally, we have to be concerned about major oil spills and the ability of the investor to deal with them efficiently and effectively. We have to be concerned about the objections from our powerful neighbour and ally, the United States of America. They can force their objections, if we fail to negotiate and satisfy them, that the environment will be protected. Any investor should be asked to guarantee such protection with a cash bond.

An oil industry would benefit our country in many ways, such as, lower fuel cost that would reduce the cost of electricity, attracting investors in manufacturing, thus creating employment.

It would be beneficial if Government could arrange a visit to the oil towns in Trinidad for environmentalist groups and media representatives. They would be able to provide information on their experiences. Visits to Point Fortin, Point-a-Pierre, Point Lisas, Labrea and other small oil towns and villages would be enlightening. They must also visit the oil wells in the Gulf of Paria. ◙

Investigation into The Ministry of Housing

As you are aware I am very close to the Royal Bahamas Police Force and will applaud its record, at every opportunity given me. I am also a defender when I think the force is being unjustly criticized. My concern of which I write to you is about the above-mentioned investigation, which is or was being conducted by the Police.

The suggestions I submit herein are based on my experience as a Police Officer and an Investigator for thirty years.

Firstly, the investigators should have visited all of the houses of which complaints were received either by the Ministry or the local media. Other house owners with complaints of defects in their houses should have been encouraged to come forward. All of these persons should have been interviewed and appropriate statements recorded with all of the necessary information relating to the payments etc. for acquiring the houses.

Secondly, Police photographers should have photographed all of the defects in each of the houses for which reports were made.

Thirdly, inquires should have been made for information about the inspectors, who were responsible for the scrutiny of the work done at each house and the eventual taking over of the houses as completed and the subsequent handing over of the houses to the owners. Fourthly, the contractors responsible for building the defective houses should have been identified.

Having obtained all of the above information the building inspectors should have been interrogated and shown the pictures of the defects. During the interrogation Detectives would have been in search of evidence of gross neglect in performing their duties and responsibilities and any evidence to suggest bribery and corruption involving the contractors. At some stage of the interrogation Detectives may have found it expedient to confront the inspectors and contractors for joint questioning.

It is my opinion that such methods of investigation would have exposed the Inspectors as either being Corrupt or grossly negligent in performing their duties. If the latter was proven they could have been relieved of their duties by the Ministry, ■

Excerpts from Letters to Ministers of Transport and The Ministry
penned by Paul Thompson Snr.

To: The Hon. C.A. Smith (8th February, 2001)

It is my opinion, that one of the most difficult problems in your new Ministry will be public transportation, in particular buses. Many countries in the Caribbean have experienced grave problems in this area and had to take drastic measures to provide reliable public transportation for residents. If we were to investigate and ascertain some of the measures implemented in other places in the region, we would be inclined to agree on what is required here in New Providence. A Public Transportation Corporation, which must include bus owners as shareholders and administrated by Government funding to get it started would be the answer to many of the problems.. The need for drivers to be racing for passengers as they will be paid weekly wages, no need for arguments over routes or cheating on routes and there will be a fare structure to include TRAVEL THROUGH ZONES AND TRANSFERS FROM ONE ROUTE TO ANOTHER. The corporation would provide season tickets, build proper bus stops and police buses as required. If Bermuda can provide such an excellent system, we can do it. Their system is similar to that of the United Kingdom.

❀ ❀ ❀ ❀ ❀ ❀ ❀

To: The Hon: Glenys Hanna Martin. (12th December, 2002)

BETTER PUBLIC TRANSPORT SYSTEM FOR NEW PROVIDENCE.
This letter was similar in content to the letter sent to
The Hon: C.A. Smith. 2nd August, 2006.

PLANS FOR DEVELOPING THE CITY OF NASSAU.
I hope that the plans for re-designing the City of Nassau includes parking as a very important consideration, as the City has outgrown the

areas and locations allocated for parking. It is time, that consideration be given to a multi-story parking building similar to the one on Paradise Island. A suitable area would be land to southwest of the General Post Office.

The building could be designed to have retail establishments outside of the ground floor with secure parking on the upper floors. Security personnel, cameras/monitors and alarms available to enhance security of persons and vehicles. Shares could be sold to the public to raise revenue for construction. It could be a public investment similar to the Paradise Island Bridge.

Parking for our Parliamentarians should be downtown on Parliament Street. The entire street should be reserved for their parking at all times. It is a secure area and adjacent to the Parliament. Stickers to be placed on vehicles of the close relatives, who may be authorised to use the parking area. This provision is made in all of the countries I have visited as a matter of respect and concern for security. The area allocated on Parliament Street would be under constant surveillance with cameras and police personnel. The parking building would eventually pay for its construction and staffing. Shareholders would all benefit from its earnings.

❀ ❀ ❀ ❀ ❀ ❀ ❀

To: Chairman Road Traffic Authority. (10th August, 2006)

SUGGESTIONS FOR THE REDUCTION
OF TRAFFIC ACCIDENTS.

It is recommended, that vehicle inspections include examination of the under carriage for faulty or worn parts and brakes. In addition to checking engine and chassis numbers to those of vehicles reported stolen.

Vehicles must be placed on a ramp for efficient and effective inspection. Qualified private agencies could be authorised by the Government to conduct inspections and provide certificates for licensing. It is done in many countries. Another area of concern is the number of accidents near school crossings. The victims are usually children or senior citizens. Installation of Manual lights for school crossings on busy thoroughfares, such as; Robinson Road, Prince Charles Drive and Carmichael Road would prove to be an asset. Strict adherance of the speed limit in school zones could be aided by hefty fines for violators.

❀ ❀ ❀ ❀ ❀ ❀ ❀

To: The Controller, Road Traffic Department (23rd December, 2006)

PLATES FOR PUBLIC SERVICE VEHICLES.

In recent months personnel of our security/investigations firm disclosed, that the system of allocating franchises to persons who do not own vehicles continues to exist. I thought that this practice had stopped when the Ingraham administration took over the Government, but this does not seem to be the case. On the 27/10/09 I was in Freeport attending a security seminar. Taxi cab drivers there confirmed, that the unethical practise continues to thrive, unabated. A taxi-cab driver at L.P.I.A. told me, that he pays $ 500.00 per week rental for his plates. The holders of the franchises are not owners of cabs or buses. It is a very unfair practise. ◙

Gambling In The Bahamas

Gambling, an action that involves a risk of losing or a chance of winning. To decide and act with the idea that somebody will be successful, that the result will be a good one. To offer money etc. in a game, a race etc. that you will lose everything if you lose the game, choose the wrong winner, or that you can increase by winning the game or choosing the right winner.

Gambling in most countries today is an industry. It is a way of life for many people. It is a form of entertainment for many and a secure livelihood for so many, who earn a good living by providing the service and/or being involved in efficiently, effectively and honestly serving those persons who wish to gamble. There are the croupiers and allied employees in casinos, jockeys at race tracks, the employees in the betting houses and of course the millions of person worldwide employed in the various forms of lotteries and other allied forms of gambling.

Many of the persons involved in the industry, as owners and/ or employees have done very well in providing for their families, their communities, with donations to charities, sports, religion, hospitals and even politics. The wages paid to employees in the industry are usually above the minimum wage and the conditions of service are above average. The proprietors in the industry demand, trust, integrity and efficiency from their employees. It is therefore in their best interest to keep their employees happy. It is said, that the industry can afford to be extravagant as the "house, never loses."

In the English speaking Caribbean the gaming industry is regulated and controlled by Government corporations and/or Government Commissions. The Government in some countries, owns and operates positions of the gaming industry, but in all instances where there is private ownership Government appointed Boards are the 'watch dogs'. These are the person, who ensure, that the regulations etc. are not contravened, customers are being fairly dealt with and the prescribed earnings of the Government are forthcoming, through licence fees and/or percentage of the revenue or profits. It differs from country to country.

In Trinidad & Tobago portions of the industry are completely under Government control. Government owns and operates the betting houses (web shops) where tickets are sold. All drawing can be witnessed live on local television. Horse raceing and other forms of gaming such as betting houses are in private hands, but are controlled by a Government board, that ensures there are no contravention of Government regulations and the laws of the country. The Trinidad & Tobago Gaming Commission has earned millions each year through its own operations and collections from private entities.

The pre-web shop years in The Bahamas involved a few person, who were engaged in what was called the 'numbers racket'. There were the street vendors and certain clandestine locations where persons were able to place their wager. The winning numbers were drawn by placing numbered balls or marbles in a bag. The bag was thrown into the air and when caught one marble or ball will be tied off, the others thrown out of the bag. The tied number was the winner. The only foreign number involved was drawn in Cuba on Saturdays. It was very well known, that some operators very often will exclude a number, that was extensively sold from the bag to avoid having to pay out large sums of money. Police intervention was frequent and persons prosecuted had to pay huge fines, which were always paid by the operators.

The industry in The Bahamas today has grown. It is modern as it engages modern technology and there is integrity. The customer is aware of the winning number and cannot be cheated. Many of the proprietors of the web shops make huge contributions to the community in the form of donations to charities, religious institutions, sports in addition to scholarships and other forms of sponsorships to communities. The industry provides employment for thousands of people. The conditions of service provided for the employees are reasonable and meets the standards of the private sector. Those employed in the industry earn a good living and provide well for their families. Discipline and integrity must prevail among the industry's employees.

For many years Governments of The Bahamas have monitored the industry and aware of the significant revenue generated. Government is at the stage where it is agreed, that the country must be made to benefit from the earnings of the industry. Many persons in The Bahamas have been lobbying for years to have the web shop operations made legal, so that Government and the people can benefit from the earnings of the industry. The Government's referendum slated for the 3rd December, 2012 is the first step towards making the industry legal. Those of us involved in the industry, in particular employees of the industry must support legalising the industry by voting "Yes". All of us must register, and vote "Yes". We all have families of voting age. Encourage them to register and vote "Yes" in support of our jobs and our ability to support ourselves and our families. Ask our families and our friends to support our cause to maintain employment and to be able to provide for ourselves and our families.

Opposition to all forms of gambling in the Bahamas existed for decades. Casino gambling in the sixties and seventies was attacked mostly by the same opposition. Government in those years ignored their attackers and casino gambling prevailed. It employs a huge number of Bahamians and is a prominent form of entertainment for our visitors.

Many of the objectors have ignored or are not enthusiastic in dealing with other major issues in our country, such as child abuse, domestic violence, corruption, crime, unemployment, poverty and immoral conduct of religious leaders.

Ask the objectors how they plan dealing with additional unemployment should they succeed in their efforts to close web shop gambling operations, how they propose to stop persons from using their personal computers to make bets in the U.S.A., sending the dollars abroad. Ask the objectors if they wish to stop all forms of gambling e.g. casinos, raffles and bingo etc. ask the objectors if they would encourage their flocks to quit their jobs in the gaming industry and ask them how many of them had received money for their enterprises from the industry; either directly or indirectly.

We as owners and employees of the industry must stand firm and vote, a resounding "Yes" for the legalising of web shop gaming. ◉

Lottery And Gaming

The Editor

During a recent visit to Trinidad & Tobago I conducted some research on the gambling industry. The information disclosed may be of public interest.

The Lotteries and Betting Industry in Trinidad & Tobago is a massive enterprise. The Government derives huge financial benefits and the industry employs thousands of people, including accountants, computer technicians administrative personnel at all levels, as well as security and investigation personnel.

Prior to 1968 it was a fluorishing underground criminal activity, led by a few affluent individuals, many of whom had a criminal history, but had the means to organise their operations and hire the personnel needed for the administration of their gambling enterprises. The particular type of gaming, known in the Bahamas as 'numbers' was called 'weh weh' by the Trinbagonian population. That form of gambling was prevalent in the ghetto areas and in the barrack type housing areas of the City of Port of Spain.

The 'weh weh' vendors frequented these areas, where they targeted the poor, the lower working classes and the lower middle class. It was very well known that many persons in the exclusive areas of the city of Port of Spain also participated. That form of gambling was also prevalent in the second City, San Fernando and the boroughs of Arima, Point Fortin (in the oil belt) and the farming town of Chaguanas. The vendors frequented their locations daily and very often could be heard interpreting dreams to their customers. Marks or signs in the dreams would be associated to a particular number, which, would be bought. The vendor even provided printed handout with marks/signs, such as scorpion, snake, deadman, policeman and jammett woman etc. each of which had an association with a particular number.

The drawing of the number was done daily at secret locations to avoid the Police. The winning number circulated by way of the underground; vendors paid the winners. One would always know when a neighbour would have won: with the loud shout "Thank you Jesus". As expected there were always allegations and suspicions of dishonesty and fraudulent conduct by some unscrupulous operators. Such operators would lose customers. During my early teens I resided in the barracks in southeast Port of Spain where crime, gangs and prostitution were prevalent. "Weh Weh" was regarded by the residents as a way out of there. My aunt played regularly. She was a religious woman. She was convinced, that God would help her, get out of that area. She finally won enough to move to another area in the city. She educated her children and lived a reasonably good life operating a food delivery service, and continued to play "weh weh".

Police intervention, with raids and arrests had no effect on the operation of "weh weh". It made the Police unpopular in the ghetto areas where it continued to flourish. People wanted to gamble, so they gambled.

In addition to the "weh weh" Trinidad had other forms of gambling and betting; the gambling clubs, with dice and card games (some of which were licensed), most of which were underground operations in houses or secret rooms in bars. There was horseracing on race tracks owned by Government, but operated by the Trinidad Turf Club, a private company of elite and affluent natives.

In the late Sixties the Government led by Dr. Eric Williams took control of lotteries, gaming and betting in Trinidad & Tobago. There was debate in the Parliament, but no referendum. The National Lotteries & Gaming Act was passed and became law in 1968. The National Lotteries Control Board was established.

The Board, appointed by the Minister of Finance controls all gaming, gambling and betting activities in the twin Island Nation. It was a complete take over of the industry by the Government. The Board re-organised the local 'numbers' game, "weh weh", which is now known as "Play Weh". Other forms of gaming, such as "scratch" (instant game of chance) were also introduced.

A renown international company that specializes in Gaming was contracted to carry out the mandates of the Board. The system has become very 'Hi Tech' over the years, with many outlets (vendors) all over the twin island nation. The whole system is managed electronically, every bet, every draw, every winning payment is recorded. Draws are conducted on National television

One will find many young person with skills in accountancy, IT and customer service engaged in the industry.

There are other forms of gaming and betting in which the Board does not actually engage, but has the responsibility to monitor and most importantly collect licence fees, taxes and any other revenue due to the Government.

Betting on horseracing is sanctioned and is carried on through numerous betting shops. There are also small casinos available to visitors and residents. The Board collects revenue from all of these establishments.

Overall policy decisions are directed to the Board by the Minister of Finance. The National Lotteries accounts and the account of the Board are Public Accounts. Revenue derived from lotteries, gaming and betting are paid into the Consolidated Fund, with the surplus made available to the Sports & Culture Fund, established by an Act of the same name.

I am told that various social welfare and cultural organisations, including churches, benefit from the Sports & Culture Account.

I interviewed a former member of the Board, who once resided in The Bahamas. He assured me that persons selected to serve on the Board are of unquestionable character and integrity.

In The Bahamas consideration could be given to having a public corporation formed for the operation, administration and control of gambling, gaming and betting: the Trinidad and Tobago model could be used as a guideline.

The corporation could offer major shares to those Bahamians presently involved in the web shop business and limited shares to he general public...

About three years ago former Deputy Commissioner of Police Mr. Keith Mason and I were on Mr. Steve Mckinney's Talk Show and we agreed that the Police raids on web shops was an "exercise in futility" I still feel that way and patiently await the decision of the Supreme Court. ◾

Agricultural Industry in The Bahamas
(Decades of Fifties & Sixties)

Rock Sound, Eleuthera was a thriving community of hardworking, sociable and happy people. The pineapple plantation and plant was a major employer. Large freighters visited to collect loads of pineapple juice, sliced pineapples and the fruits.

The business owned by the Bakers and Sawyers thrived. The owners were reportedly a part of the Bay Street Boys, that became the U.B.P. Hatchet Bay. Eleuthera was another thriving community with full employment at the Hatchet Bay Plantations. The plantation supplied milk, ice cream, chicken and eggs to New Providence and The Bahamas. In New Providence the firm had "Milk Stands" where the products were sold. Eleutherans were able to purchase beef on weekends only. In the later Sixties the plantation was bought by Government. Not long after the purchase and the departure of the previous management, it went bankrupt and closed. A police investigation was started, but discontinued.

Abaco and Andros had SML Farms of the U.S.A., farming, vegetables and fruits of various types which were exported to markets in the U.S.A. by large transport planes. There was full employment. Overseas workers were imported to work on the farms. The business closed in the late Sixties.

We received a gift of quality cattle for breeding and developing cattle farming. The project started well, but in the ensuing years it was discovered that the animals were not being properly maintained and subsequently died.

Abaco Sugar Cane Factory & Plantation. It was started by an overseas investor. Acres of sugarcanes planted, a factor for making sugar built and homes built for overseas workers. Years later Government purchased the business. Years later the factory and equipment became junk, weeds outgrew the sugarcane, the building and rolling stock rotted.

Cat Island produced quality tomatoes and we canned and exported tomato paste. It is puzzling how the agricultural industry we had, just disappeared and or did not progress as the Country progressed. We should not be importing avocados, citrus fruits, vegetables, corn, pigeon peas, mangoes, peppers, bananas, sweet potatoes and other underground foods. We have the land. Crops such as Mangoes, Avocadoes, Citrus fruits and ground provisions do not require the care needed for vegetables etc. Large plantations should be encouraged on Family Islands.

Political Violence in Grand Bahama

The 'Dissident Eight' consisted of eight high profile, respectable citizens, who won seats in the House of Assembly as members of Sir Lynden Pindling's Progressive Liberal Party (PLP). For some reason they broke away from the Party and in some circles were called Free PLPs and UBPs (United Bahamian Party). The breakup became national news and was reported in the local media for several months. As expected, there was a lot of anger among the PLP politicians and party supporters, The group eventually became the Free National Movement (FNM). It was publicised, that the group would visit Grand Bahama for meetings with supporters and residents there. Their first public meeting was to be held in the settlement of Pinder's Point.

The late Sir Albert Miller, Deputy Commissioner of Police was the police officer in charge of Grand Bahama District. Sir Lynden Pindling and the PLP had very strong support in Freeport, Grand Bahama where there was a huge Jamaican population, who would always refer to him as 'plenty man day'. It was disclosed, that the police Special Branch Unit had advised, that any gatherings or meeting by the group be adequately policed, in particular if held in Freeport. The group travelled to Pinder's Point and convened the meeting before a fair crowd of residents of the community and of the City of Freeport. There were no Police personnel present, except for an Inspector, who was known to be an open supporter of the PLP. As the meeting was about to begin there was outburst of verbal noises and threats, followed by banging of chairs and physical attacks on the group (Dissident Eight/Free PLP), which resulted in injuries to some of the group and the cancellation of the meeting.

On the group's return to New Providence, a complaint was made to the Commissioner of Police. I was instructed by the Commissioner to conduct a thorough investigation into the incident. I proceeded to Grand Bahama, with details of the incident as reported by the group. Inquiries at Pinder's

Point disclosed the identities of six men from the City of Freeport, who were the principals in the disturbance and the physical attacks. The Police Inspector had departed the room and the area. He was not present during the incident, but according to witnesses he left at a time when he should have anticipated, that there was going to be disorder. The six perpetrators of the incident were arrested and charged, with various offences, including assault and battery, causing harm and disorderly conduct. In my report I recommended that disciplinary action be instituted against the Police Inspector. Nothing happened. We all knew him to be a man of tremendous political influence. Mr. Kendal Nottage was the attorney for the accused persons, all of whom were respected residents of Grand Bahama, with no arrest or criminal record.

The leader of the group was a very close friend and admirer of Sir Lynden Pindling, a prominent businessman, respected family man, charitable and with a great sense of humour, that endeared him to many people. He was also my very close friend, who supported my policing efforts when I was in charge of the CID. in Freeport, at an earlier period. Magistrate Wilton Hercules was sent to Freeport for the trial. The accused person pleaded guilty.

The address by Mr. Kendal Nottage was very eloquent. He talked about the good character of the men, their personal contributions to society, their loyalty to the cause of freedom and their strong Christian beliefs. At one time during the address Mr. Hercules stopped him and said; Counsel, congratulations on your most eloquent plea, but I am thinking of a sentence of imprisonment for a period of at least six months, unless you can convince me why it should be less.

Upon completion of the hearing the group received a severe warning, they were bonded over to keep the peace etc. and heavy fines imposed. I had never seen the leader of the group without his dark shades since I had known him. When Magistrate Hercules mentioned six months in prison, his shades fell from his eyes to the floor. He told me later it was due to cold sweat. He never lived that down with me. He was murdered during an armed robbery at one of his business establishments in Freeport. He was Mr.Lofton Cooper, a great Bahamian. ◙

Conversation with:
The Hon. Clarance A. Bain, M.P.

Clarance Bain (CB) and his brother were very close friends, whom I could rely on when in need. His brother Edgar Bain was one of a few coloured, Bay Street merchants. He was also the owner of the Silver Slipper night club on East Street where the great Freddie Munnings and his Band performed before the Cat & Fiddle night club.

Edgar was one of a few, who peacefully opposed the Bay Street Boys and later the United Bahamian Party (UBP). Others included prominent citizens such as Gerald Cash, Milo Butler, Cleveland Eneas, Clifford Darling and others. They protested on sites where racial discrimination was being practiced. Royal Bank of Canada where the only coloured staff were the messenger and a cleaner, as well as the Registry and the Grand Central Restaurant where coloured persons were not served. The Savoy Theatre was for white persons only.

Clarance Bain on his return to the Bahamas got involved. There were several others involved in peaceful protests, i.e. taxi drivers and hotel employees such as 'Boose' Rodgers.

Party politics arrived and we had the Progressive Liberal Party and the United Bahamian Party. Most Police Officers supported the PLP The support increased when Lynden Pindling became leader of the party.

Clarence and Edgar Bain got involved. H.M. Taylor and Cyril Stevenson continued to be involved and use the Herald newspaper as a means of getting people support for the PLP. We began to see some changes in the governance of the country as the PLP support began to grow. The Police Force under British command was also supportive of the PLP It was a silent movement within the service as public political discussions were not permitted. The Police Barracks was removed from the city constituency due to the number of officers residing there, who each had a vote.

Lynden Pindling and Orville Turnquest won the seat in the constituency, that included the Police Barracks. Clarence A. Bain and

Cyril Stevenson won seats in Andros. The UBP won the election.

Clarence Bain and I met very often. He lived in my neighbourhood, Lewis Street where he owned a guest house and restaurant.

Our conversations were usually about measures to improve the country. He wanted more educational opportunities, more schools and scholarships. He resented the merchant monopoly and the mailboat monopoly and looked forward to the day when all Bahamians would be able to compete in these businesses.

He hoped for major improvement in the living conditions in Bain Town and Grants Town where there was outdoor toilets and water faucets, with landlords getting rich off poor people.

I discussed with him the Rent Assessment & Control Board, that existed in Trinidad where houses and apartments being rented must have bathrooms indoors and all other utilities and the Board decides the rental fees.

Bain was in favor of the repatriation of the British Officers, who were here on contract and replacing them with local officers, such as Messrs Wenzel Grainger, Augustus Roberts, Bernard J. Nottage, George Knowles, Conrad Knowles, Salathiel Thompson, Albert Miller and John Crawley.

The British officers were brought here on contract when a new Commissioner of Police Lt. Col. Colchester Wemyss came to develop the Police Force. Many of our senior and junior officers went abroad to the United Kingdom on training courses and were ready to take over the administration of the Police Force.

Lt. Col. Colchester Wemyss resigned after a UBP Commission of Inquiry He was replaced by Mr. Nigel Morris from the U.K.

The PLP won the 1967 Elections and the changes in the Force's command gradually began, local officers had taken over the command of the force. A British Commissioner of Police remained in place until after Independence when Salathiel Thompson was appointed. Commissioner Hindmarsh was brought in by the PLP Government to replace Nigel Morris.

The 1972 General Elections was about eighteen months away. The campaigning had slowly began.

Clarence Bain asked me a question which took a while to provide him with the full answer. He wanted to know why there was a change in Policemen's attitudes towards the PLP. He told me, that there were reports, that some Police Officers did not welcome PLP campaigners on their premises as they did before and it appeard, that Police support for the PLP. had waned.

The response was simple. Prior to the arrival of the contract officers from the United Kingdom, two story cottages were built in areas around the Police Barracks to accommodate them. On arrival these officers were accommodated in two bedroom apartments in the cottages. Other existing accommodation were renovated and furnished for the same purpose. The arriving British contract officers received free accommodation and utilities, even telephones were free and they were also provided with a Police Car, that was cleaned and serviced daily by personnel from the Police Garage. They also got a two week annual vacation in the United Kingdom, with the airfare paid for by the Government.

When they departed the accommodations were made available to local gazetted officers. Those gazetted officers, who moved in had to pay rent, utilities and for the car. Deductions were made from their wages. The PLP Government had changed the arrangement. Another change, that hit the pockets of the lower rank policemen was the elimination of allowances for special skills. We received allowances for driving (qualified to drive any Police vehicle, including fire engines), tradesmen including carpenters and mechanics in the Police Carpenter shop and the garage, Fingerprint experts and Photographers in the Criminal Records Office.Clerical allowance to officers, who were able to type and properly prepare case files for forwarding to the Attorney General's Office and an Education allowance to officers, who acquired Associate Degrees etc. Clarence Bain understood what caused the change in attitudes. He did mention the problem to his party officials and we soon got a small increase in wages. The allowances were never returned.

Clarence and Edgar Bain were great Bahamians. ◙

Policing The Bahamas 1951 & Beyond
THE FINAL CHAPTER

The contents of this chapter is not intended to be political, but factual, informative and honest. Neither is it intended to be critical of persons or organisations, but to offer constructive advice and observations from the past and present.

An annual conference on Crime, for Commissioners and Senior Officers is held at Police Headquarters, which is usually opened by an address from the Prime Minister. I have had the privilege of participating in sevral conferences where I had the opportunity to make many recommendations and observations, some of which are contained in the following paragraphs.

I proudly recall making a speech in the presence of Sir Lynden O. Pindling, in which I criticised Government's decision to appoint Commissioners of Police from Britain, when we had well trained and experienced senior officers here, in the persons of Wenzel Grainger, Augustus Roberts and Bernard Nottage. That plea was eventually successful when Mr. Salathiel Thompson was appointed Commissioner, after our Independence.

I also recommended the formation of the Police Staff Association and made my plea to Sir Lynden, which after years of seeking an answer was told by Commissioner Thompson, that the Prime Minister was not in favour. However I continued in my pursuit, lobbying Cornelius Smith, Minister of National Security.

Then entered, Commissioner Bartlette who recognized the benefit of an Association. The current Government approved and it became law. Bartlette provided office space and personnel.

Conditions of service for the Force improved remarkably, which enhanced the morale and performance of the officers: the Association continues to be an integral part of the Force.

The information, advice and constructive criticism to be documented in the paragraphs of this chapter are based on my qualifications as a Police Officer, my knowledge of the governance of the Country, my love for the people of this Country and my hope to see The Bahamas being the leader in the Caribbean. (The Singapore of the West.)

Allow me to quote from the Progressive Liberal Party 'Our Blue Print for Change' as follows :-

"The New Day beckons the Economic Revolution. A Revolution that encourages and supports new ideas, ingenuity and creativity etc"

New Ideas are to be found in these paragraphs :

THE APPOINTMENT OF AN INTEGRITY COMMISSION
Proposed Composition

- Bishop Drexel Gomez
- Former Chief Justice & President of the Court of Appeal.
- Mr. Paul Farguharson, Commissioner of Police Retired
- Mr Ellison Greenslade, Commissioner of Police Retired
- Head of the Government Audit Department
- Senior Official of the Public Treasury
- Head of the Financial Intelligence Unit
- Head of the Public Disclosure Commission
- Attorney from the Department of Legal Affairs.

Responsibilities to include:
a) Investigation of criminal activity & corruption in the Public Sector.
b) Persue and act on reports received from the Auditor, that merits Police investigation or departmental action.
c) Make recommendations to enforce the collection of taxes, loans and all monies owed to Government institutions, in particular; real property & corporate taxes, Bank of The Bahamas, Bahamas Development Bank, Ministry of Education and the Public Treasury.
d) Introduce a special Court for Government debtors.
e) Enforcement of the Public Disclosure Laws. (Use staff from the Financial Unit to Investigate suspicious disclosures.)
f) Enforcement of the Seizure & Forfeiture of the Proceeds of Crime Act. (Use staff from the Financial Intelligence Unit to investigate and report.)

Assistance is available from the Metropolitan Police (Scotland Yard), The Royal Canadian Mounted Police, the Federal Bureau of Investigation and The Drug Enforcement Administration of the U.K., Canada & U.S.A. Personnel from all of our Law Enforcement Agencies must be made available to the Commission as required.

Information: Public Expenditure.

An audit of the funds reportedly spent by Government for the first two Junkanoo Carnivals are long overdue. The cost was reportedly $21M. (for what? and with whom?). The media disclosed that $900K was paid to band leaders and musicians. Information was received from a reliable source, that $750K was reportedly paid to a U.S. citizen, who built the three stages. Other expenses included; foreign artists, travel expenses, performances at Grand Bahama. There were purchases of generators and the fencing for the venue. It was revealed that $12M was spent on the first carnival and $9M. on the second.

Ministry of Tourism reportedly spent $650K on an International Music Festival, that did not occur (for what? and with whom?)

Financial controls in Government used to be efficient, effective and demanding. In recent years an employee of the Public Treasury was able to steal $500K. He was convicted of stealing $250k+. An employee of the College of the Bahamas was convicted of stealing close to $1M. from that institution over a period of time.

Whatever happened to these persons in Government departments, who are responsible for financial controls. I recall as a young detective being sent out on investigations to the Islands. I was given an allowance at the Treasury. Upon my return I had to account for every penny spent, with receipts (No booze allowed).

The Passport Office was a part of the Criminal Investigation Department. The office closed at 4:00 p.m. to enable the Superintendent to check the cash, the receipts and the blank passports, before sending the proceeds with a report to the Treasurer. Any suspicion of criminal misappropriation of Government money was reported directly to the Police, by the senior civil servant. Very often the politician would only be told after our investigation began. I recall being involved in investigations at the Broadcasting Corporation of The Bahamas, credit card fraud by an M.P., The National Insurance Board, stealing by reason of employment by an M.P., Postal Service employees at the Post Office Saving Bank,

Nassau and Governor's Harbour; stealing and falsification of accounts. These prosecutions and more, not mentioned, kept public servants honest. Dishonesty in the public service was not condoned.

National Insurance Fraud

Employers, who deduct National Insurance contributions from their employees and fail to submit payments to the National Insurance Board, are committing a criminal offence, to wit, Fraudulent Breach of Trust. Employees discovering the failure to make the payments should report the matter to the Police.

Government Rentals vs. Ownership

Government rentals in The Bahamas, in particular, New Providence, is very costly. Our City between Elizabeth Avenue and east to Deveaux Street has died. Abandoned old derelict buildings (a danger to pedestrians) and wide unused spaces could become an attractive and thriving part of our city again.

The suggestion is, that Government acquire these derelict abandoned buildings and with Government/Public financing, design and build a multi story complex to accommodate Ministries (presently in rental space), the General Post Office, Bahamas Immigration Office, a Police Station and docks. Abundant parking would be made available on a couple of the upper floors to the public, generating income and easing congestion. The ground floors to accommodate entertainment centres, restaurants, and retail stores.

The project would save Government's rental expenditure in addition to earning rental income. The idea should be considered by our Town Planners, engaging experts in the legal and financial fields (cost of legally acquiring the properties). It would be a huge project, creating lots of employment, that would make our city alive again.

Rent Assessment & Control Board

It was first proposed by the Hon. Clarance A Bain. He was a very close friend and I had discussed the idea with him. It did not reach the Parliament. The Board would have been responsible for the inspection of properties being rented to ascertain suitability, including the upgrade of water and sewage systems. Bain wanted to eliminate the street faucets and the outdoor toilets. He confided in me, that the idea failed due to the fact, that there were so many landlords, who were either politicians or political cronies, who did not wish to upgrade their rental properties, due to the cost. The Board would have provided legislation relevant to the collection of rent by landlords, which is very time consuming and problematic in our Courts.

Public Transportation

New Providence needs a Government controlled Public Transportation System administrated by a Public Transportation Corporation, such as those, that exist in many foreign countries. For decades I have suggested that The Ministry of Transport and Road Traffic Authority executives visit their counterparts in London, Bermuda and Barbados that provide an efficient service; most noticeable are the uniformed drivers, sheltered bus stops and timely schedules. Revenue is also generated from advertising spaces at the various bus stops.

Present bus owners would be invited to be shareholders in the Corporation. There would be no need then, for speeding and dangerous overtaking as the revenue derived would be for the Corporation. Finances would have to be discussed as it relates to the payment of corporation staff, maintenance of vehicles, bus stops, ticketing and shareholders.

Government Vehicles

A large number of Government vehicles are allocated to public servants in New providence. An audit should be undertaken to determine which job classifications, necessitates the allocation of a Government vehicle. Instead, I had recommended a cost-cutting measure, in which I suggested, that the audit may have found it more expedient, to allocate a vehicle(s) and driver(s) arrangement for Ministries and Departments, to transport staff, to and from, out of office assignments.

The responsibility for the care and maintenance of the vehicles would be that of the drivers. The vehicles would remain at the various Ministries, when closed i.e., after office hours, weekends & public holidays.

Bahamas Correctional Services

Fox Hill prison has always been a major concern. We can now add to that the Detention Centre. Conditions for the inmates and even the guards are a human rights disaster, really a health disaster in waiting.

The Government, the Bar Association and The Bahamas Christian Council are all aware. Public awareness of the deplorable conditions is derived from reports published by international organisations, in particular those based in the U.S.A. Former Commissioner of Police Mr. Salathiel Thompson was very concerned about the conditions of our prisons and the fact that our most dangerous criminals are all incarcerated on the island of New Providence, our major tourists mecca.

From as early as the 1970s, when he was appointed, he recommended to Government, that a maximum security prison be built on either Inagua or Ragged Island. He had anticipated that at some time the Royal Bahamas Defence Force would have to construct a mini-base on one of the two Islands, which would provide added security for the prison. My choice was Andros. The island is very large with fertile soil for farming, rearing or animals and poultry for use in the prison

I was also concerned about the distances to travel in the event of a riot or other incident needing quick response. It was recommended, that the prison in New Providence be administrated and operated as a Borstal, similar to those in the United Kingdom. He had not visited any Borstals himself, but was very interested in their functioning.

I had the opportunity to visit a Borstal in Scotland while training at the Scottish Police College. As I entered the premises, although I knew it was a prison, the environment and the atmosphere seemed to be that of an educational institute. The waiting area was like a hotel lobby with books and magazines. Upon further entry on tour of the premises we were shown offices, with furniture produced by the inmates. Visiting the various work areas we saw young men in uniforms that looked more like school uniforms than prison uniforms. All of the young offenders seen, were well groomed and appeared to be content with their situation.

At that Borstal, various trades and occupations are taught: furniture making and repairs, tailoring (the clothing worn by the inmates and the guards are tailored there), vehicle repairs and auto body work to name just a few.

We were told, that maintenance to Government offices, such as minor electrical and plumbing requirement are carried out by the inmates. The Government Departments are charged for all work done.

A portion of the payment received goes to the institute. The reminder is deposited into the inmates accounts and held until they are discharged. There is a committee working on the outside, that finds employment for the inmates upon discharge from the institute.

The proposal to build a maximum security prison on an island was never considered. A Borstal could not be implemented on the present site.

The Shanty Towns

Commissioner Salathiel Thompson was very concerned about illegal immigration, in particular from Haiti. He was even more concerned about the Shanty Towns on our islands. The security risk of not knowing, who is in your country, knowing nothing about them and unaware of the numbers, bothered him.

We eventually decided on a plan to rid the country of the Shanty Towns. The plan was to start with Immigration, Police and Defence Force raids. We planned to start with Pigeon Pea and The Mub Abaco Islands,where the large populations were residing.

Apart from arresting the illegal immigrants, he planned to prosecute the builders of the Shanty Towns and the landlords, who collected the rent. The plan did not find favour with the Government, so we did not proceed. Shanty Towns and illegal immigration continue to be a costly and annoying exercise. We have failed to deal with illegal immigration and Shanty Towns, effectively.

Unlawful Imprisonment

Actions taken in the Courts are costing our country millions of dollars. The supreme Courts are awarding hundreds of thousands of dollars to victims in civil actions. The problem has been ongoing with persons being held unlawfully for as long as seven years. The problem continues unabated. Our Constitution and Laws of our country are very clear. It should be very well known to all Law Enforcement Officers, that persons arrested must be taken before a court and formally charged with an offence before they can be detained in any prison or detention centre. Such persons can be held by Law Enforcement for a period of 48 hours, after which, application must be made to the Courts for an extension of up to 72 hours. We have held persons for as long as seven years.

I had brought this matter to the attention of the former Minister of National Security, advising that he appoints a committee to conduct a census of the inmates at the prison, detention centre and any other place of detention to audit the records, to determine how many more person are being held illegally. We must take immediate steps to stop the drain on the Treasury for unlawful imprisonment. ■

Name Index of Persons Mentioned in this Book

Name Index of Persons Mentioned in this Book